STATES OF IMITATION

Studies in Social Analysis
General Editor: Martin Holbraad
University College London

Focusing on analysis as a meeting ground of the empirical and the conceptual, this series provides a platform for exploring anthropological approaches to social analysis while seeking to open new avenues of communication between anthropology and the humanities, as well as other social sciences.

STATES OF IMITATION
Mimetic Governmentality and Colonial Rule

Edited by

Patrice Ladwig and Ricardo Roque

berghahn
NEW YORK · OXFORD
www.berghahnbooks.com

First published in 2020 by

Berghahn Books

www.berghahnbooks.com

© 2020 Berghahn Books

Originally published as a special issue of *Social Analysis*, volume 62, issue 2.

Library of Congress Cataloging-in-Publication Data

Library of Congress Control Number 2020007096

British Library Cataloguing in Publication Data

A catalogue record for this book is available from the British Library.

ISBN 978-1-78920-737-8 (hardback)
ISBN 978-1-78920-738-5 (paperback)
ISBN 978-1-78920-739-2 (ebook)

CONTENTS

ILLUSTRATIONS

ACKNOWLEDGMENTS

This volume results from a collaboration between researchers based at the Max Planck Institute for Social Anthropology (MPI), Halle/Saale, Germany, and the Institute of Social Sciences, University of Lisbon (ICS-UL), Portugal, in the context of the joint project "Colonialism and Mimetic Processes in Historical and Anthropological Perspectives" funded by the German Academic Exchange Service (DAAD) and the Portuguese Acções Integradas Luso-Alemãs (FUP/CRUP) (project reference A-07/2011). It is also a product of the research project entitled "Colonial Mimesis in Lusophone Asia and Africa" funded by the Foundation for Science and Technology (FCT), Portugal (reference PTDC/CS-ANT/101064/2008) and based at the Institute of Social Sciences, University of Lisbon. Between 2010 and 2013, the group members held several workshops and conference panels on the topic, in which the theories and historical data for this publication were extensively discussed. We are especially grateful to all workshop participants at Halle and Lisbon for important comments and stimulating debates, and to Carmo Daun e Lorena for exchanges at an initial stage of this project.

We also want to acknowledge the help of numerous friends, administrative staff, and people who gave us access to private and public archives and their expertise in many of the historical and ethnographic field sites where we work in Europe, Africa, and Southeast Asia.

We also received valuable and generous critical feedback from the anonymous reviewers for the special issue of Berghahn's journal *Social Analysis*, in which most of the pieces presented here were first published in 2018. Early Portuguese-language versions of the chapters by Cristiana Bastos, Ricardo Roque, and Tiago Saraiva first appeared in a special issue on colonial mimesis in the Portuguese empire published in the journal *Etnográfica* in 2014. We thank *Etnográfica* for permission to reuse these materials here. Tiago Saraiva's chapter and Patrice Ladwig's final essay were not originally included in the special issue of *Social Analysis*. During the past year, it was a great pleasure to work with Amanda Horn and Sulaiman Ahmad at Berghahn.

Patrice Ladwig and Ricardo Roque

INTRODUCTION
Mimetic Governmentality, Colonialism, and the State

Patrice Ladwig and Ricardo Roque

When Claude Lévi-Strauss undertook fieldwork in Brazil among the Nambik-wara in 1938, his ethnographic writing became an object of imitation by his ethnographic subjects. Especially the chief of the non-literate Nambikwara mimicked the ethnographer's act of writing by drawing wavy horizontal lines on papers that Lévi-Strauss had distributed. Then the chief pulled out another piece of paper, inspected a series of objects he received from his people, and with a grand gesture checked each item on his imaginary list by pretending to read it. When Lévi-Strauss's (1961: 290) description and interpretation of this event was published as a chapter in *Tristes Tropiques*, the anthropologist concluded that the Nambikwara chief had made a crucial discovery:

> So the Nambikwara had learnt what it meant to write! But not at all, as one might have supposed, as the result of a laborious apprenticeship. The symbol had been borrowed, but the reality remained quite foreign to them. Even the borrowing had had a sociological, rather than an intellectual object: for it was not a question of knowing specific things, or understanding them, or keeping them in mind, but merely of enhancing the prestige and authority of one individual or one function at the expense of the rest of the party.

Lévi-Strauss's account can be seen as part of a broader historical sequence of colonial contact situations in which mimetic exchanges between European

Notes for this section begin on page 20.

and indigenous peoples become the preferred object of writing and reflection (cf. Taussig 1993: 70–79). Moreover, this ethnographic scene—thereafter highly debated (see Doja 2006; Geertz 1989)—encapsulates critical themes in wider discussions on mimesis and imitation: the appropriation of the power of the other; the tensions between original and copy, as well as between similarity and difference; the relationship between form and content, bias and verisimilitude, and so on. Lévi-Strauss's reading of this scene, however, emphasizes one further theme that is of particular relevance for the current collection. Lévi-Strauss interpreted the Nambikwara event within his wider reflections on writing as a tool of power and domination, urbanization and state building. Writing, Lévi-Strauss (1961: 293) concluded, "seems to favour rather the exploitation than the enlightenment of mankind ... the primary function of writing, as a means of communication, is to facilitate the enslavement of other human beings." In this sense more than just an epistemic gesture, mimetic practices can have a productive 'political' significance. Imitative gestures in cross-cultural (including colonial) encounters, such as those of the Nambikwara chief, bear the potential to enhance authority, establish hierarchies, and articulate power with regard to specific forms of political and social organization. Without doubt, many themes in Lévi-Strauss's rendering of this encounter resonate with numerous reflections on mimesis and imitation as a concept and as practice in human history. Yet the latter theme, we believe, indicates a zone of mimesis in theory and history that particularly requires further reflection. The current book endeavors to shed light on this historical and conceptual zone by drawing attention to three connected topics: colonialism, the state, and their entanglements with mimetic processes.

Main Themes

Although we acknowledge and address the resistance aspects of mimesis and imitation on the part of the colonized, our main aim is to investigate, on the one hand, how the colonial state sought to manage, control, and incorporate its indigenous subjects through mimetic strategies of governance and, conversely, how indigenous polities resorted to imitative practices in order to either engage with or oppose the presence of the colonial state. Each chapter in this collection elaborates on the conceptual insights of mimesis differently and independently; each work adopts distinct approaches to state and government in colonial settings. Yet all of them share a similar trajectory of encountering the conceptual insights of mimetic theory with issues of colonial governmentality, its forms of rule and statehood. The chapters draw on archival data and ethnographic research concerning the colonial expansion of Europe from the 1800s to the mid-twentieth century and principally cover the history of French and Portuguese colonization in West Africa and in Southeast Asia. However, rather than trying to offer a comprehensive geographical coverage of European imperialism in these regions, this volume presents a set of case studies that demonstrate the potential for addressing issues of mimesis, colonial rule, and state formation together in the context of broader historical and anthropological research on colonial histories in the modern world. In colonial studies, the intersections between anthropology and history have become well established in the last decades (Axel 2002b; Cohn 1987; Comaroff and Comaroff 1992; Dirks 1992; Stoler and Cooper 1997). Building on this scholarship, this book focuses on three general themes for exploring the complex (and at times concealed) web of relations connecting mimesis and colonial rule.

The first theme considers the potentials and dangers of mimesis as a practice and as a strategy of colonial government. It addresses the ways in which the agents of the colonial state may govern through imitation and how this can become part of the techniques, theories, and materialities through which the colonizers have attempted to control the lives of indigenous peoples. We claim that in certain specific contexts the imitation of indigenous cultural, social, and political patterns by colonial regimes became an essential part of the workings of colonial statecraft and governmentality. These mimetic processes were open to change, manipulation, and distortion, and several contributions also emphasize the partial and fragmentary nature of such processes. We propose that these forms of mimetic governmentality contributed to the development and stabilization of colonial states and regimes of governance, while, conversely, often producing 'states'—both as situational configurations and collective political and social assemblages—that were temporary and inherently fragile. Picking up on the interplay of fragility and stabilization, the second theme revisits the trope of colonial mimicry by indigenous actors, this time as an object of colonial anxiety and state regulation. It considers how the copying and reproduction of colonial authorities' behaviors, costumes, and ideas by indigenous people could become the object of state anxiety and organized forms of control. Mimetic connections by Europeans with indigenous customs and social practices are further positioned in relation to wider discussions concerned with assessing their legitimating and practical value in terms of political organization and state formation in the colonies. The third theme explored here deals with the ways in which indigenous communities and minorities themselves have related to the colonial state through practices of imitation. In particular, we aim not only to highlight the antagonistic and subversive aspects of these imitative practices—as much previous research has already tackled—but also to explicitly draw out how such gestures can become modes of productive appropriation, and how these imitations become meaningful with regard to indigenous peoples' attempts at recreating their own identities and even enhance some forms of relatively autonomous 'indigenous' political power in colonial situations.

Overview of the Chapters

Each of these themes—resistance, governmentality, and appropriation—is explored in one or more of the chapters included in this collection. Looking at the case of a colonial governor accused of being complicit in 'headhunting barbarities' in East Timor, Ricardo Roque explores colonial government as a set of problematic—yet politically productive—mimetic and parasitic transits with indigenous traditions of violence in East Timor. Patrice Ladwig investigates how the French colonial regime in Indochina attempted to recreate and re-enact indigenous traditions of Buddhist statecraft and kingship, by affectively 'rematerializing' ancient Buddhist architecture, temples, and relic shrines. Cristiana Bastos explores the strategic, and inventive, use of African architectural forms in Portuguese colonial hospitals, showing how a vision of the creation of 'hut-hospitals' in twentieth-century colonial medical practice revealed an emerging mimetic form of biopower for managing and intervening in the population's health. Oliver Tappe's chapter brings out the double-sided political productivity of mimesis in colonial encounters in the Lao-Vietnamese frontier region. He discusses the mimetic relationships that the French colonial state maintained with local forms of authority in the frontier highlands, while also describing how the same hill peoples established reciprocal ties of mimesis with the colonial state. Tiago Saraiva explores the significance of colonial mimesis within the entangled histories of science, animal breeding, and settler violence associated with the establishment of the Karakul Experimental Station by the Portuguese colonial state in Angola, in the 1940s. Saraiva approaches the Station as a 'laboratory' of colonial 'mimetic operations'. There, the colonizers' desire to imitate the supposed 'modernity' of other European empires was accompanied by a mimesis of indigenous social life and the reproduction of idealized forms of Portuguese sociability. Christoph Kohl's chapter re-examines the significance of imitation as a multi-dimensional form of opposition to the colonial state in carnival rites in colonial Guinea-Bissau, bringing into light the ways through which the Portuguese authorities tried to cope with the perceived subversive nature of indigenous mimicry by exerting control and issuing prohibitions. The final piece by Patrice Ladwig investigates the themes of mimesis and imitation from a more theoretical and genealogical perspective. By placing theories of mimesis and imitation into the historical context of the Enlightenment (Kant and Hegel), early anthropology (Frazer and Lévy-Bruhl), and the works of the Frankfurt School of critical theory, he outlines a conceptual, transcultural history of mimesis that oscillates between civilizational hegemony and critiques of modernity.

In the following, we seek to outline two main contexts within which to read the contributions in this book. First, we will draw attention to the significance of looking at mimesis, primitivism, and colonialism together in the context of the latest anthropological and historical research on the topics. We then revisit the theme of resistance. Pointing to its critiques, we contextualize these as part of a larger skepticism that followed the resistance boom in anthropology in the 1990s. Beyond resistance, we point to the relevance of studies that have explored issues of identity building via mimetic processes and the associated integration of foreign elements into local cosmologies and political organizations. We then review anthropological research on state formation and its potential for the analysis of colonial contexts. A significant proportion of these approaches employ Foucauldian themes such as governmentality and bio-power, while others reveal an interest in the imaginary dimensions of the state. Here, we propose that an additional focus on mimesis and imitation can open up new avenues for understanding colonial state formations and their regimes of governmentality, especially as regards the vulnerable, partial, and contested nature of state imaginaries and governance practices.

Mimesis, Colonialism, and 'the Primitive'

From Plato's and Aristotle's original formulations to contemporary developments in literary theory, psychology, social theory, evolutionary biology, social anthropology, and so forth, many have fed on the prolific literature and intellectual debates regarding mimesis since the classical age.[1] Beyond the classical applications of the mimesis concept in the arts and aesthetics, this extensive scholarship has signaled the wide-ranging applicability of mimetic theorizing in contemporary thought, drawing attention to the social, cultural, and political implications of mimesis as a human activity. The ideas of mimesis, mimicry, and imitation share a common genealogy and an overlapping problematic. Although Patrice Ladwig's final contribution examines the at times diverging genealogies of these concepts, and each term has evolved at times distinctly over time, we believe that it is most productive to conceptualize these terms in a Wittgensteinian sense as being marked by a 'family resemblance' beyond hierarchical taxonomies (see Wittgenstein [1953] 2001: §66–§71); or, as Gebauer and Wulf (1995: 309) influentially suggest, they can be treated as a connected whole—as a "thematic complex."[2] Over time, this 'thematic complex' has accumulated a historical and conceptual depth that leaves one gasping for breath. It first enters central philosophical discussions in Greek antiquity, then penetrates Roman models of rhetoric. During the Renaissance it becomes revitalized and transformed as *imitatio*—to remain dominant in studies of art and literature for centuries. Mimesis also took on an unprecedented importance in the critical theory of modernity (Horkheimer and Adorno [1944] 2002) and later on in approaches to media and simulacra (Baudrillard 1994). Together with the imitation and the copy, it remains a reference in contemporary discussions surrounding digital copies, copyright, and authenticity (Ribeiro 2013). Even if according to Lempert (2014: 380) mimesis and imitation are rarely addressed explicitly within anthropological theory, the universe of meanings and applications surrounding them attests that as concepts they continue to spur innovative approaches (see Walker 2010; Willerslev 2007: 9–27).[3] We can here merely allude to the long trajectory of mimesis within Western intellectual traditions, but we nevertheless think that this brief account speaks to its intellectually variable, sometimes subterranean, yet rich condition as a conceptual and thematic complex.

Theories of Mimesis in Colonial History

In examining the distinct conceptual histories and changing historical semantics behind the terms that compose this thematic complex, we consider it important to emphasize the imprint of colonial history on the contents of theories of mimesis themselves. Both as human phenomena and as analytical categories, mimesis and colonialism share a long common history inscribed into the asymmetric power relationships of colonial encounters. Since the Renaissance, but especially since the Enlightenment, European intellectual traditions have come to devalue existing notions of imitation as socially and epistemologically uncreative.[4] Renaissance writers saw imitation as a central concept, but not as original and creative behavior. Instead, as in Cervantes's *Don Quixote*, imitation became a topic for parodies of outdated mechanical behavior (Foucault [1966] 1994: 46–48). In colonial discourse, we believe that a similar procedure was at work and that the Enlightenment, with its self-proclaimed rationality, intensified this semantic shift. Accordingly, colonial reports, travel accounts, and early ethnographies often described the mechanical, non-innovative, and fake character of imitative acts among 'primitives' and colonial subjects. Imitation thus gained negative connotations and became associated, for example, with the behavior of 'uncivilized' and 'primitive' colonial subjects. In that way, the presence of allegedly irrational imitative practices also legitimized the exercise of colonial rule by agents coming from (Western) societies that proclaimed to have freed themselves from imitation, societies that with the coming of the Enlightenment saw themselves leaving imitation behind, progressing toward innovation and rationality (Ladwig 2017). Therefore, although not always acknowledged, the development of Western theories of mimesis has also been intertwined with colonialism and with the new cross-cultural connections brought into being by the overseas expansion of European influence since the sixteenth century.

Intensified contact with distinct cultures confronted Europeans with alternative forms of mimesis as practice and as concept. A clear example is the meeting of European self-professed rationality and materialism with the 'primitivism' of

indigenous magical systems. James Frazer's famous classical theory of 'sympathetic magic' set out in the last decades of the nineteenth century is exemplary
of this point. Frazer's viewpoint was grounded on a pejorative evolutionary
imagery of 'primitive imitation'. "Magic is a spurious system of natural law,"
Frazer (1894: 39) concluded, "as well as a fallacious guide of conduct; it is a
false science as well as an abortive art." Later anthropological accounts written during the colonial period were at times more balanced, but nevertheless
exposed a tendency to exoticize imitation and magic as properties of the 'primitive'. Lucien Lévy-Bruhl's (1935) concepts of 'primitive mentality' and 'mystical
participation' assumed that imitation was at the heart of cognitive and cultural
differences between scientific rationality and pre-logical systems of thinking. He
reasoned that, in 'primitive societies', "the reality of the similitude is of the same
kind as the original—that is, essentially mystic" (ibid.: 52). European theories
of mimesis also came to incorporate these imageries of primitive magic. Walter
Benjamin's (1935) writings on mimesis, for example, were partially inspired by
his readings of Lévy-Bruhl. In primitive ritual, madness, drug-induced states of
mind, and surrealist art, Benjamin ([1933] 1986) saw creative possibilities for
the return of mimetic capacities that, in his view, were already lost in modern
society. The ambivalence of 'primitive mimesis', located between rejection and
redemption, is also present in Lévi-Strauss's (1961) encounter with the Nambikwaras' appropriation of writing. His description is a good example of the
sense of uncanniness that 'primitive' mimetic behavior could invoke among
Europeans. The Nambikwaras' imitative behavior irritated and haunted him,
making him feel "tormented by th[e] absurd incident" and giving him a bad
night of sleep (ibid.: 290).

Anthropology's entanglement with colonialism and its forms of power, government, and knowledge has been a subject of constant critical reflection within
the discipline since the 1970s (e.g., Asad 1973, 1991; Cohn 1996; Dirks 1993;
Pels and Salemink 1994, 1999; Stocking 1991; Stoler 2002; Thomas 1994). The
notions of 'discourse' and 'representation' have figured importantly in this literature, notably increasing in the wake of Edward Said's (1978) classic study
Orientalism. Said's arguments and subsequent post-colonial literary approaches
to colonial discourse have been criticized for reductionist overemphasis on text
and representation.[5] Anthropological approaches to colonialism, in contrast, call
for a thicker ethnographic understanding of both the textual and material aspects
of colonialism and its inner fractures, struggles, contradictions, resistances, and
negotiations (e.g., Pels and Salemink 1999; Stoler and Cooper 1997). Literary
understandings of mimesis—including that of Said (2003), an admirer of Auerbach's (1953) classic work *Mimesis*—see it straightforwardly as little more than
a synonym for image and representation. However, it should be clear at this
point that our heuristic focus on mimesis encompasses a broad range of social,
cultural, and political practices, material as well as textual. The very notion of

mimesis, as Gebauer and Wulf (1995) rightly observe, is not limited to issues of representation. Hence, to reduce the study of colonial mimesis to mental or literary imageries would but repeat the pitfalls of colonial discourse analysis. In contrast, we suggest that the anthropology of colonialism's embroilment with mimetic action and ideas requires a flexible heuristics, with a view to capturing the manifold modes of mimesis making in practice.

Following this sustained wave of critical studies, various themes related to mimesis, mimicry, and imitation have also been approached from the perspective of their inscription into colonial processes. However, rarely have these studies articulated reflections on mimesis with consideration of the colonial state and its forms of governmentality. In the context of an anthropology of colonial rule, the chapters collected herein point toward the significance of studying colonialism as a political field of cross-cultural mimetic relations. To lay focus on mimesis allows one to further explore the hypothesis that colonialism is not equal to 'Western culture'—that it is not merely a case of the imposition of external (Western) models on (indigenous) local realities, but rather a complex relational process of mutual exchanges and struggles from which "alternative governmentalities," in Peter Pels's (1997: 177) suggestive words, can come into being. The current collection builds on these insights, challenging anthropologists of colonialism to think beyond 'Western governmentality' itself. It illuminates the fact that, in several circumstances, colonialism's 'alternative governmentalities' resulted from generative engagements with indigenous rather than European models. Colonial state building could rest on mimetic interactions with autochthonous cultures that did not flow simply from the colonizer to the colonized; often they could take a reverse direction. Moreover, indigenous agents could turn the imitation of European government structures to their own political purposes, thereby transforming and sometimes even subverting colonial intentions. Looking at the colonial state from the angle of mimesis requires one to discard descriptions of colonial governmentality under the category of 'Western' alone. For governmentality, we hypothesize, became colonial to the extent that it surrendered itself to, or was appropriated by, what was local and indigenous—to the extent that self-referential ideas of 'Western' and 'European' were partially or even integrally abandoned.

As Roque (2014, 2015a) has argued more extensively elsewhere, anthropological and historical literature on mimesis and colonialism has explored the insights of mimetic theory principally within and across three related themes: indigenous resistance and anti-colonialism; the making of identity and alterity in colonial encounters and post-colonial relationships; and, finally (although secondarily), theories and practices of colonization and cross-imperial relations. By and large, however, debates about colonial power and forms of government during the last decades have theorized imitative practices as expressions of anti-colonial resistance and subversion. Although acknowledging the importance of these approaches, the present volume intends to take a step further. In particular, we propose to reassess the potentials of mimesis with regard to the most cherished topics in anthropologically informed studies of colonialism: the colonial state, its forms of governmentality, and its practices for ruling *other* peoples overseas.

Beyond Mimesis as Resistance and Subversion

The concepts of mimicry and imitation have been central to post-colonial studies and the study of anti-colonial resistance. Frantz Fanon's (1965) critique of the desire for the imitation of Europe in his concluding remarks of *The Wretched of the Earth* is an early instance of the centrality of the imitation trope in anti-colonial thought. Later, the concept of 'colonial mimicry' took one of its most distinctive turns in the work of literary critic Homi Bhabha. In a widely cited article, Bhabha (1984) conceptualized colonial mimicry as an ambivalent process through which colonial authority can be subverted and resisted. Although Bhabha's emphasis on subversive mimicry was widely criticized due to its crude textual reductionism, it resonated strongly with a growing interest in social and cultural anthropology in the counter-hegemonic nature of imitation as a form of 'cultural resistance' to colonialism. In the wake of Jean Rouch's (1955) fascinating and controversial ethnographic film *Les maîtres fous* (The Mad Masters), anthropologist Paul Stoller (1984) influentially interpreted the Hauka movement in West Africa as a 'horrific comedy' (see also Henley 2006; Taussig 1993). Later, Stoller (1995: 90) rearticulated and refined his interpretation: "The Hauka spirit possession is very much an embodied opposition to colonial rule; it was an exercise in mastery through mime."

The equation 'mimesis as resistance' became a dominant interpretive framework based on two presuppositions (see Roque 2015a): first, that mimesis and mimicry in colonial and post-colonial contexts were principally indigenous (re) actions oriented toward European models; second, that these (re)actions were meaningful—principally and almost exclusively—in the context of an emancipatory politics of cultural resistance, opposition, and criticism of colonialism. Despite this rather narrow focus, these works call attention to the subversive potentials of mimicry with regard to colonial authority. The fact that indigenous mimicries of Europeans in rituals and masquerades could be the object of special laws and prohibitions issued by state authorities not only stands as historical evidence of the disruptive and unruly nature of mimicry, but moreover allows us to shed light on the workings of the colonial state. Countermeasures such as control, regulation, prohibition, punishment, and general state surveillance procedures are important occasions for the manifestation of colonial governmentalities and the expression of (at times paranoiac) state imaginaries (but see

Dias 2005: 9; Saada 2005: 30). In this book, Kohl's chapter on carnival in colonial Guinea-Bissau offers a further example of state anxieties surrounding indigenous masquerades. Kohl observes how, throughout the twentieth century, the Portuguese colonial government showed discomfort with African parodies of colonial authorities, to the point of occasionally issuing legal instructions to regulate the (mis)use of Portuguese costumes and state uniforms in local carnivals. Interestingly, such accounts of the colonial regulation of mimesis seem to echo Plato's (1992) early call for the policing of mimesis by the state. In his *Republic*, uncontrolled and 'chaotic' mimesis is seen critically and is subject to control by the guardians of the *polis* (ibid.: books 2, 3; see also Gebauer and Wulf 1995: 25–30).

Later critiques of resistance studies led to shifts in favor of more nuanced and ethnographically informed readings (see Ortner 1995, 2016). Concerning imitation in particular, these critiques call attention to the wider complexity of cultural meanings behind mimetic ritual performances and other appropriations. Indeed, indigenous imitations of Europeans can be seen as productive and positive modes of incorporation, which are meaningful in relatively autonomous cultural terms, beyond political opposition (see Trajano Filho 2006). In the wake of these critiques, emerging work at the juncture of anthropology and history has explored mimesis as a concept that illuminates dynamics of identity and alterity in colonial and post-colonial contexts (e.g., Ferguson 2002).

Looking beyond mimesis as merely a form of resistance, anthropologist Michael Taussig (1987, 1993) opened up new paths for an alternative conceptualization of mimesis as a constitutive aspect of colonial power.[6] Seeking inspiration in Benjamin ([1933] 1986), Horkheimer and Adorno ([1944] 2002), and Frazer (1894), Taussig sees colonial mimesis as associated with a reciprocal magical mastery of the powers of alterity. His insights on mimesis as a forceful instance of colonial terror and violence reveal that, rather than serving merely to resist, counter, or disrupt colonial power, mimesis is also a European activity that can act productively on the workings of colonialism. "In the colonial mode of production of reality, as in the Putumayo," Taussig (1987: 134) observes, "such mimesis occurs by a colonial mirroring of otherness that reflects back onto the colonists the barbarity of their own social relations, but as imputed to the savagery they yearn to colonize." As a recent study argues (Roque 2015b), and as Ladwig's, Roque's and Saraiva's chapters in this book further explore, Taussig's work can be used for developing new readings of the history and anthropology of mimesis and the colonial state.

Indigenous Appropriations of the Outsider State

As much as they call for an (always incomplete) quest for similarity, mimetic processes involve a dynamic of differentiation and individuation. As an indigenous praxis, the imitation of colonial outsiders can express a transformative desire for difference and individuation. Consequently, more than simply being a gauge of anti-colonial resistance, mimesis can be approached as modes of performing identities through appropriation of the foreign Otherness of colonizing Europeans (Walker 2010; see also Harrison 2006: 38–64). These insights can be usefully explored in the context of indigenous forms of political authority. The necessary reference to an initial 'outside' and its subsequent incorporation through processes of imitation plays a crucial role in larger political arenas, their imaginaries and foundation mythologies. A focus on the sources of political authority and state formation in indigenous polities—in pre-colonial, but also in colonial and post-colonial periods—is thus crucial. In parts of Asia, the Pacific, and Africa, the creation of political authority was often based on modes of incorporation and usurpation of outsider or foreign models and resources. The 'stranger-king' theme exemplarily postulates that order, vitality, and indeed the establishment of political units need an impetus from the outside. The imitation of colonial intruders (and other foreigners) played a central role in the formation of political authority. As Marshall Sahlins (2008: 189) puts it: "During the early colonial period in Polynesia, local ruling chiefs became stranger-kings—by assuming foreign identities. This tactic of taking on the personae of European greats was practiced particularly by ambitious chiefs who could not claim by ancestry the authority to which they now aspired by power and wealth—through means largely acquired in trade with the foreigners they were pleased to imitate" (see also Candea and da Col 2012: S7; Hocart 1953: 82–86).

This emphasis on the significance of mimesis in the formation of Asian, Pacific, and African indigenous polities has rarely been extended to an analysis of indigenous polities under European colonial rule. Some studies are just beginning to examine the roles of mimesis and mimicry as analytical concepts in the context of indigenous state formation, political organization, and national identity in Africa and Asia after decolonization (see, e.g., Hoehne 2009: 259). In the context of mainland Southeast Asia, Oliver Tappe's chapter in this collection serves as an example of the movement of scholarship in this direction (see also Jonsson 2010). Tappe reflects on the historical role of mimetic interactions with colonial rulers in shaping indigenous minorities' political formations in the peripheral Lao-Vietnamese highlands of colonial Indochina. Importantly, Tappe moves beyond a simplistic reading within the resistance idiom. Subtly using the notion of 'mimesis', he formulates a critique of James Scott's (2009) sweeping argument that Southeast Asian highland societies are fleeing the state. The highland societies discussed in Tappe's chapter can be seen to expose features of what Pierre Clastres (1987) has labeled 'societies against the state'. Yet the mimesis of outsider states explored by Tappe also points to the diversity of outcomes of mimetic processes, far beyond a mere tendency to avoid the state (see also Tappe 2015).

The shift from resistance to identity has led to more nuanced and sophis-ticated interpretations of indigenous imitative appropriations of modernity, outsider states, and colonial rule more broadly. Still, many of these approaches tend to follow a definition of colonial mimicry as indigenous actions of rep-etition (or representation) of European (or other) foreign models. Concep-tual developments of mimesis, identity, and alterity should also be extended beyond 'native' mimicries in order to explore European imitative practices in imperial and colonial settings. Through this orientation, imitation can also be approached as a faculty of the European colonizer—as a meaningful dimension of the praxis of colonization. Several studies, including Saraiva's contribution to this volume, have already proposed that European colonialisms and forms of state rule have developed over time through the imitation of each other (cf. Adelman 2015; Eskildsen 2002; Fuchs 2001). Complementarily, Europeans in the colonies can become mimetic agents, active subjects of imitative behavior, rather than just objects of and models for indigenous reproduction. Imitating indigenous worlds was a practical possibility that, in spite of its risks, could in certain circumstances result in political benefits. In reshaping the authority and administration of the colonial regime, indigenous societies—their states and forms of rule—could become models for colonizing strategies.[7]

Mimesis and the Colonial State

By the mid-nineteenth century, 'modern' statehood and the nation-state had already become a 'naturalized' characteristic of most European powers at home. However, these forms and features of the state were largely absent in the colonies. At the same time, this absence or partialness of statehood also served to legitimate the expansive drive of colonial rule, especially beyond coastal areas. Fueled by eighteenth-century ideologies, statehood was consid-ered a crucial marker of civilization. As Hegel ([1837] 1956: 39) expressed it: "The Universal is to be found in the State, in its laws, its universal and rational arrangements." Following from this axiom, Hegel proposed that "the State is the Divine Idea as it exists on Earth" (ibid.). From this viewpoint, societies that had weak centralized structures, or were organized around acephalous principles (like segmentary societies) (Sigrist 1994), were understood to be entrapped in a state of nature. As victims of a sort of 'Hobbesian war', they had to be pacified and integrated into the state. In the words of historian Eric Hobsbawm (1994: 46), this type of alleged socio-political barbarism was con-ceptualized as "the reversal of what we may call the project of the eighteenth-century Enlightenment, namely the establishment of a universal system of such rules and standards of moral behaviour, embodied in the institutions of states dedicated to the rational progress of humanity." Hence, established on these visions, the colonial *mission civilisatrice* was also a mission toward state for-mation—and specifically toward the creation of states that, in principle, were primarily to become replicas (or extensions) of Western states.

However, these ideals and discourses could be seen to contribute little to the practical management of colonial subjects. A regular 'problem' many colo-nial authorities encountered was the lack of functional, centralized institutions and of bureaucratic staff capable of implementing in the colonies forms of ruling deemed to be equivalent to European or metropolitan administrations. Informed by visions of modern bureaucratic states, colonial administrators were frequently unable to simply replicate these European models. In practice, in fact, European states in their colonies often had to turn to the resources at hand. Already existent and functioning indigenous forms of power, intelligence gather-ing, and authority were crucial resources that could be imitated or appropriated (see Bayly 1996). Early modern imperial formations give evidence that these entanglements were intentionally procured. In many cases, when late-colonial European states actually sought to extend territorial control, such pragmatism came to the fore.

In addition to these practical considerations, it is crucial to mention that imitation as an interpretive framework occupied an important place in colonial epistemologies. Imitation was an essential tool for thinking through norms of social and intercultural behavior in the colonies, but it was also relevant in wider debates on colonial policy and sciences, especially from the nineteenth century onward (see Bastos, this volume; Grandmaison 2009; Roque 2015b; Saada 2005; Singaravélou 2011). Whether or not they were consciously making use of notions of imitation, colonial administrators could pragmatically and parasitically look to local structures and indigenous realities as examples and models for establishing their own peculiar forms of rule—especially in backwa-ter settings, where reliance on local resources became critical for the survival of the usually fragile and isolated 'white' colonial communities (Roque 2010a, 2010b). It should come as no surprise, therefore, that colonial states—espe-cially but not exclusively in these circumstances—often built their effective power mimetically on indigenous foundations and might therefore take the character of what we designate as states of imitation.

Contributions in this volume attest to the fact that the fragility of colonial states in general lends itself to intersections between mimesis and government. This focus is particularly present in the chapters by Bastos, Kohl, and Roque, all of which emphasize the significance of colonial vulnerability in prompting a productive endorsement of mimesis either as an object of control and regulation or as a calculated political strategy of government. In such contexts, the colonial state at times shifted to locations in cultural and social space that were very far from expected European referents. Like the stranger-kings mentioned before, colonial rule could seek its foundations beyond the replication of European statecraft and norms, in realms that pertained to the perceived Otherness of local and indigenous structures. Mimesis, in other words, was integral to the decentered location of the colonial state—an issue that the anthropology of the state has only recently begun to tackle.

Locating the (Colonial) State

The elusiveness of the presence of the 'state' in much anthropological research reveals the difficulties of addressing it as an analytical entity, especially outside Western societies. *A priori* Western imageries of modern statehood, as mentioned above, possibly hindered recognition of the 'state' as an effective empirical object in colonial contexts and in societies outside Europe (cf. Abrams 1988; Asad 1973: 105–106; Radcliffe-Brown 1940: xxiii). Yet since the 1990s, the anthropology of the state has undergone an unprecedented and ongoing renaissance, from which the study of the colonial state has also been benefiting (see Reeves 2014; Sharma and Gupta 2006; Thelen et al. 2015). Recent approaches in anthropology describe the state as more than simply a rational centralized entity that is limited to taxing and conscripting populations and monopolizing legitimate violence within a given territory—as, for example, in Max Weber's (1978) classical account. In addition, recent perspectives also emphasize the state's multiple, competing, and contradictory features (Comaroff 1998; Ferguson and Gupta 2002). The state is constantly created through practices and discourses, performed in institutions and bureaucracies, that end up impinging on the everyday lives of its subjects and their perceptions of it (Gupta 2012; Hull 2012). Although dispersed into diversified fields and actors, the state can often appear as if it were a single entity. Following Foucault's plea for exploring the micro-politics of rule, Timothy Mitchell (1991: 94) proposes that the state "should be examined not as an actual structure, but as the powerful, metaphysical effect of practices that make such structures appear to exist." Other approaches point to the significance of state imaginaries (Hansen and Stepputat 2001; Kapferer 2005) and to the fantasies and emotions of state subjects (Aretxaga 2003; Navaro-Yashin 2002) that can find their expression in narratives and rumors (Gupta 2005; Ladwig 2013). Despite their heterogeneity, these recent approaches have in common an emphasis on state formation as an ongoing, never complete process marked by conflict, power negotiations, and efforts to establish order in a more or less clearly defined territory (Krohn-Hansen and Nustad 2005a: 4).

These points have been developed in dialogue with colonial history. Hansen and Stepputat (2001), for instance, actually argue that only a dialogue with colonial history can shed light on contemporary and post-colonial processes, while also alluding to the relevance of imitation in this context. "Instead of seeing state formation in the postcolonial world as a flawed imitation of a mature Western form," they write, "we need to disaggregate and historicize how the idea of the modern state became universalized and how modern forms of governance have proliferated throughout the world" (ibid.: 6; cf. Stoler and Cooper 1997: 32). This calls attention to the fact that the 'diffusion' of Western values and state models in colonial contexts drew not so much on mechanical and dualistic ideas of imitation but instead on more complex mimetic processes. The material of mimetic processes, as Lempert (2014: 386) notes, does not "come from just two things called original and copy, but rather from a highly distributed assemblage of signs." Be it in the domain of a citizen's subjectivity or of larger state institutions, reproductions are not simple copies of one pre-existing 'whole', but an assemblage of fragments that become appropriated and translated into different contexts. Mimetic strategies can emerge in a variety of places, but they are likely to have very different and unpremeditated outcomes. Therefore, one way of tackling the challenge of the 'diffusion' of Western states might be to explore the fragmented nature of imitation by looking at the bits and pieces that are extracted from a 'model' and seeing how they are again transformed through a variety of local practices and state imaginaries. Such kinds of evocative states of imitation—in the double sense of the word as a situation and as a form of political rule and collective social organization—are therefore always changing and inherently unstable. Oliver Tappe's chapter in this collection provides an excellent example of this point. By taking a perspective that resonates with the recent emphasis on the fragility and contested sovereignty of the state, Tappe shows how the multiplicity of starkly differing and competing state models (French, Lao, Vietnamese, and those of state-building ethnic minorities) can also imply a creative and unexpected cross-fertilization of imitative processes of state making in peripheral areas.

The chapters on mimesis, colonialism, and the state contained in this volume work through, and disturb, these recent streams of scholarship on the state from two main directions. On the one hand, they articulate a growing and solid focus on issues of state governmentality and biopolitics. On the other hand, they express an emerging concern with the relationships between the state and forms of imagination and affect. In both instances, we propose to employ mimesis as a crucial conceptual supplement in order to enhance discussions on the state and its colonial manifestations.

Governmentality, Biopolitics, and State Imaginaries

Much of the literature on state formation and rule has taken its inspiration from Michel Foucault's (2007) notion of governmentality. In general, the concept can on a simple level be described as the 'art of government' (ibid.:

87–114). However, throughout his career Foucault developed an increasingly complex notion of governmentality that encompasses the institutions, the (micro-)processes, and the strategies and forms of analysis that are employed for the management of the state, its population, and the economy (ibid.: 108–110; see also Dean 2004: 9–39; Lemke 2011). Foucault virtually ignored colonialism in his entire oeuvre. Yet as Stoler (1995: 1) observes: "No single analytic framework has saturated the field of colonial studies so completely over the last decade as that of Foucault." In fact, the impact of Foucault's approaches seems to have been more prominent in the historical study of colonial states than in the study of their coeval 'non-colonial' counterparts (see Pels 1997).[8] Despite the rich mass of studies already produced, the topic continues to attract scholars of colonialism, and innovative ideas continue to emerge. Nevertheless, the lack of an explicit combination of mimetic theory with notions of governmentality represents a gap that the chapters assembled in this collection aim to address.

Inspired by Foucault's work, Paul Rabinow (1989: 289) has argued that colonies often constituted laboratories "of experimentation for new arts of government capable of bringing a modern and healthy society into being." New policies could first be tested in the colonies and later applied, in modified form, 'at home', for example, in relation to surveys and population censuses (Cohn 1987; Hacking 1990). The travel of technologies and concepts from the colonies to the metropole points to another striking connection between imita-tion, colonialism, and state formation. European colonies could themselves become experimental hubs in their own right: they could be the origin for the development of new power technologies and the creation of new forms of state governance. The results could later be reused and replicated back in metropoli-tan settings. In this vein, in an article that gained from exchanges with authors in this collection, Roque (2015b) merges perspectives from governmentality studies and imitation to propose the notion of 'mimetic governmentality' as a broader conceptual framework for the combined study of mimesis and govern-ment (see also Ladwig 2011). Roque (2015b: 69) suggests that we have to take into account "the theories, techniques, and tactics concerned with the 'gov-ernment of others' whose underlying principle of action is the incorporation and reproduction of the perceived Otherness of so-called 'native' or 'primitive' populations, with a view to rule and conduct their existence." This point is developed further in Roque's contribution to this book, calling attention to mimesis as regards also the government of the colonial self. In this sense, colonial mimetic governmentality not only could engineer societies but also could enter the private lives of its subjects—including the very lives of colonial agents of the state. Roque argues that imitative interactions with indigenous social forms entailed a dangerous potential for disarranging European boundar-ies of identity and selfhood. However, they also represented an advantageous point for the colonial state, one from which colonial rulers could exert a sort of parasitic colonial command of indigenous worlds.

This volume offers further original and productive engagements with the significance of mimesis for colonial governmentality, exploring, for example, its comparative dimensions. Research on colonial governmentality has signaled its heterogeneous and localized features (cf. Pels 1997: 176, see also D. Scott 1995: 193). We certainly recognize the validity of this argument, but we also think that one should consider comparatively the circulatory and cross-colonial nature of governmentality.[9] In this context, a focus on mimesis can become one way of conceptually approaching how in different places colonial state regimes could produce (or aim at producing) similar, and therefore comparable, outcomes. In his contribution, Tiago Saraiva makes clear that, in order to understand the violent histories of colonial mimesis in the Angolan backland, one needs to consider the Portuguese and German white settler colonialisms as a connected ensemble. In a similar vein, Patrice Ladwig's chapter makes use of the comparative potential of imitation in colonial government, alluding to the translocal character of French colonial politics. Ladwig shows how architects working for the École française d'Extrême-Orient actually implemented very similar architectural policies in the colonies of Indochina and North Africa. Several of the architects working on the renovation of Buddhist monuments in Laos had been posted to Morocco before then. In both countries, their work contributed to the material revitalization of indigenous forms of governance within the colonial state and the French 'politics of association'. Although the places and results differed, the French colonial regime was able to use these building works as an affective strategy that aimed at pacifying colonial subjects.

Like Ladwig's contribution, Tiago Saraiva's analysis of the model 'native neighborhood' for African shepherds and Cristiana Bastos's study of hut-hospitals in Mozambique in Angola signal a similar drive toward the affective dimension of colonial governmentality, occurring at a cross-colonial level in Portuguese Africa. In the early twentieth century, the architectural design of colonial hospitals in the Portuguese African colonies revealed—similarly to the colonial 'indigenous neighborhoods' that mimicked 'native' housing, as examined by Saraiva—a sort of predatory mimicry within biopolitics, a mode of state rationality oriented toward enrolling and seducing 'native populations' into colonial health networks through the creation of replicas of indigenous housing. Employing Foucault's notion of biopolitics, Bastos argues that special hut hospitals "were designed as fenced compounds with a main building and a variable number of smaller, hut-like constructions." As such, they have to be understood as "an exercise of power in the governance of life, or, in other words, as a technique of colonial biopower." Imitation is here aimed at integrating the population step by step into a health system that is at the same time part of a larger biopolitical colonial order created to keep the body politic and its workforce effective—a point that can be usefully articulated with Mitchell's (2006) readings of the state as emerging via repetition in closed social spaces, or with David Arnold's (1993) approach to colonial medicine as a form of power knowledge within institutional enclaves.

Tiago Saraiva's contribution to this volume expands the notion of a colonial biopolitical order further into the realm of human-animal relations. Saraiva persuasively argues that the colonial governmentality of human populations (both of 'white settlers' and 'natives') in Angola implied the government of non-human animals. As the author writes, "The breeding of the Karakul sheep was meant to reproduce Portuguese settlers." Karakul sheep were inextricably interconnected with settlers' lives. This colonial society of people and animals thus mirrored the social worlds formed by African nomad shepherds attached to their herds of oxen. "The life of the white settlers in the colonial reservation of Karakul," Saraiva observes, "was no less organized in the function of animal breeding than the life of the Kuvale tribe with their herds of oxen."

Beyond Foucauldian-oriented approaches, an emphasis on state imaginaries has also been a characteristic of recent literature on the state. For instance, anthropologist Bruce Kapferer (2005: ix) has stated that the "reality of the state is to be grasped ethnographically both in its imaginary and in the concreteness of practices that have a state relation or reference" (see also Thelen et al. 2015). The imaginary, far from just being a fantasy, is here conceptualized as a kind of horizon, a matrix for decisions and expectations that is therefore socially effective (see Castoriadis [1975] 2005: 160–165 ; Taylor 2002: 106).[10] In Ladwig's chapter we find a good example of how a political imaginary produced by imitation that mainly works with the 'symbolic' and its underpinnings in Buddhist cosmology can become an effective means of colonial statecraft and create a temporary, yet powerful, state imaginary representing the French as sponsors of Buddhism. French Orientalists were thus probably aware that imitation also figured prominently in Southeast Asian indigenous polities (cf. Tambiah 1985: 266).

Conclusion

Mimesis and colonialism, as both human phenomena and analytical categories, share a long history. Nonetheless, the reciprocal significance of the concepts of mimesis and colonialism has only recently been addressed. Both as a theory and as a practice, mimesis was constitutive of colonial history during the five centuries of European imperial expansionism. It became one relevant mode of relating between Europeans and non-Europeans in colonial encounters, while after decolonization it continued to be constitutive of the transits between Africa, Asia, Europe, America, and Oceania. The concrete processes and practices through which indigenous people could appropriate and imitate (and potentially subvert) the colonial foreigners have become a fertile area of anthropological study. Yet, this volume argues, it is time for anthropologists, historians, and students of colonialism in general to turn the concept away from the colonized and back onto the colonizers themselves. The mimetic faculty, for long ascribed crudely to the 'primitive', we suggest, is in reality constitutive of modern forms of colonial state government.

Mimesis and imitation are discussed here in relation to several specific scenarios of colonialism and the state. But state building, rule, and governmentality are not limited to colonial contexts. They refer to historical and social phenomena of wider relevance. As such, the studies herein may also help the analysis of forms of state rule and power relations that are beyond the scope of modern Western colonialism. Of course, contemporary aspects of governance relating to neo-liberalism, security apparatuses, law, risk, and new technological forms of biopower, for example, are not the same as the ones discussed in this volume. However, we believe that these are scenarios where the complicities between mimesis and state rule can also be put to analytical test. It is therefore our hope that the essays in this volume will inspire further research, not only on the manifold dimensions of colonialism and its states of imitation, but on the general mimetic character of power and governance as well.

Patrice Ladwig studied social anthropology and sociology and obtained his PhD from the University of Cambridge. He has worked at the University of Bristol, the Max Planck Institute for Social Anthropology, and the University of Zurich. His work focuses on the anthropology of Buddhism (Laos and Thailand), death and funeral cultures, colonialism, the link of religion to communist movements, and general social theory. He currently works at the Max Planck Institute for the Study of Religious and Ethnic Diversity and carries out research on economic modernization, religion, and ethics in the context of the Max Planck Cambridge Centre for the Study of Ethics, Human Economy and Social Change. E-mail: ladwig@mmg.mpg.de

Ricardo Roque is a Research Fellow at the Institute of Social Sciences at the University of Lisbon (Instituto de Ciências Sociais da Universidade de Lisboa). He is also an Honorary Associate in the Department of History at the University of Sydney. He works on the history and anthropology of colonialism, human sciences, and cross-cultural contact in the Portuguese-speaking world from 1800 to the twentieth century. He has published widely in Portuguese and English on the history of physical anthropology and colonial encounters in East Timor, Goa (India), and Angola. He has also published on the theory and ethnography of colonial archives. He is the author of *Headhunting and Colonialism* (2010) and co-editor of *Engaging Colonial Knowledge* (2012), *Crossing Histories and Ethnographies* (2019), *Lusotropicalism and Its Discontents* (2019), and *Resistance and Colonialism* (2019). E-mail: ricardo.roque@ics.ulisboa.pt

Notes

1. For literary theory, see Auerbach (1953); for a more synthetic approach, see Spariosu (1984). In philosophy and the human sciences more widely, Wulf (2014), Gebauer and Wulf (1995), Melberg (1995), and especially Potolsky (2006) explore the genesis and application of the concept through different historical periods. For approaches in anthropology, see Dias (2005), Taussig (1993), and Walker (2010: chap. 1). For theories of imitation and mimesis in psychology and the natural sciences, Donald (2005) and Garrels (2011) provide good overviews.

2. For approaches that differentiate between these terms and concepts mainly according to grades of intentionality and reflexivity, see, for example, Spariosu (1984: 33) and Donald (2005: 286).

3. For a classical approach to these concepts, see Tarde (1903); for new developments, see Candea (2010).

4. The translation of mimesis into the Latin *imitatio* emphasizes the mechanical and 'fake' character of mimesis that, according to Halliwell (2002: 13), has become a dominant connotation.

5. See Roque and Wagner (2012) for an analysis of Said's positions.

6. For critiques of Taussig's works, see Baud (1997) and Huggan (1997).

7. For a discussion on the differences between strategy (based on structures of power, institutions, and knowledge) and tactics as potential subversion in the sense of Michel de Certeau (1984), see Tappe's chapter in this volume.

8. For studies on colonial governmentality, see Bennett et al. (2014), Kalpagam (2014), Legg (2007), and Lemke (2001).

9. This also resonates with Gabriel Tarde's (1903) application of imitation to empire making and colonialism. Tarde understood colonization as the product of repetition transplanted into a variety of locations (ibid.: 217–224; see also Toscano 2007: 603–604).

10. Strauss (2006) has unpacked various concepts and ideas surrounding the use of the term 'imaginary' in anthropology. See also Axel (2002a: 248–253; 2002b: 25) for a novel account of the imaginary in historical anthropology.

References

Abrams, Philip. 1988. "Notes on the Difficulty of Studying the State (1977)." *Journal of Historical Sociology* 1 (1): 58–89.

Adelman, Jeremy. 2015. "Mimesis and Rivalry: European Empires and Global Regimes." *Journal of Global History* 10 (1): 77–98.

Aretxaga, Begoña. 2003. "Maddening States." *Annual Review of Anthropology* 32: 393–410.

Arnold, David. 1993. *Colonizing the Body: State Medicine and Epidemic Disease in Nineteenth-Century India.* Berkeley: University of California Press.

Asad, Talal. 1973. "Two European Images of Non-European Rule." In *Anthropology and the Colonial Encounter,* ed. Talal Asad, 103–119. New York: Humanities Press.

Asad, Talal. 1991. "Afterword: From the History of Colonial Anthropology to the Anthropology of Western Hegemony." In Stocking 1991, 314–324.

Auerbach, Erich. 1953. *Mimesis: The Representation of Reality in Western Literature.* Princeton, NJ: Princeton University Press.

Axel, Brian Keith. 2002a. "Fantastic Community." In Axel 2002b, 233–266.

Axel, Brian Keith, ed. 2002b. *From the Margins: Historical Anthropology and Its Futures.* Durham, NC: Duke University Press.

Baud, Michiel. 1997. "Imagining the Other: Michael Taussig on Mimesis, Colonialism and Identity." *Critique of Anthropology* 17 (1): 103–112.

Baudrillard, Jean. 1994. *Simulacra and Simulation.* Trans. Sheila F. Glaser. Ann Arbor: University of Michigan Press.

Bayly, C. A. 1996. *Empire and Information: Intelligence Gathering and Social Communication in India, 1780–1870.* Cambridge: Cambridge University Press.

Benjamin, Walter. (1933) 1986. "On the Mimetic Faculty." In *Reflections: Essays, Aphorisms, Autobiographical Writings.* Ed. Peter Demetz; trans. Edmund Jephcott, 333–336. New York: Schocken Books.

Benjamin, Walter. 1935. *Probleme der Sprachsoziologie: Ein Sammelreferat* [Problems of language sociology: A collective presentation]. http://www.textlog.de/benjamin-kritik-probleme-sprachsoziologie.html.

Bennett, Tony, Ben Dibley, and Rodney Harrison. 2014. "Introduction: Anthropology, Collecting and Colonial Governmentalities." *History and Anthropology* 25 (2): 137–149.

Bhabha, Homi. 1984. "Of Mimicry and Man: The Ambivalence of Colonial Discourse." *October* 28: 125–133.

Candea, Matei, ed. 2010. *The Social after Gabriel Tarde: Debates and Assessments.* London: Routledge.

Candea, Matei, and Giovanni da Col. 2012. "The Return to Hospitality." *Journal of the Royal Anthropological Institute* 18 (S1): S1–S19.

Castoriadis, Cornelius. (1975) 2005. *The Imaginary Institution of Society.* Trans. Kathleen Blamey. Cambridge: Polity Press.

Certeau, Michel de. 1984. *The Practice of Everyday Life.* Trans. Steven F. Rendall. Berkeley: University of California Press.

Clastres, Pierre. 1987. *Society Against the State: Essays in Political Anthropology.* Trans. Robert Hurley and Abe Stein. New York: Zone Books.

Cohn, Bernard S. 1987. *An Anthropologist among the Historians and Other Essays.* Delhi: Oxford University Press.

Cohn, Bernard S. 1996. *Colonialism and Its Forms of Knowledge: The British in India.* Princeton, NJ: Princeton University Press.

Comaroff, John L. 1998. "Reflections on the Colonial State, in South Africa and Elsewhere: Factions, Fragments, Facts and Fictions." *Social Identities* 4 (3): 321–361.

Comaroff, John L., and Jean Comaroff. 1992. *Ethnography and the Historical Imagination.* Boulder, CO: Westview Press.

Dean, Mitchell. 2004. *Governmentality: Power and Rule in Modern Society.* London: Sage.

Dias, Nélia. 2005. "Imitation et Anthropologie" [Imitation and anthropology]. *Terrain* 44 (1): 5–18.

Dirks, Nicholas B., ed. 1992. *Colonialism and Culture.* Ann Arbor: University of Michigan Press.

Dirks, Nicholas B. 1993. "Colonial Histories and Native Informants: Biography of an Archive." In *Orientalism and the Postcolonial Predicament: Perspectives on South Asia*, ed. Carol A. Breckenridge and Peter van der Veer, 279–313. Philadelphia: University of Pennsylvania Press.

Doja, Albert. 2006. "The Kind of Writing: Anthropology and the Rhetoric Reproduction of Postmodernism." *Critique of Anthropology* 26 (2): 157–180.

Donald, Merlin. 2005. "Imitation and Mimesis." In *Perspectives on Imitation.* Vol. 2: *Imitation, Human Development, and Culture*, ed. Susan Hurley and Nick Chater, 283–300. Cambridge, MA: MIT Press.

Eskildsen, Robert. 2002. "Of Civilization and Savages: The Mimetic Imperialism of Japan's 1874 Expedition to Taiwan." *American Historical Review* 107 (2): 388–418.

Fanon, Frantz. 1965. *The Wretched of the Earth.* Trans. Constance Farrington. London: MacGibbon & Kee.

Ferguson, James. 2002. "Of Mimicry and Membership: Africans and the 'New World Society.'" *Cultural Anthropology* 17 (4): 551–569.

Ferguson, James, and Akhil Gupta. 2002. "Spatializing States: Toward an Ethnography of Neoliberal Governmentality." *American Ethnologist* 29 (4): 981–1002.

Foucault, Michel. (1966) 1994. *The Order of Things: An Archaeology of the Human Sciences.* New York: Vintage Books.

Foucault, Michel. 2007. *Security, Territory, Population: Lectures at the Collège de France 1977–1978.* Trans. Graham Burchell. New York: Palgrave Macmillan.

Frazer, J. G. 1894. *The Golden Bough: A Study in Comparative Religion.* 2 vols. New York: Macmillan.

Fuchs, Barbara. 2001. *Mimesis and Empire: The New World, Islam, and European Identities.* Cambridge: Cambridge University Press.

Garrels, Scott R., ed. 2011. *Mimesis and Science: Empirical Research on Imitation and the Mimetic Theory of Culture and Religion.* East Lansing: Michigan State University Press.

Gebauer, Gunter, and Christoph Wulf. 1995. *Mimesis: Culture, Art, Society*. Trans. Don Reneau. Berkeley: University of California Press.

Geertz, Clifford. 1989. *Works and Lives: The Anthropologist as Author*. Stanford, CA: Stanford University Press.

Grandmaison, Olivier Le Cour. 2009. "De l'assimilation à la politique d'association" [From assimilation to association policy]. In *La République impériale: Politique et racisme d'État* [The imperial republic: Politics and state racism], ed. Olivier Le Cour Grandmaison, 107–211. Paris: Fayard.

Gupta, Akhil. 2005. "Narratives of Corruption: Anthropological and Fictional Accounts of the Indian State." *Ethnography* 6 (1): 5–34.

Gupta, Akhil. 2012. *Red Tape: Bureaucracy, Structural Violence, and Poverty in India*. Durham, NC: Duke University Press.

Hacking, Ian. 1990. *The Taming of Chance*. Cambridge: Cambridge University Press.

Halliwell, Stephen. 2002. *The Aesthetics of Mimesis: Ancient Texts and Modern Problems*. Princeton, NJ: Princeton University Press.

Hansen, Thomas Blom, and Finn Stepputat. 2001. "Introduction: States of Imagination." In *States of Imagination: Ethnographic Explorations of the Postcolonial State*, ed. Thomas Blom Hansen and Finn Stepputat, 1–40. Durham, NC: Duke University Press.

Harrison, Simon. 2006. *Fracturing Resemblances: Identity and Mimetic Conflict in Melanesia and the West*. New York: Berghahn Books.

Hegel, Georg F. W. (1837) 1956. *The Philosophy of History*. Trans. J. Sibree. New York: Dover Publications.

Henley, Paul. 2006. "Spirit Possession, Power, and the Absent Presence of Islam: Reviewing *Les maîtres fous*." *Journal of the Royal Anthropological Institute* 12 (4): 731–761.

Hobsbawm, Eric. 1994. "Barbarism: A User's Guide." *New Left Review* 206 (1): 44–54.

Hocart, A. M. 1953. *The Life-Giving Myth and Other Essays*. Ed. Lord Raglan. New York: Grove Press.

Hoehne, Markus V. 2009. "Mimesis and Mimicry in Dynamics of State and Identity Formation in Northern Somalia." *Africa* 79 (2): 252–281.

Horkheimer, Max, and Theodor W. Adorno. (1944) 2002. *Dialectic of Enlightenment: Philosophical Fragments*. Ed. Gunzelin S. Noerr; trans. Edmund Jephcott. Stanford, CA: Stanford University Press.

Huggan, Graham. 1997. "(Post)Colonialism, Anthropology, and the Magic of Mimesis." *Cultural Critique* 38: 91–106.

Hull, Matthew S. 2012. *Government of Paper: The Materiality of Bureaucracy in Urban Pakistan*. Berkeley: University of California Press.

Jonsson, Hjorleifur. 2010. "Mimetic Minorities: National Identity and Desire on Thailand's Fringe." *Identities* 17 (2): 108–130.

Kalpagam, U. 2014. *Rule by Numbers: Governmentality in Colonial India*. London: Lexington Books.

Kapferer, Bruce. 2005. "Foreword." In Krohn-Hansen and Nustad 2005b, vii–xi.

Krohn-Hansen, Christian, and Knut G. Nustad. 2005a. "Introduction." In Krohn-Hansen and Nustad 2005b, 3–26.

Krohn-Hansen, Christian, and Knut G. Nustad, eds. 2005b. *State Formation: Anthropological Perspectives.* London: Pluto Press.

Ladwig, Patrice. 2011. "Buddhist Relics and Mimetic Colonial Governmentality in French Laos." Paper presented at the workshop "Colonialism and Theories of Imitation," Lisbon, ICS-University Lisboa, 12–13 April.

Ladwig, Patrice. 2013. "Haunting the State: Rumours, Spectral Apparitions and the Longing for Buddhist Charisma in Laos." *Asian Studies Review* 37 (4): 509–526.

Ladwig, Patrice. 2017. "Mimetic Theories, Representation, and 'Savages': Critiques of the Enlightenment and Modernity through the Lens of Primitive Mimesis." In *The Transformative Power of the Copy: A Transcultural and Interdisciplinary Approach*, ed. Corinna Forberg and Philipp W. Stockhammer, 37–77. Heidelberg: Heidelberg University Publishing.

Legg, Stephen. 2007. *Spaces of Colonialism: Delhi's Urban Governmentalities.* Oxford: Wiley-Blackwell.

Lemke, Thomas. 2001. "The Birth of Bio-politics: Michel Foucault's Lecture at the Collège de France on Neo-Liberal Governmentality." *Economy and Society* 30 (2): 190–207.

Lemke, Thomas. 2011. *Foucault, Governmentality, and Critique.* Boulder, CO: Paradigm.

Lempert, Michael. 2014. "Imitation." *Annual Review of Anthropology* 43: 379–395.

Lévi-Strauss, Claude. 1961. *Tristes Tropiques.* Trans. John Russell. New York: Criterion Books.

Lévy-Bruhl, Lucien. 1935. *Primitives and the Supernatural.* Trans. Lilian A. Clare. London: Allen & Unwin.

Melberg, Arne. 1995. *Theories of Mimesis.* Cambridge: Cambridge University Press.

Mitchell, Timothy. 1991. "The Limits of the State: Beyond Statist Approaches and Their Critics." *American Political Science Review* 85 (1): 77–96.

Mitchell, Timothy. 2006. "Society, Economy, and the State Effect." In Sharma and Gupta 2006, 169–186.

Navaro-Yashin, Yael. 2002. *Faces of the State: Secularism and Public Life in Turkey.* Princeton, NJ: Princeton University Press.

Ortner, Sherry B. 1995. "Resistance and the Problem of Ethnographic Refusal." *Comparative Studies in Society and History* 37 (1): 173–193.

Ortner, Sherry B. 2016. "Dark Anthropology and Its Others: Theory Since the Eighties." *HAU: Journal of Ethnographic Theory* 6 (1): 47–73.

Pels, Peter. 1997. "The Anthropology of Colonialism: Culture, History, and the Emergence of Western Governmentality." *Annual Review of Anthropology* 26: 163–183.

Pels, Peter, and Oscar Salemink, eds. 1994. "Introduction: Five Theses on Ethnography as Colonial Practice." *History of Anthropology* 8 (1–4): 1–34.

Pels, Peter, and Oscar Salemink, eds. 1999. *Colonial Subjects: Essays on the Practical History of Anthropology.* Ann Arbor: University of Michigan Press.

Plato. 1992. *Republic*. Trans. G. M. A. Grube. Indianapolis: Hackett Publishing.

Potolsky, Matthew. 2006. *Mimesis*. London: Routledge.

Rabinow, Paul. 1989. *French Modern: Norms and Forms of the Social Environment*. Cambridge, MA: MIT Press.

Radcliffe-Brown, A. R. 1940. "Preface." In *African Political Systems*, ed. M. Fortes and E. E. Evans-Pritchard, xi–xxiii. Oxford: Oxford University Press.

Reeves, Madeleine. 2014. *Border Work: Spatial Lives of the State in Rural Central Asia*. Ithaca, NY: Cornell University Press.

Ribeiro, Gustavo Lins. 2013. "What's in a Copy?" *Vibrant* 10 (1): 20–39.

Roque, Ricardo. 2010a. *Headhunting and Colonialism: Anthropology and the Circulation of Human Skulls in the Portuguese Empire, 1870–1930*. Basingstoke: Palgrave Macmillan.

Roque, Ricardo. 2010b. "The Unruly Island: Colonialism's Predicament in Late Nineteenth-Century East Timor." *Portuguese Literary and Cultural Studies* 17–18: 303–330.

Roque, Ricardo. 2014. "Mimetismos coloniais no império português" [Colonial mimesis in the Portuguese empire]. *Etnográfica* 18 (1): 101–109.

Roque, Ricardo. 2015a. "Mimesis and Colonialism: Emerging Perspectives on a Shared History." *History Compass* 13 (4): 201–211.

Roque, Ricardo. 2015b. "Mimetic Governmentality and the Administration of Colonial Justice in East Timor, ca. 1860–1910." *Comparative Studies in Society and History* 57 (1): 67–97.

Roque, Ricardo, and Kim A. Wagner, eds. 2012. *Engaging Colonial Knowledge: Reading European Archives in World History*. Basingstoke: Palgrave Macmillan.

Rouch, Jean, dir. 1955. *Les maîtres fous* [The mad masters]. Documentary film, 36 min. Produced by Les Films de la Pléiade; distributed by Icarus Films.

Saada, Emmanuelle. 2005. "Entre 'assimilation' et 'décivilisation': L'imitation et le projet colonial républicain" [Between 'assimilation' and 'decivilization': Imitation and the republic colonial project]. *Terrain* 44: 19–38.

Sahlins, Marshall. 2008. "The Stranger-King or, Elementary Forms of the Politics of Life." *Indonesia and the Malay World* 36 (105): 177–199.

Said, Edward W. 1978. *Orientalism: Western Conceptions of the Orient*. London: Penguin.

Said, Edward W. 2003. "Introduction to the Fiftieth-Anniversary Edition." In *Mimesis: The Representation of Reality in Western Literature*, Erich Auerbach, ix–xxxii. Princeton, NJ: Princeton University Press.

Scott, David. 1995. "Colonial Governmentality." *Social Text* 43: 191–220.

Scott, James C. 2009. *The Art of Not Being Governed: An Anarchist History of Upland Southeast Asia*. New Haven, CT: Yale University Press.

Sharma, Aradhana, and Akhil Gupta, eds. 2006. *The Anthropology of the State: A Reader*. Oxford: Blackwell.

Sigrist, Christian. 1994. *Regulierte Anarchie: Untersuchungen zum Fehlen und zur Entstehung politischer Herrschaft in segmentären Gesellschaften Afrikas* [Regulated anarchy: Investigations on the absence and emergence of political rule in segmented African societies]. Hamburg: Europäische Verlagsanstalt.

Singaravélou, Pierre. 2011. *Professer l'Empire: Les 'sciences coloniales' en France sous la IIIe République* [Professing the empire: The 'colonial sciences' in France under the Third Republic]. Paris: Publications de la Sorbonne.

Spariosu, Mihai, ed. 1984. *Mimesis in Contemporary Theory: An Interdisciplinary Approach*. Vol. 1: *The Literary and Philosophical Debate*. Philadelphia, PA: John Benjamins Publishing.

Stocking, George W., Jr., ed. 1991. *Colonial Situations: Essays on the Contextualization of Ethnographic Knowledge*. Madison: University of Wisconsin Press.

Stoler, Ann L. 1995. *Race and the Education of Desire: Foucault's History of Sexuality and the Colonial Order of Things*. Durham, NC: Duke University Press.

Stoler, Ann L. 2002. *Carnal Knowledge and Imperial Power: Race and the Intimate in Colonial Rule*. Berkeley: University of California Press.

Stoler, Ann L., and Frederick Cooper. 1997. "Between Metropole and Colony: Rethinking a Research Agenda." In *Tensions of Empire: Colonial Cultures in a Bourgeois World*, ed. Frederick Cooper and Ann L. Stoler, 1–56. Berkeley: University of California Press.

Stoller, Paul. 1984. "Horrific Comedy: Cultural Resistance and the Hauka Movement in Niger." *Ethos* 12 (2): 165–188.

Stoller, Paul. 1995. *Embodying Colonial Memories: Spirit Possession, Power and the Hauka in West Africa*. New York: Routledge.

Strauss, Claudia. 2006. "The Imaginary." *Anthropological Theory* 6 (3): 322–344.

Tambiah, Stanley J. 1985. *Culture, Thought and Social Action: An Anthropological Perspective*. Cambridge, MA: Harvard University Press.

Tappe, Oliver. 2015. "A Frontier in the Frontier: Sociopolitical Dynamics and Colonial Administration in the Lao-Vietnamese Borderlands." *Asia Pacific Journal of Anthropology* 16 (4): 368–387.

Tarde, Gabriel. 1903. *The Laws of Imitation*. Trans. Elsie Clews Parsons. New York: Henry Holt.

Taussig, Michael. 1987. *Shamanism, Colonialism, and the Wild Man: A Study in Terror and Healing*. Chicago: University of Chicago Press.

Taussig, Michael. 1993. *Mimesis and Alterity: A Particular History of the Senses*. London: Routledge.

Taylor, Charles. 2002. "Modern Social Imaginaries." *Public Culture* 14 (1): 91–124.

Thomas, Nicholas. 1994. *Colonialism's Culture: Anthropology, Travel, and Government*. Princeton, NJ: Princeton University Press.

Thelen, Tatjana, Larissa Vetters, and Keebet von Benda-Beckmann. 2015. "Introduction to Stategraphy: Toward a Relational Anthropology of the State." *Social Analysis* 58 (3): 1–19.

Toscano, Alberto. 2007. "Powers of Pacification: State and Empire in Gabriel Tarde." *Economy and Society* 36 (4): 597–613.

Trajano Filho, Wilson. 2006. "Por uma Etnografia da Resistência: O Caso das *Tabancas* de Cabo Verde [For an ethnography of resistance: The case of the *tabancas* of Cape Verde]." *Série Antropologia* 408: 1–36.

Walker, Iain. 2010. *Becoming the Other, Being Oneself: Constructing Identities in a Connected World*. Newcastle: Cambridge Scholars Publishing.

Weber, Max. 1978. *Economy and Society*. 2 vols. Trans. and ed. Guenther Roth and Claus Wittich. Berkeley: University of California Press.

Wengrow, David. 2010. *What Makes Civilization? The Ancient Near East and the Future of the West*. Oxford: Oxford University Press.

Willerslev, Rane. 2007. *Soul Hunters: Hunting, Animism, and Personhood among the Siberian Yukaghirs*. Berkeley: University of California Press.

Wittgenstein, Ludwig. (1953) 2001. *Philosophical Investigations*. Hoboken, NJ: Blackwell.

Wulf, Christoph. 2014. "The Mimetic Foundation of Social Life: Historical and Anthropological Perspectives." *Paragrana* 23 (2): 15–24.

Chapter 1

DANCES WITH HEADS
Parasitic Mimesis and the Government of Savagery
in Colonial East Timor

Ricardo Roque

In this chapter, I investigate the colonial trade between 'civilization' and 'savagery' through the relations that the representatives of the colonial state maintained with indigenous ritual violence. I explore this topic on the basis of a revealing case study: the historical episode of Portuguese Governor Afonso de Castro's polemical participation in 1861 in a customary ceremony associated with the celebration of headhunting raids and war victories in East Timor, a remote Portuguese colony in Southeast Asia. These rites went by the name of 'dance' or 'feast of the heads' (*festa das cabeças*, in Portuguese) in the colonial discourse of the time, or by the name of the *lorosa'e* (rising sun) in its widespread indigenous designation in the Tetum language. Despite a presence dating back to the sixteenth century, the eastern half of the island of Timor was then but a small remote and forgotten possession of Portugal. The colonizing community was small; most Europeans resided in the capital city Dili and its surroundings.

Notes for this chapter begin on page 47.

As there was virtually no regular European army, the governors had to rely on collaboration with indigenous irregulars, creating close ties with Timorese ruling classes and their warrior customs.[1] The approach of Governor Afonso de Castro to the 'feast' needs to be understood in the context of these local structures and constraints. However, it also provides for a case study of wider significance.

By following the governor's writings concerning both the advantages and disadvantages of his compliance with these 'barbaric' rites, I propose to conceptualize colonial transits with savagery within government praxis as a form of parasitic mimesis. Drawing on archival documents, I develop an ethnography to suggest that savagery—both of others and of the self—could become the object of a parasitic form of mimetic governmentality in a double sense: as a form of governing others, an art of managing and exploiting the perceived barbarism of indigenous alterity; and as a form of governing the self, an art of managing colonial identity in the tropics by fine-tuning differences from and resemblances to savagery. As such, this chapter expands on the concept of mimetic governmentality originally explored by the author in an earlier study (Roque 2015) and also discussed in the introduction to this volume. It argues that the colonial trade with images, sites, and rites of otherness and savagery could be framed productively within mimetic and parasitic relations, but also that it demonstrates the profound moral, symbolic, and identity-based tensions and problems that such trade entailed. My goal is to test analytical tools of general and comparative reach that are capable of understanding the production of colonial relations at the exact points where 'civilization' and 'barbarism' intersect, fertilize, and collide, regardless of the nationality of the empires in question. By testing this approach herein, I do not intend to limit it to the specificities of Timor or those of Portuguese colonialism. Instead, I think that it may open up paths of interpretation into the connected histories of mimesis, government, and savagery in European colonialism in general. I begin by describing some analytical dimensions of my approach to this shared history. In the pages that follow, I will seek to further explore them conceptually and illuminate them empirically.

Mimesis and the Government of Savagery

First in *Shamanism, Colonialism, and the Wild Man* (1987) and then in *Mimesis and Alterity* (1993), Michael Taussig approaches mimesis as a constitutive aspect of the history of European colonial expansion. In studying the exploitation of rubber on the Colombian border, Taussig argues that the savagery attributed by the colonial settlers to the indigenous other fueled the violence pursued by the settlers in a game of mirrors whereby the imagined savagery of the Indian as a 'wild man' became inscribed in the practice of terror against the Indian body. Taussig develops on original ideas by Horkheimer and Adorno

([1944] 2002: 137–173), for whom the brutality imposed on the Jews during Nazism was a form of organized mimesis—the excess of the Nazis' material (re)action to the deep fear induced by the anti-Semitic representation of the Jew as an inhuman and demonized being (see Taussig 1993: 45–46, 59–63; cf. Benjamin ([1933] 1986).[2] In Taussig's (1993: xiv) phrasing, "the felt relation of the civilizing process to savagery" traverses the colonial phenomenon. The latter is inconceivable without a "net of passionful images spun for several centuries by the colonial trade with wildness that ensures civilization its savagery" (ibid.: xviii; see also Kramer 1993). Civilization and savagery—the central diptych of European imperialism's 'self-consciousness' since the Enlightenment (Elias 1989)—form an integrated and dynamic duality around which the political and epistemic history of colonial expansion of the Western world in the modern age is played out. They are central to understanding the shared histories of mimesis and colonialism and, I will add, reflect on the formation of modern forms of colonial governmentality both as regards the colonized Other and the colonizer Self. In colonial interactions on the ground, savagery was not simply a static property of the Other; it was a dynamic condition of others and of the self that had to be managed in practice. For those who held responsibilities within the machinery of the colonial state, savagery could also become a key matter of colonial administration.

This chapter follows these lines of inquiry but seeks to open up some alternative conceptual routes. In contrast with Taussig—for whom colonizing mimesis acts primarily as a destructive force set upon 'colonized' bodies—what interests me here is the political productivity (extractive and non-destructive) of mimesis as a practice carried out by self-proclaimed colonizers. Mimesis is a complex notion with ancient origins and varied intellectual expressions in Western thought (see Gebauer and Wulf 1995; Potolsky 2006). I mobilize a broad heuristic notion of mimesis to encompass mimetic processes—such as the one made manifest in Castro's account of his experiences in Timor—that refer to both symbolic representation and social experience, and that can elicit potentially disruptive as well as potentially generative political, subjective, and moral effects. Thus, I here approach colonial mimesis and mimicry as connected phenomena that belong to the realm of the mimetic (cf. Walker 2010: 31). In fact, as we shall see, Governor Afonso de Castro's story of colonial contact with savagery interchangeably evokes and articulates, and often juxtaposes, what in other contexts appear to be distinct meanings of the mimetic.[3] In my reading of the mimetic in the archival material, I will use Roger Caillois's and Michel Serres's innovative insights on mimicry as a bodily, cultural, and social relation to space. In their wake, I conceptualize mimetic processes in connection with parasitism as both an imagined and actually experienced relation of contact to a ritual environment perceived to be Other, to be 'savage', as a practical and experienced mode of being possessed by, and of assimilating to, the circumstances.

In exploring these notions, I am interested in capturing the mimetic impulse that underlies colonial forms of rule. Following up on one of my previous works, I intend to call attention to mimesis as a manifestation of the administrative rationality and action of colonial agents; as intrinsic to the claims of colonial authority; as an art of government; and as a mode of 'mimetic governmentality' (Roque 2015).[4] Consequently, colonial mimesis can be addressed, first, as a strategy of government of (indigenous) others, whose principle of action is the incorporation and reproduction of the perceived otherness of 'native' or 'primitive' populations, with a view to ruling over their conduct and existence. In addition, I argue herein that colonial forms of mimetic governmentality can be understood in relation to the government of the (colonial) self, that is, a form of management of European identity through the handling of similarity and difference as regards the indigenous world and its perceived otherness and savagery. Therefore, unlike Foucault (2007: 132), who could treat these two types of government as being distinct—"the government of oneself, which falls under morality" and "the 'science of governing well' the state, which belongs to politics"—I would like to read them together as co-existing and overlapping expressions of the government of savagery. The mimetic government of others challenged colonial agents to creatively articulate and regulate their identities through various forms of self-discipline and government of the self. To set the inclusion of the Other as a principle of colonial action could threaten the self-proposed 'civilizing' project of colonialism—at the scale either of the colonizer as subject or of the imperial collective as a whole. Self-discipline and moral regulation could thus also constitute a domain that encompasses more than the strict jurisdiction of individual morality: in certain contexts, its regulation and its exercise belong to the specific sphere of governance of the state.

Insofar as colonial agents were invested with representation of state authority—as in the case of the Portuguese governor of Timor discussed herein—the problems of government of the self easily extrapolated to individual morality and subjective discipline, becoming conflated with the regulation of the imperial order itself. To play on a famous saying by Homi Bhabha (1984), becoming 'almost native, but not quite', that is, to administer the will to become the Other while simultaneously being anxious to deny similarity, constituted a difficult art for those who risked triggering imitation of the primitive as a government strategy. This was even more so when the same mimetic gesture—making the native a model and the European a copy—foreshadowed a 'bad imitation' that could dangerously reverse the expected effect of civilizing intervention (see Xavier 2014). Such dangers of decline and loss of identity were closely linked to the idea of 'going native', a striking topic within the colonial imagination of Europeans in the period covered by this chapter. Understanding the mimetic movement toward governing others, therefore, implies attention to the tensions that are inherent to the possibility of subjective production of similarity with otherness. In some contexts, such as the one analyzed herein, the problem of the colonial government of others as savages could correspond to the problem of the government of savagery as a manifestation within the colonial civilizing process itself.

The fact that the case study discussed in this chapter concerns the highest authority and representative of the Portuguese imperial state and Crown in the colony—the district governor—is thus especially significant for my argument. This case brings to light how mimetic interactions at the level of the individual could correspond to issues of a wider, collective imperial scale. As a colonial agent and representative of Portugal's imperial government, the governor and his actions did not remain solely at the level of the individual. In Timor, the governor lived the life of national, imperial, and state collectives. In a sort of Durkheimian correspondence between the individual and the collective, the problems (as well as the solutions) of the governor's contact with savagery were perceived as broader problems of state and imperial governance. Accordingly, in managing his identity as regards his contact with 'wild rituals', the governor was also compelled to manage a wider sense of morality and collective identity.

The chapter elaborates on these analytical topics through a narrative strategy. It begins with Afonso de Castro's response to criticism from the imperial authorities in Lisbon with regard to his participation in Timorese headhunting rites. On the basis of the correspondence between Lisbon and Dili, I will explore the literary descriptions made by the governor concerning the feast of the heads. These accounts were circulated between 1860 and 1862 in various circuits and textual genres. I focus in detail on the particular accounts that sparked controversy with the metropolitan authorities to conceptualize the governor's relationship with the ritual as a mode of mimetic parasitism. In other words, it was perceived as a mimetic relation marked by a tension between assimilation to the environment and the reflexive demarcation of difference, while also being inscribed in a parasitic political rationality aimed at converting the assimilation of otherness into a fruitful gesture of state government. In this way, colonial mimesis as an art of government of others as well as of oneself found political productivity in parasitism. The chapter concludes by articulating these themes in relation to the governor's pragmatic theories of government that guided his administration of East Timor and that were also consequential for future administrative approaches to similar savage events in the colony.

Reporting the Feast of the Heads

On 23 June 1862, Afonso de Castro, the district governor of Timor and an army captain, sent a lengthy letter to Lisbon in response to reprimands he had received from Carlos Bento da Silva, the minister of trade and overseas affairs.

The Confidential Ordinance to which Castro was replying incorporated the vision of the king of Portugal, the young King Luís. The subject was awkward and delicate. The governor justified his actions in the face of criticism made by the minister and the royal authority regarding certain acts of his administration, which occurred during the recent celebrations of the Portuguese victory over the 'rebel' Timorese kingdoms of Lacló and Ulmera.[5] The 'War of Lacló and Ulmera' lasted from March to September 1861. As had been the custom in the colony, the governor had to subdue a Timorese uprising through recourse to allied Timorese warriors, under the designations of irregular companies of *arraiais* and *moradores*, who served military service as auxiliary troops in the form of a tribute to the government.

The Confidential Ordinance resulted from the interpretation made by the imperial authorities of one among many letters and reports sent by Castro concerning this 1861 campaign. In one of his writings, Castro had provided a detailed description of his direct experience of the headhunting rites performed in Dili in September 1861. "The governor justifies himself," stated a note handwritten at the ministerial office on Castro's (1862a) letter of response, "for having permitted, within Dili, the staging of the solemn barbaric event called the *feast of the heads.*" The exact contents of the minister's critique sent from Lisbon to Timor in January 1862 is unknown, as the aforementioned Confidential Ordinance was not preserved in the Portuguese archives. However, we know its subject and contents indirectly due to the defensive response sent from Dili by the governor. In it, Castro (1862a; underlining in the original; emphasis added) began his 'letter of justification' as follows:

> With all due respect and submission, I received the gentle reprimand that Your Excellency sent me, in the name of His Majesty, regarding the solemn event that occurred here last September [1861] called the feast of the heads, which His Majesty never wants to take place again within the Praça [Dili settlement].
>
> Your Excellency, please allow me to justify my behavior, which may appear to suggest that I harbor feelings that do not stand in harmony with the ideas of civilization and piety that I must set as an example to the people whom I have the honor to govern.
>
> The event that I attended, forced by compelling circumstances, which I will mention shortly, disgusted me as they should disgust any civilized man. *I would have to be infected by the savagery of these people with whom I mingle* in order to willingly observe the scenes that I have described to Your Excellency solely as a historian.

What scenes witnessed by Castro, presumably "solely as a historian," would have aroused the indignation of the king and invective criticism from Lisbon? What words and documents must have come to the attention of the minister that were now capable of forcing the governor to provide an extended justification of his system of administration? And, if true, what were the reasons for this governor of Timor—praised in the subsequent literature as a pioneer of civilization and modernization of the colony—to have succumbed to contact with savagery? To answer these questions, let us go back some months before the letter of justification and review Castro's earlier writings about the campaign and, more generally, Timorese warrior customs.

Celebrating a Portuguese Victory

Afonso de Castro (1824–1885) ruled the district of Timor between 1859 and 1863. His reputation as a dynamic, visionary, and modernizing governor—the founder of the new structures of the colonial state in the territory in the mid-nineteenth century—has appeared in literature concerning Timor up to the present day.[6] A key factor underpinning his reputation was the fact that his published work about Timor was based on the experience and knowledge he had acquired in situ during his governmental duties. Castro is still the most influential nineteenth-century Portuguese author on Timor, to the point that his writings about the country's history and Timorese uses and customs were reproduced, quoted, discussed, or otherwise referred to in the literature on East Timor until well into the twentieth century.[7] The history of these publications, as we shall see, reveals that their origins were intertwined with Castro's administrative work. These published texts, however, are only the visible part of his entire written works. Castro's expositions of the history and customs of Timor—including his accounts about the feast of the heads that took place in 1861—circulated solely in the form of official letters and reports to his immediate superior, the overseas minister, in Lisbon.[8] It was in these official letters that Castro reported in detail about local history, events, uses, and customs among the Timorese. It was also in one of these letters that the episode of his involvement in the feast of the heads came to the attention of the imperial authorities.

In September 1861, Afonso de Castro dispatched a report to his superiors in Lisbon about the feast of the heads that was organized in the colony after the victory over the rebels of Lacló and Ulmera. In the center of this account was his own direct, personal experience of the ceremony on 12 September 1861 in the square of Dili. Just like the censorship imposed by the Ministry over his previous reference to the feast as a historical custom in the colony (Castro 1860b), this description was never allowed to be published by the imperial authorities and subsequently remained restricted to the archival circuits of administration. This was a first-hand account of a ceremonial event that relied on the authority of the governor's bodily participation. The report did not state that the ceremony belonged to an undated past, as if it were a distant ancient custom from bygone days. It was presented as an event entirely contemporaneous with the civilized presence of colonial governance, as a ceremonial occasion that was prepared and held as an integral part of the state-sponsored celebrations of the Portuguese victory in the war. As is clear from Castro's subsequent letter of justification, it was explicitly the reading of this report that led the king and the minister to reprimand the governor, issuing categorical instructions for the ceremony never to be repeated. So what were the details of this uncomfortable account of 1861 that caused the royal authorities to treat one ceremony in the empire's most remote colony as a serious matter of state? With literary verve, Castro (1861; underlining in the original) described the details as follows. The account is worth quoting in full:

On the 12th, the so-called *feast of the heads* took place, of which I will make a brief description to Your Excellency in order to give an idea of the customs of these people. At eight o'clock, the irregular Companies of the government, of around 200 men, formed in the public square of Dili next to the triumphal arch, which had been erected in that square, on top of which the following two verses, in large letters, could be read:

You will go down in the annals of Lusitanian history
For your laurels of victory.

An official guard of the Battalion was placed in front of the arch and on the side of a tent. At nine o'clock, I headed with some officers to the tent and positioned myself in front of the Royal Pavilion that had been raised there. Many Ladies of Dili sat in the tents. I then gave the order for the *arraiais* [village irregulars] to enter, which advanced as follows.

Ensign Xavier rode in front of fifty horses ridden by the chiefs, and this squadron was followed by the military encampment, waving their flags. The *assuaes* (brave warriors) came with an unsheathed sword in their right hand and a rifle in their left, dancing, expressing a thousand grimaces and ugly faces, and making loud cries, which were matched by the *arraial*. Once this group of soldiers arrived thirty paces from me, they dismounted and greeted me. All members of the *arraial* stood in front of me, and then Ensign Xavier asked for three cheers for His Majesty, the Nation, and the Governor, which the *arraiais* responded to.

Until that point, the spectacle had been amazing and was very interesting, but from that point onward, it became disgusting and horrible for a European.

After the greetings had terminated, the [indigenous] companies of *moradores* broke ranks and took part in the dances, while the *arraial* formed a circle and two *asua'ins* from Caiman advanced, each holding up a head in one hand by its long hair. My Secretary then handed two sticks to these two Commanders of the residents, with two red handkerchiefs tied to their tips, together with two silver circles that are called *luas* (moons). Each commander took his stick and started jumping in front of the *asua'ins*. The latter also jumped and pulled ugly faces, trying to divert their body.

After a few jumps, the Commanders threw the sticks, and the *asua'ins* grabbed them, removing the moons, which they hung around their neck, and putting the head next to the base of the Royal Pavilion. This was repeated twelve times—corresponding to the number of severed heads. Then the *asua'ins* who had captured the prisoners arrived—there were three women, two men, and a child—and after receiving the moons, these *asua'ins* put the prisoners next to the heads. Once this was completed, the *tabedaes* [groups of male and female Timorese dancers] entered who danced round the heads. Then something occurred that Your Excellency will certainly find it difficult to believe and will be horrified to hear: A large soldier jumped in a circle around the *tabedaes*, grabbed the head that he had cut and held it by the hair with his teeth, and then began to dance like a madman with that trophy in his mouth!

On the basis of this fact, Your Excellency can judge the state of savagery of this people!

This vivid description was written just two days after Castro had witnessed the ceremony, in a mixture of pomp and horror. Using these words, the governor transmitted to the minister the collective effervescence of the occasion. He presented the feast as an act of the colonial government—as part of the official celebrations of the Portuguese victory over Lacló that took place under the aegis of his government. In other words, Castro described the barbaric ritual as if it were a rite of the colonial state. The presence of the governor, of European officials, and of commanders and ladies communicated the idea of a colonial ceremony in which the Europeans acted in festive communion with the Timorese but, at the same time, were also separated from them. Attracted by the magnetic allure of extreme otherness, the representatives of civilization observed as spectators—as if purely separate and untouched—an eccentric theater of barbarity (see also Castro 1864: 402–404). Thus, the same account also reveals the governor's concern to establish boundaries between the participants in this collective situation. It reveals his rhetorical effort to distance himself in the text from what he posits as the savagery of Timorese actions, highlighting his passive position as a European official who did not play an effective role in the fervent amalgam of the ritual. The account was offered to the minister as evidence of "the state of savagery" of the Timorese. Castro's colonial self thus strove to distance himself from the savagery that was attributed to the Other, but in which he nevertheless saw himself immersed. However, as we will see, this rhetorical othering was not enough to extract Castro from the savagery of the rite.

The governor presented himself to the reader as a passive, silent persona, an outsider detached from the ceremonial setting. As a prototypical European, he adopted the flawless skin of a distant spectator, a gaze, a mere ocular presence that remained untouched by the event. In what concerns the governor's position in the rite, these records thus contrast with an earlier historical description

Rua do " Commercio ", Dilly. — TIMOR.

ILLUSTRATION 1.1: Postcard showing the Rua do Comércio in Dili in the 1870s to 1890s. The governor's palace is on the left. The 1861 celebrations of the feast of the heads in Dili probably took place in this setting. Reproduced courtesy of João Loureiro.

of the feast (Castro 1860b), and in which the figure of the governor appeared as a historical and customary ritual 'agent', who presided over the dance and rewarded the headhunters. In any case, there is an important point to retain from Castro's textual renderings of the feast of the heads. Wherever it was that his texts located himself and European officials in the feast of the heads, there was no way to avoid creating the impression for his readers that the governor was situated in rather than out of the ritual space—that he, too, was implicated in the so-called Timorese savagery. There was no way to set himself apart. There was no way of avoiding being perceived as having been possessed by the circumstances of the ritual. There was no way, finally, of escaping the traps of a mimetic relationship. The next section conceives of this tension as a mimetic drama and brings forth Castro's colonial mimesis of savagery as a particular relationship to space.

The Governor and the Mimetic Drama

In Lisbon, the descriptions sent from Timor aroused the perception of a problem of an imperial scale. This concern was expressed by the sense of threat and loss through dilution within the surrounding space of the privilege of distance between the 'civilized man' and the 'savage', the foundational duality of the nineteenth-century colonial project. The problem, in short, was that within the space of the rite, Governor Afonso de Castro had become the Other, had become a savage—and with him, the imperial state and its civilizing process were also immersed in savagery. By merely exposing his presence in the space of the feast, Castro seemed to create continuities of substance between civilization and savagery where only discontinuities were morally permissible. This perception configured a mimetic drama, "a drama," to borrow from Taussig (1993: 34), as expressed in a sensuous relation to circumstances, an attraction for space "in which the self is but a self-diminishing point amid others, losing its boundedness." As such, Castro's participation in the headhunting rite equaled succumbing to the mimetic temptation of "depersonalization by assimilation to space," as described by the French anthropologist and surrealist Roger Caillois (1984: 30) in an illuminating essay originally written in 1935 (see also Cheng 2009; Taussig 1993: 34–43). For Caillois, the ultimate principle of mimetic action (in the human world and also in non-human living organisms) is less the search for similarity than the individual's orientation to assimilate itself within the environment, the impulse to be tempted and possessed by that which surrounds it/him.

Mimicry, following Caillois's inspiration, can thus be seen as a 'temptation' by the space in which the self allows itself to be possessed by its surroundings. In mimetic relationships, the drama of the individual is the attractiveness of the surroundings, to the point that his/her existence and personality disappear, diluted in the same space. In the words of Caillois (1984: 28; emphasis in the original):

> It is with represented space that the drama becomes specific, since the living creature, the organism, is no longer the origin of the coordinates, but one point among others; it is dispossessed of its privilege and literally *no longer knows where to place itself* ... The feeling of personality, considered as the organism's feeling of distinction from its surroundings, of the connection between consciousness and a particular point in space, cannot fail under these conditions to be seriously undermined.

In the case at hand, the tension above suggested by Caillois between being possessed by the environment and dispossessing oneself of oneself will find an empirical echo in the idea of subjecting the colonizer to the circumstances—in the twin meaning of a 'contingency' and 'everything around'. We will see below that this idea was repeated in Castro's attitude toward government and in his justificatory discourse. Caillois's insights thus illuminate the mimetic tensions caused by the governor's participation in the ceremony. By attending the feast of the heads and succumbing to its circumstances, the Portuguese governor risked a kind of de-individuation by becoming a constituent participant indistinct from that which surrounded him, nothing more than one point among many—simply a savage among savages.

The mimetic drama that seemed to emerge in the complaints from Lisbon was due to the governor's incapacity to substantiate the colonizers' privilege of difference. The drama sensed in Lisbon also indicated another metropolitan concern, which was politically motivated. Through immersion in the Other, there was the risk of losing the moral mandate of the civilizing mission that legitimized the modern colonial vocation of the Europeans and, with it, their mandate of power. Unable to sustain difference toward barbarism, it was feared that the governor would become unable to exercise the colonial mandate of governmentality and domination. Indeed, how could a governor continue to be an agent of civilization if his position was indistinguishable from that of his native subjects, if in this manner his place and his state of consciousness and feelings became indistinguishable from the savages? How could the imperial administration that he represented avoid falling, too, into a state of savagery?

These issues eventually influenced Castro's (1862a) attempt to cope with this mimetic drama in his letter of justification. In responding to the minister's Confidential Ordinance of 1861, the governor rehearsed an argumentative refutation of the charge that he was annulling his subjective condition as a colonial European and thereby undermining the identity of the entire empire. This refutation involved two lines of arguments. First, Castro challenged the idea that the contact implied the simple dissolution of difference. He argued that although his presence in the rite induced similarity, his positioning in the midst of the party did not entail absolute denial of European identity. The second argument was that his inclusion in the ritual was a politically virtuous administrative procedure, to the advantage of the colonial state. It was presented as an event in the context of a political rationality of parasitic power, which enriched the Portuguese domination. In this context, the governor theorized his praxis of colonial governance in Timor as an art of surrendering to the force of circumstances. This allows us to interpret his presence in the feast of the heads as a pragmatic gesture of assimilation within his surrounding environment, in pursuit of his overall political guideline: the calculated parasitic exploitation of otherness. I begin with an examination of his first argument—that contact did not equal similarity.

Contact and the Return to the Self

"I would have to be infected by the savagery of these people with whom I mingle," wrote Castro (1862a) at the start of his letter of justification. This phrase exemplarily conveys the governor's strategy to circumvent the dramatic allures of his mimetic relation to the headhunting rite. He claimed that the existence of physical contact did not correspond to the production of similarity and that the events of 1861 in Dili did not amount to a case of mimetic de-individuation.

Castro denied that the colonial civilizing project could be undermined by "magical-sympathetic" principles of transmission of qualities or substances. He denied, given that this would be opposed to modern reason, that mere contact with things, people, or circumstances of the savage world, for example, would oblige a civilized man to commune with the substantive qualities of this Other world, thenceforth transforming himself into a similarly savage creature.[9] Appealing to such an elementary materialistic logical reasoning, the governor thus rejected the possibility of suffering the effects of a magical relationship of imitative contagion.[10] The ritual conjunction between Portuguese and Timorese bodies was not sufficient to produce a nexus of transubstantiation. To think, therefore, that a civilized being could become a copy of a savage being through contact and contagion—to think that savagery could be transmitted or 'caught' like a disease—corresponded to falling into the absurdity of magical, primitive, irrational, or pre-modern thinking. However, the fact that Castro felt the need to evoke these materialistic principles is indicative enough that, de facto, in Lisbon it was feared that some kind of principle of sympathetic transubstantiation had been triggered by the contact between the governor, the Portuguese empire, and the barbarity of the rites.

This statement of principles—rejecting the irrationality of the idea of sympathetic-mimetic contagion—did not constitute sufficient justification for concern. In addition, while accepting that he took an active part in the feast of the heads, Castro claimed that his contact with the feast could not produce similarity *without* differentiation. His alleged surrendering to savagery implied neither dissolution of identity nor loss of the colonial position of power. 'Contact' and 'presence' were not in their own right capable of stripping the governor's European, Christian, and colonial individuality from his personal identity. As a result, the moral nature of the colonial state was not distorted. Accordingly, although "forced by circumstances" to immerse himself in the ritual, the governor claimed that a reflexive double act was sufficient to guarantee difference and individuality: this entailed, first, the suspension of beliefs and, second, the subsequent return to himself.

In this manner, Afonso de Castro sought to assuage the concerns of the king and the minister, stating that his permission and personal immersion in the ritual did not impede him from continuing to embrace Christian affections, feelings, and values. He claimed that his involvement in the feast was caused by the "imperious force of circumstances" and was not "voluntary" (Castro 1862a), adding that the denial of Oneself to which he had been forced did not prevent him from preserving his distinctly European and civilized identity. "From my love of progress and civilization, from my inner feelings of religiosity," stated Castro, "I think I have given enough evidence to enable Your Excellency to be certain of them." The feast, he reiterated, "disgusted me, just as it should disgust all civilized men." He declared to the Minister: "Filled with revulsion, sorrowful and almost ashamed of my role as a spectator in such an intense act of savagery, I overcame those revulsions, stifled my feelings of respect for the dead and my feelings of humanity, and I watched that act ... But in light of my account, I hope that Your Excellency will not judge that I am indifferent to these acts of ferocity and much less that I share the feelings of these people" (ibid.).

One thus seems to be before a peculiar management of civilizing identity through a mimetic trade with savagery. "Mimesis involves a manipulation of the world," Iain Walker (2010: 33) observed in his reanalysis of Taussig, "in order to remain, in important respects, the same" (cf. Taussig 1993: 113–116). As such, Castro's (1862a) mimetic relation to the feast's perceived savagery was also articulated as a performance of civilized identity. Becoming the Other was offered as compatible with becoming the same—as if crossing paths with head-hunting rites was never contradictory to Castro's orientation toward remaining himself. Although acknowledging the dispossession caused by contact with the feast of the heads, which made him stifle his feelings, the governor remained able to "reposition himself" as distinct from the savages and the "feelings of the people." This ability, on the one hand, to suspend his own self and, on the other, to be able to return to his original feelings after contact with the ritual event allowed Castro to justify and ultimately control his momentary mimetic relation. For this reason, he considered that his actions did not undermine the privilege of difference in any way. Hence, it seems that Castro's reflections on his relation to the feast of the heads were meaningful in what Willerslev (2007: 12) calls a "double negative field" of self-denial and rejection of non-self—the field of "not me, *not* not-me" (ibid., citing Richard Schechner), in which the imitation of the Other implies a denial of oneself that never becomes complete dissolution in the Other. Castro's mode of becoming the same therefore presumed that he could deny the self and share the savagery of the ritual space with the Timorese, but that, by a conscious effort, he would be able to reject full assimilation to other-ness and preserve his civilized inner being. His feelings, affections, values, and emotions remained completely European. They were suspended for only a few moments, and he later returned to them, unscathed, the same person.

The governor thus allegedly maintained a sense of distinction in relation to the environment, as above referred to by Caillois, that prevented the death of colonial individuality. In sum, in the condition of exercising his reflexivity, the governor's participation in the feast of the heads preserved the privilege of difference for himself and for the Portuguese empire in Timor. Moreover, as we shall see next, Castro saw this exercise of self-control as a guarantee of the colonial exercise of the government of others, a prerequisite for a parasitic form of governing the natives. It is time, then, to turn to Afonso de Castro's second argument in his letter of justification—the claim that the authorization he had granted, as well as his participation, was a strategic form of parasitic appropria-tion of savagery, a pragmatic move at the service of Portuguese rule.

The Parasitic Governor

For Castro, his experience of the rite was a gesture of patriotic sacrifice, a martyr-like surrender of the individual to barbarism carried out in the name of higher collective values. As such, he sought to demonstrate that his active participation in a ritual role constituted a calculated political move, a rational and premeditated act of governance with the objective to "safeguard our rule in these parts" (Castro 1862a). This second justification points to the political rationality inscribed within the governor's act of surrender to the ritual. In fact, the self-control and ability to temporarily switch off his own identity, reflexively suspending his civilized values, was subordinated to a political purpose—gaining power over the rite itself and over the Timorese people. To take part in the space of otherness, therefore, had a strategic meaning. It allowed Castro and the empire to claim a position of sovereignty in Timor, expressed in a relation of parasitic exploitation of the forces of barbarism imputed to the Timorese.

French philosopher Michel Serres's (1982) study on parasitism provides me with the conceptual grounds for analyzing this form of connection.[11] By attending the headhunting ritual, by taking place in the middle of the warriors' dances, the governor behaved as a parasite, using his dissolution with and among the Timorese dances, soldiers, prisoners, and human heads in order to extract from them the energy that was needed for the weak Portuguese colonial settlement in Timor. Castro's parasitism in this context was therefore also, like his mimetic condition, a particular relation to space. "Power," writes Serres, "is nothing but the occupation of space" (ibid.: 142). "The parasite gets power," he adds, "less because he occupies the center than because he fills the environment" (ibid.: 95). In Serres's uses, the notion of milieu carries a double meaning, not only of the environment, but also of a between-space (see Connor 2002). Thus positioned in this middle domain, the parasite "takes part of the products of others for his own profit or for the profit of the state to whom he respectfully defers. He is a veritable impostor" (Serres 1982: 5).

From this perspective, Castro's colonial parasitism of this headhunting ritual expressed a relationship to the milieu in two ways: first, in the sense of a relationship with the space or surrounding environment of the ritual; second, in the sense of a relationship in the middle, a way of occupying the between-space, a parasitic (and thus abusive) mediation of the transit between civilization and savagery, between Timorese warriors and Portuguese authorities, fostered by the feast. In this light, the *topos* of the parasitic power evoked by Serres corresponds to the *topos* of the mimetic relationship described above by Caillois. The position of the parasite is not in the center, but rather in the interstices, in the between-space. And just as mimicry is formed via association with that which is around us, parasitism is also manifested in the abusive exploration of the environment and of the transactions that take place therein. Between parasitic and mimetic orientations, one may say, there is a mutually productive relationship. Indeed, it is in the mimetic logic of assimilation to the environment that the parasite finds the prerequisite for its activities of interception and theft of the energies of its host. Writes Serres (1982: 202): "I don't know if mimicry is entirely parasitic, but it is a necessary trick for the robber, the stranger, the guest; it is a disguise, a camouflage in local colors, when the locale is a host, an other ... It is an erasure of individuality and its dissolution in the environment; it is a good means of protection in both defense and attack."

In Serres's view, the parasite's fundamental 'subterfuge' emerges here as the mimetic dissolution in the environment, a "deletion of individuation" in a space *other*—an idea similar to the one alluded to by Caillois. Given that this environment is the other world of the host, the parasite's association with space corresponds to a mimetic association with otherness. In this light, Castro's attendance at the feast of the heads emerges as a stratagem of the parasite. A colonial political rationale is thus added to the governor's immersion in the feast. While his presence could serve to protect himself from the Other, it could also serve to take advantage of it. The mimetic assimilation of the individual to the environment simultaneously configured a relationship of parasitic exploitation of the savagery of the ceremony.

The Force of Circumstances: A Pragmatic Theory of Action

Afonso de Castro surrendered himself to the power of circumstances in ritual space. At the heart of his justifications for this action we finally find a tactical sense and a pragmatic theory of colonial action (see also Roque 2010: 47–59). In this context, the key expression of this praxiology, of this practical theory of colonial rule, is the term 'circumstances'. In the appeals made by the governor to the force of circumstances, the expression evoked a double meaning that partially overlaps with Serres's spatial visions of milieu. First, it designated that which was in the surrounding space, which existed around the governor—that is, an environment. Second, it referred to that which was *temporally* contingent, unexpected, and unpremeditated, to the point of determining the course of events. Granting the command of colonial government to the impersonal force of circumstances, Castro seemed to strip the subject-governor from his position at the center, delegating the control of his governmental approach to the multiple and unexpected elements of the Timorese space that surrounded him.

The idea that local Timorese circumstances effectively governed the course of colonial action appeared on a regular basis in the governor's discourse. In 1860, for example, in open opposition to metropolitan general instructions recommending peaceful mediation, Castro explained to the minister that he had decided to attribute special importance to the use of violence in the repression of conflict in Timor, giving as his reason the force of circumstances. "I will not turn away from the general instructions that the Government of His Majesty gives me," Castro (1860a) wrote, "in relation to the frequent wars afflicting these peoples, but there are cases in which I will have to proceed as warranted by the circumstances." In this defense of the use of violence, we are therefore faced with a similar appeal to being possessed by the space, by the surroundings—a call for a colonial state configured as a response adapted to the local and the indigenous, rather than being defined beyond it.

This same force of circumstances was dominant in the overall formatting of Castro's government as regards the headhunting rites. In 1859, shortly after his arrival in Timor, he quickly decided on behalf of the effectiveness of governance to forego the prohibition on the feast of the heads ritual that had been imposed by his predecessor (Castro 1862a). Admittedly—Castro confessed rhetorically—he would have preferred to prohibit altogether this "savage solemnity." Instead, he retrenched in relation to his idealistic goal and even terminated some regulatory measures introduced by the former governor, Luís Augusto Macedo, who had tried (to no avail) to ban the "macabre" practice of kicking the decapitated heads.[12] Thus from the outset, in a calculated manner, Afonso de Castro gave free rein to the feast of the heads. The pragmatic justification offered for the festive episodes of 1861 in Dili followed the same line of argument. In his concluding justificatory remarks to the minister, Castro explained that his part in the feast was not an act of will, but rather a pragmatic decision forced by the "circumstances" of Timor and the war in 1861. "Even so, if there had been other circumstances in September [1861], I would have tried to abolish any spectacle similar to the *feast of the heads*. But what," Castro (1862a) asked rhetorically, "were those circumstances?" He explained:

> The *arraiais* had just conquered, i.e., attacked Lacló, and after a five-month campaign, they had to undertake another against Ulmera (to the west of Dili). If I wished to prohibit the ceremony, the *arraiais* warriors would interpret this, first, as an affront, as a show of contempt for the value of their *asua'ins* (brave warriors) and ... in light of the ban on their ancient traditions and their styles, they would be disturbed and no one would be able to have persuade them that the campaign that they were about to undertake would not be fatal. The result would be that the ceremony would not occur, but the *arraiais* would disappear and no one would be able to reunite them ... Now without the *arraiais* there would be no way for me to quell the revolt ...
>
> If due to an imprudent act, due to an innovation, doubtless due to laudable sentiments, I provided the pretext whereby a situation that was favorable to us became dangerous, I would merit a severe punishment.
>
> Given that my first duty was to uphold our rule in these parts, support our sovereignty, this duty makes me sacrifice any considerations and forge a compromise with all the customs and traditions of these peoples, unless such a compromise would be shameful. That is what I did.

The priority given to the continuity of the feast of the heads embodied the pragmatic principle of adjustment to the circumstances of the colony, even at the expense of the moral standards of the empire. The governor succumbed to temptation by the surrounding space: the pragmatic advantage of including warriors within the colonial armies enabled the Portuguese to secure a military victory and, ultimately, preserve their sovereignty in the territory. Similarly, in surrendering to the powers of the feast of the heads amid the Timorese, Castro helped to overcome the vulnerabilities of the colonial state in Timor, extracting from the savage ceremony the strength that the Portuguese empire seemed unable to generate on its own. He was not the first governor to do so, nor the last. In Timor, the feast of the heads continued to be both a problematic and productive space for the Portuguese colonial authority, with governors and army officers in regular attendance up to the East Timorese rebellion of 1911–1912. Perhaps, then, as Afonso de Castro suggested, savagery was not 'caught' by the Europeans; instead, the Europeans clung to it.

Conclusion

In this chapter I have explored the mimetic transactions between civilization and savagery through the links that the representatives of colonial authority maintained with spaces and practices of ritual violence, as was the case with the so-called feast of the heads in Timor during the governance of Afonso de Castro in the mid-nineteenth century. Drawing inspiration from Roger Caillois and Michel Serres, I have conceptualized colonial mimesis as a spatial relationship of contact by the colonizer with the savage environment—a practical and experienced mode of possession by means of, and through assimilation to, the 'circumstances'. As such, savagery emerged as an object of mimetic governmentality and state administration, not just in relation to the government of others (the indigenous), but also with regard to the government of oneself, that is, the management of savagery as a threatening condition of the colonial self. This study reveals that colonial mimesis of savagery can be framed within a parasitic form of government, but it also demonstrates the profound moral, symbolic, and identity-based tensions that such mimetic trade also entailed. To conclude, I would briefly like to highlight two general points of the analysis, although I am simultaneously aware that a comparative test lies beyond the scope of this chapter.

The first point concerns the dynamic tension between assimilation and reflective preservation of difference that seems to mark mimesis as a colonial praxis. I have guided the analysis through a conception of the mimetic as a felt, experienced relation to a space that is perceived to be Other, as a practice of assimilation to the surrounding space, and as a relationship *to* and a position *in* the milieu in which the environment and the subject become mutually possessed. In the context of colonial practices, this makes it necessary to consider the issue of difference, in addition to the modes of government of the self, at the level of both the subject and the state. This point is especially significant in relation to the issue of colonial contact with things, places, and activities that are classified as barbaric, abject, and impure and that pose symbolic threats to European settlers, such as barbaric rites of headhunting. In this chapter, I have followed this sort of tension and peril in the governor's efforts to resolve the allegations of loss of identity and subsequent conversion (either individually of himself or collectively of the whole empire) to barbarism as a result of attending the feast of the heads. A reflexive gesture of self-suspension served the goal of maintaining the moral integrity of the civilized self, preventing similarity, and sustaining symbolic contamination. Addressing colonial mimesis in this and other similar situations implies understanding the forms of *governing oneself* that are activated in order to deal with the effects posed by mingling with worlds that are perceived to be utterly Other.

The second point concerns the fact that mimetic processes can entail a political gesture legible in a parasitic rationality oriented to the *governing of others*. The case of the relationship maintained by Governor Afonso de Castro with the feast of the heads has made it possible to consider a mimetic practice as being inseparable from what I have dubbed a parasitic relationship, that is, a relationship presided over by a political rationality of abusive (albeit subtle) extraction of the energies of otherness for one's own benefit. The colonial yielding to the Other articulated a desire for power. The mimetic principle of subjection to the circumstances is in this case united to the parasitic principle of subtle extraction of the forces of this same circumstance. In the case that I have analyzed here, the governor authorized and took part in a ritual that he knew was barbaric in the expectation that his tolerance, presence, and participation would increase the power and authority of the colonial state that he represented. By prioritizing the force of circumstances, by taking part in the ceremony of the feast of the heads, the colonial administration aimed at possessing the savagery of its hosts in order to produce a power that it was unable to generate by itself.

The sovereign, as Candea and da Col (2012) have recently reminded us, begins to take form as a 'usurping guest'. It may be that Afonso de Castro's take on his pragmatic cohabitation with headhunting ceremonies in Dili stands as an emic colonial theory of the usurping stranger, one expressed in his eloquent formulation of an approach, at once mimetic and parasitic in my reading, to colonial governmentality. To participate in Timorese savagery was thus much more than a random occurrence, a momentary slip. It constituted the usurping stratagem of the colonial parasite—a calculated political strategy conceived as a good and effective art of government.

Acknowledgments

Research for this chapter was funded in part by a grant from the Foundation for Science and Technology, Portugal, as part of the project "Colonial Mimesis in Lusophone Asia and Africa" (PTDC/CS-ANT/101064/2008) at the University of Lisbon's Institute of Social Sciences. Support was also provided to the author by the Race and Ethnicity in the Global South Laureate Program (REGS) as a recipient of an Australian Research Council Postdoctoral Fellowship (FL 110100243) and later as an Honorary Associate in the Department of History at the University of Sydney. I would like to thank Christoph Kohl, Patrice Ladwig, and Oliver Tappe for their companionship and fruitful intellectual dialogue as participants in DAAD/CRUP Exchange Grant A-07/2011. For comments on earlier drafts, I am grateful to Cristiana Bastos, Ananya Chakravarti, Tiago Saraiva, and Ângela Barreto Xavier. Materials discussed herein have also appeared in a modified Portuguese version in 2014 in *Etnográfica* 18 (1). Thanks are extended to Martin Dale for help with translation and editing.

Ricardo Roque is a Research Fellow at the Institute of Social Sciences at the University of Lisbon (Instituto de Ciências Sociais da Universidade de Lisboa). He is also an Honorary Associate in the Department of History at the University of Sydney. He works on the history and anthropology of colonialism, human sciences, and cross-cultural contact in the Portuguese-speaking world from 1800 to the twentieth century. He has published widely in Portuguese and English on the history of physical anthropology and colonial encounters in East Timor, Goa (India), and Angola. He has also published on the theory and ethnography of colonial archives. He is the author of *Headhunting and Colonialism* (2010) and co-editor of *Engaging Colonial Knowledge* (2012), *Crossing Histories and Ethnographies* (2019), *Lusotropicalism and Its Discontents* (2019), and *Resistance and Colonialism* (2019). E-mail: ricardo.roque@ics.ulisboa.pt

Notes

1. For the wider implications of headhunting rites within colonial warfare and the complexities of the possible Timorese meanings of these rituals, see Roque (2010).
2. The generic relationship between mimesis and violence has also been explored, in different directions, by René Girard (1972) in his theory of mimetic desire.
3. Ideas of mimesis, imitation, and mimicry have followed interconnected, although distinct, trajectories as concepts within the human sciences. In the context of my

analysis here, I do not distinguish *a priori* between mimesis as 'symbolic representation' and mimicry as 'disruptive imitation' (Huggan 1997); or between mimesis as a mental act and mimicry as a purely physical act (Gebauer and Wulf 1995); or, still, between mimicry as a disruption of authority and mimesis as a claim to authority (Bhabha 1984).

4. Cf. chapters in this volume by Bastos and Ladwig and the introduction by Ladwig and Roque.

5. For this episode and the revolt of Lacló, see Oliveira (1950: 33–35) and Pélissier (1996: 42–50).

6. Born into an aristocratic family in the north of Portugal and educated at the Colégio Militar and the Polytechnic School of Porto, Castro was quickly destined for a military career in the army. After vigorous involvement in the September faction in the liberal riots of the 1840s, he maintained prolific journalistic and political activity in the metropolis. He was a member of Parliament for the Timor Circle in 1854 and finally governor (appointed in 1858, but only assuming the position de facto in 1859). Later, he was appointed lieutenant colonel and also civil governor in Madeira and the Azores. He never returned to Timor.

7. For a sampling of his publications on Timor, see Castro (1860a, 1860b, 1861, 1862a, 1862b, 1863, 1864, 1867). In this chapter, Castro's texts have been translated by Martin Dale.

8. Contrary to that which was and would continue to be the norm in the nineteenth century, Castro ran the government of Timor with formal autonomy, independently from Macao. He held broad powers and corresponded directly with Lisbon.

9. Castro thus communicated his adherence to the 'modern' materialistic rationality of the seventeenth-century Scientific Revolution, which rejected ideas of contact and theories of sympathetic connection as explaining action and transmission of qualities between material bodies (Shapin 1996).

10. These considerations by the governor precede and almost overlap chronologically the other developments in the theory of magic and mimicry. Shortly thereafter, in 1862, Henry W. Bates disclosed his ideas on biological mimicry, which had a relevant impact on Darwin's theory of evolution. Several years afterward, anthropologist James Frazer systematized his reflections on magic and sympathy. Castro was not aware of any of these developments.

11. For more on parasitism in colonial interactions, see Roque (2010: chap. 1).

12. To my knowledge, the actual occurrence of the feast had not been subject to any other prior state regulation or ban. Some attempts at regulation appeared later in 1896 in some instructions for military commanders (see Silva 1896).

References

Benjamin, Walter. (1933) 1986. "On the Mimetic Faculty." In *Reflections: Essays, Aphorisms, Autobiographical Writings*. Ed. Peter Demetz; trans. Edmund Jeph-cott, 333–336. New York: Schocken Books.

Bhabha, Homi. 1984. "Of Mimicry and Man: The Ambivalence of Colonial Discourse." *October* 28: 125–133.

Caillois, Roger. 1984. "Mimicry and Legendary Psychastenia." Trans. John Shepley. *October* 31: 16–32.

Candea, Matei, and Giovanni da Col. 2012. "The Return to Hospitality." *Journal of the Royal Anthropological Institute* 18 (S1): S1–S19.

Castro, Afonso de. 1860a. "To the Minister of the Navy and Overseas Territories, June 1860." Official Letter No. 67. Lisbon, Arquivo Histórico Ultramarino, Macau e Timor, AHU_ACL_SEMU_DGU_005, Caixa 26.

Castro, Afonso de. 1860b. "To the Minister of the Navy and Overseas Territories, 1 November 1860." Official Letter No. 112. Lisbon, Arquivo Histórico Ultramarino, Macau e Timor, ACL_SEMU_DGU_005, Caixa 26.

Castro, Afonso de. 1861. "To the Minister of the Navy and Overseas Territories, 14 September 1861." Official Letter No. 63. Lisbon, Arquivo Histórico Ultramarino, Macau e Timor, ACL_SEMU_DGU_005, Caixa 28.

Castro, Afonso de. 1862a. "To the Minister of the Navy and Overseas Territories, 23 June 1862." Official Letter No. 44. Confidential. Lisbon, Arquivo Histórico Ultramarino, Macau e Timor, ACL_SEMU_DGU_005, Caixa 28.

Castro, Afonso de. 1862b. "Résumé historique de l'établissement portugais à Timor, des us et coutumes de ses habitants" [Historical summary of the Portuguese establishment in Timor, the habits and customs of its inhabitants]. *Tijdschrift voor Indische Taal-, Land- en Volkenkunde* 11: 465–506.

Castro, Afonso de. 1863. "Notícia dos usos e costumes dos povos de Timor" [News of uses and customs of the people of Timor]. *Anais do Conselho Ultramarino*. Unofficial section: 29–31.

Castro, Afonso de. 1864. "Une rébellion à Timor en 1861" [A rebellion in Timor in 1861]. *Tijdschrift voor Indische Taal-, Land- en Volkenkunde* 13: 389–409.

Castro, Afonso de. 1867. *As Possessões Portuguezas na Oceânia* [The Portuguese possessions in Oceania]. Lisbon: Imprensa Nacional.

Cheng, Joyce. 2009. "Mask, Mimicry, Metamorphosis: Roger Caillois, Walter Benjamin and Surrealism in the 1930s." *Modernism/Modernity* 16 (1): 61–86.

Connor, Steven. 2002. "Michel Serres's Milieux." Extended version of a paper presented at the ABRALIC (Brazilian Association for Comparative Literature) conference on "Mediations," Belo Horizonte, 23–26 July. http://www.stevenconnor.com/milieux.

Elias, Norbert. 1989. *O Processo Civilizacional* [The civilization process]. Lisbon: D. Quixote.

Foucault, Michel. 2007. *Security, Territory, Population: Lectures at the Collège de France 1977–1978*. Trans. Graham Burchell. New York: Palgrave Macmillan.

Gebauer, Gunter, and Christoph Wulf. 1995. *Mimesis: Culture, Art, Society*. Trans. Don Reneau. Berkeley: University of California Press.

Girard, René. 1972. *La violence et le sacré* [Violence and the sacred]. Paris: Grasset.

Horkheimer, Max, and Theodor W. Adorno. (1944) 2002. *Dialectic of Enlightenment: Philosophical Fragments*. Ed. Gunzelin S. Noerr; trans. Edmund Jephcott. Stanford, CA: Stanford University Press.

Huggan, Graham. 1997. "(Post)Colonialism, Anthropology, and the Magic of Mimesis." *Cultural Critique* 38: 91–106.

Kramer, Fritz. 1993. *The Red Fez: Art and Spirit Possession in Africa*. Trans. Malcolm R. Green. New York: Verso.

Oliveira, Luna de. 1950. *Timor na História de Portugal* [Timor in the history of Portugal]. Vol. 2. Lisbon: Agência Geral das Colónias.

Pélissier, René. 1996. *Timor en Guerre: Le Crocodile et les Portugais (1847–1913)* [Timor at war: The crocodile and the Portuguese (1847–1913)]. Orgeval: Pélissier.

Potolsky, Matthew. 2006. *Mimesis*. London: Routledge.

Roque, Ricardo. 2010. *Headhunting and Colonialism: Anthropology and the Circulation of Human Skulls in the Portuguese Empire, 1870–1930*. Basingstoke: Palgrave Macmillan.

Roque, Ricardo. 2015. "Mimetic Governmentality and the Administration of Colonial Justice in East Timor, ca. 1860–1910." *Comparative Studies in Society and History* 57 (1): 67–97.

Serres, Michel. 1982. *The Parasite*. Trans. Lawrence R. Schehr. Baltimore: Johns Hopkins University Press.

Shapin, Steven. 1996. *The Scientific Revolution*. Chicago: University of Chicago Press.

Silva, José Celestino da. 1896. *Instrucções para os Commandantes Militares* [Instructions for military commanders]. Macau: n.p.

Taussig, Michael. 1987. *Shamanism, Colonialism, and the Wild Man: A Study in Terror and Healing*. Chicago: University of Chicago Press.

Taussig, Michael. 1993. *Mimesis and Alterity: A Particular History of the Senses*. London: Routledge.

Walker, Iain. 2010. *Becoming the Other, Being Oneself: Constructing Identities in a Connected World*. Newcastle: Cambridge Scholars Publishing.

Willerslev, Rane. 2007. *Soul Hunters: Hunting, Animism, and Personhood among the Siberian Yukaghirs*. Berkeley: University of California Press.

Xavier, Ângela Barreto. 2014. "'Parecem indianos na cor e na feição': A 'lenda negra' e a indianização dos portugueses" ["They seem to be Indians in color and form": The "black legend" and the Indianization of the Portuguese]. *Etnográfica* 18 (1): 111–133.

Chapter 2

VARIANTS OF FRONTIER MIMESIS
Colonial Encounter and Intercultural Interaction
in the Lao-Vietnamese Uplands

Oliver Tappe

The history of upland ethnic groups in mainland Southeast Asia shows that they adopted a variety of mimetic practices with the aim of negotiating a beneficial relationship with lowland empires (Jonsson 2014; Tappe 2015b). State actors from the lowlands also demonstrated a 'mimetic faculty' (Benjamin [1933] 1986; see also Taussig 1993) in dealing with the different people living in the upland fringes of empires, for example, by modeling frontier administration on local forms of political organization. This chapter investigates these two fundamentally different yet at times complementary variants of mimesis in the context of nineteenth- and early-twentieth-century upland Southeast Asia. In particular, I will focus on the ethnically heterogeneous Lao-Vietnamese upland frontier before and during French colonial administration. I will explore

Notes for this chapter begin on page 69.

processes of interaction and the manifold entanglements between lowland empires and different upland societies.

Mimesis is first of all a way to create relations. Second, mimetic processes characterize the trajectories and contingencies of these relations. Agents of mimetic appropriation aim to establish mutually beneficial relations (Roque 2015a). Both sides try to shape, to control, or at least to negotiate these relations. Within such encounters and interactions, mimetic practices appear as tactics, in Michel de Certeau's (1984) sense. In contrast to strategies, tactics are adopted in an unknown, potentially hostile setting as flexible and opportunistic responses to specific power configurations (ibid.: 34–39).

During colonial encounters in the Southeast Asian uplands, mimetic practices of both colonizer and colonized appear as tactics, I would argue, because these encounters imply uncertainty, fear, and ignorance on both sides. Local elites would now have to reckon with a new power, while the colonial administrator might find himself remote from the foundations and structures of this power. If state actors and state subjects constitute the opposing poles in such mimetic relations, their respective aims, interests, and mutual representations might collide (cf. Pels and Salemink 1999). How are such inherent power relations perceived and negotiated by the respective actors? This question is particularly acute in a colonial context where state control of mountainous frontier regions gradually increased.

French colonial rule aggravated a process of administrative transformations and rationalization of governance that had already been triggered in nineteenth-century Vietnam and Siam and in their respective upland fringes (Davis 2015; Poisson 2004; Winichakul 1995). Mimetic tactics played a significant role in frontier encounters between lowland state formations and diverse upland societies (Jonsson 2005, 2010, 2014; Salemink 2003). The much-debated concept of 'frontier' describes "a pre-modern and zonal form of boundary" (Imamura 2015: 96), or a social space where "cultures interpenetrate in a dynamic manner" (Leach 1960: 50). Frontier rhetoric often implies an expansive force. According to the well-known views of Frederick Turner (1921) regarding the American West, a shifting frontier demarcates the expansion of civilization or a civilization yet to come—a perspective in contrast to that of James C. Scott (2009) with his idea of a purposefully 'state-repelling' upland frontier in mainland Southeast Asia.

Expansionist connotations of the frontier concept render it epistemologically problematic. Nevertheless, even if the term 'borderlands' appears more suitable in Asian contexts (cf. Giersch 2006), the situation in late-nineteenth-century Southeast Asia was indeed located in a context of imperial expansion. The Siamese and Vietnamese courts were vying with each other for political influence in the uplands, while later the British and French colonial powers intervened and confronted each other in the Golden Triangle (Grabowsky 2003;

A. Walker 1999). Upland societies were increasingly facing a variety of external political actors who interfered in local socio-political configurations to different degrees. Frontier encounters gained intensity in imperial and colonial contexts, resulting in considerable frictions and transformations, along with dynamics of inclusion, appropriation, and gradual enclosure (Cooper 2005; Scott 2009).

In this chapter I will analyze two parallel strands of mimetic appropriation within the relationship between the colonial administration and the upland population: first, the French colonial appropriation and transformation of local forms of governance; second, local mimetic tactics of adaptation to the changing political economy and increasing state enclosure. My discussion is inspired by the recent debate about James Scott's interpretations of the Southeast Asian uplands—or *zomia* (see Schendel 2002)—as a zone of deliberate "state evasion and state prevention" (Scott 2009: 8).

Contrary to Scott's main argument about state-repelling uplanders, I would like to emphasize tactics of self-empowerment through mimetic adaptation to, and appropriation of, external sources of power—here represented by various state actors such as French colonial administrators. Even if power inequalities and hierarchy may characterize intercultural relations in upland Southeast Asia, this does not necessarily entail a crude dialectic of domination and resistance. Rather, I would like to illuminate the room to maneuver that was available to upland political actors within colonial state enclosure. Uplanders experienced 'the state' not as a mere imposition of external political models but as a relational process from which "alternative governmentalities" (Pels 1997: 177; see also Ladwig and Roque, this volume) might emerge.

As Oscar Salemink (2015) argues, Scott (2009) does indeed point at interaction and exchange, but gives it less attention than revolt and other means of state avoidance. Scott indicates the attraction of certain elements of the lowland state for upland populations and refers to the economic and symbolic reach of the state. Uplanders aspired to acquire items of economic (salt, silver, tools) as well as symbolic (titles, regalia, costumes) value, which in the end served local empowerment and "left a deep impression in the hills" (ibid.: 35). Scott does not elaborate on the character of this impression, nor does he explore its consequences. He neglects the aspects of interaction and exchange in order to emphasize anarchy and revolt as the main characteristics of upland societies (Jonsson 2012).

Instead of focusing on the binary of domination and resistance, I argue that we should pay more attention to networks of mutual exchange, to relations and interdependence. The French colonial administration of the mountainous hinterlands of Annam and Tonkin and the local elites in those areas arguably constituted each other through processes that Ricardo Roque (2010: 18) describes as "mutual inclusion and asymmetric balances," a form of symbiosis that held colonial and indigenous worlds together. While Roque focuses on the juridical realm in his analysis of mutual parasitism during colonialism (ibid.; 2015b), French Indochina is an example of colonial collaboration for economic gains: both the French and the indigenous elites aimed to exploit resources and control trade routes, often to the detriment of peasant livelihoods (Brocheux and Hémery 2009).

The Lao-Vietnamese borderlands provide ample opportunity to test Scott's hypothesis of state-repelling upland societies. In particular, upland Tai societies refute simplistic upland-lowland binaries, since their own social structures resemble lowland state formations but are also adapted to upland livelihoods. Scott misconstrues upland Tai polities (*muang*) as mimic states that imitate lowland empires of the Tai-speaking world. We should, rather, assume an encompassing heterogeneous, hierarchized social space, a continuum linking coastal and mountain communities characterized by manifold economic, political, and cultural relations. According to Karl Izikowitz (1969: 142), "interaction then depends on the nature of the relations ... and can lead to war, rebellion, persecution, flight, the imitation of customs, peaceful trade, and many other types of action." Mimesis here provides a useful lens through which to view any social and political relations in Southeast Asia.

Most studies on mimesis focus on the subversive agency of subaltern peoples facing hegemonic colonial powers (see Ladwig and Roque, this volume). However, as indicated above, mimetic tactics can also be observed with dominant actors such as colonial state representatives. As my analysis will illustrate, French administrators in the Lao-Vietnamese uplands tried to implement strategies devised by the colonial administration—based on structures of power, institutions, and knowledge (Certeau 1984: 38)—to co-opt local elites in order to make frontier administration more cost-efficient. Yet on the local level—on potentially perilous terrain—colonial administrators often resorted to ad hoc tactics in everyday negotiations with the Other. Mimetic tactics of mutual appropriation shaped the interdependent relationship—at least in the formative years of French colonial rule—between colonizers and colonized in what Roque (2010: 17–18) describes as "mutual parasitism."

This gamble within the colonial encounter implies mimetic processes that Michael Taussig (1993) summarizes as exploring difference and becoming Other—a dialectical politics of identity and alterity marked by a shifting interplay of identity and difference, proximity and distance (cf. Ladwig and Roque, this volume; Melberg 1995). However, rather than a road to complete assimilation, mimesis aims at "absorbing the outside and changing world in order to stay the same" (Taussig 1993: 131), that is, self-assertion instead of transformation (cf. Gebauer and Wulf 1995). Nonetheless, as the case studies below will illustrate, the colonial encounters of the late nineteenth century definitely initiated processes of socio-political transformation within the apparent continuity of upland-lowland relations.

Following Roque (2015a: 206), "mimesis involves processes of resemblance that are always partial and selective; as such, it calls for parallel processes of differentiation and individuation" (cf. Harrison 2006). Colonial and indigenous actors were able to relate through this specific mode of human interaction, both aiming at mutual appropriation of the power of the Other and thus at self-empowerment. The local elites tapped into the emergent power source of the colonial administration, and the colonial administrators capitalized on local nodes of political and economic power. If we understand statecraft as *Staats-kunst*—as an 'art of governance'—Fritz Kramer's (1993) discussion of ritual efficacy through mimetic appropriation of the Other's power provides another useful perspective on mimesis in the colonial situation.

This study is an attempt to combine historical and anthropological approaches in order to attain a long-term perspective of socio-political relations in *zomia* and to rethink upland-lowland dynamics beyond the dominance-resistance narrative through the lens of mimetic interaction. Archival ethnography aims to trace the transformations of socio-cultural configuration in the course of state-making projects in the Lao-Vietnamese borderlands in pre-colonial and colonial times.[1] My approach is intended to provide a corrective to Scott's inspiring but one-sided discussion of state-repelling upland societies. I shall emphasize the tacit rapprochement and mutual interdependence of upland and lowland groups, including the French colonial state in its formative years at the turn of the twentieth century. After a short historical overview of the Lao-Vietnamese borderlands, I will present my case studies on different aspects of mimetic entanglements in *zomia*.

Houaphan and Sipsong Chau Tai: Political and Cultural Trajectories of the Lao-Vietnamese Upland Frontier

The mountainous regions that today constitute northwestern Vietnam and northeastern Laos historically formed a natural frontier between the Indian-ized and the Sinicized cultural worlds of Southeast Asia (see Arnason 1997; Coedès 1968). Different Tai-speaking groups (Lao, Lü, Black and White Tai, etc.) inhabit the upland river valleys and once entertained tributary relations to other peoples such as the Khmu of the Mon-Khmer language family—pejo-ratively called 'Kha' (slaves) by the Lao—and the Hmong, who migrated from China in the nineteenth century (Michaud 2006). In particular, the Tai of the Black River region acted as intermediaries between different upland popula-tions and, for example, Chinese merchants (Davis 2011, 2017; Le Failler 2014).

The jagged, densely forested, and ethnically heterogeneous uplands were often remote from the imperial lowland centers, in both a geographical and an administrative sense. Direct conquest was the exception. The Vietnamese and

Lao rulers relied instead on tributary and trade relations with local elites to achieve at least a certain economic control of their resource-rich hinterlands. While the Vietnamese reduced their presence to a minimum, relying almost fully on local alliances (in particular with Muong and Tai groups), the Lao constituted a politically dominant minority in some upland valleys. The upland Lao principalities in Houaphan were small and isolated and entertained only loose tributary relations with the Lao imperial centers by the Mekong River (see Lorrillard 2008; Tappe 2015a).

In the pre-colonial upland frontier of contemporary northern Laos and northwestern Vietnam, the main interest of lowland empires was safeguarding the flow of trade and tribute. Small principalities of upland Lao and Tai people, mirroring the *muang* system of the larger Buddhist lowland empires, controlled the fertile upland river valleys and the trade with different upland groups such as the Hmong, acting as intermediaries between Lao, Vietnamese, or Chinese lowland centers and the resource-rich uplands. When the French arrived in the region and attempted to establish their colonial administration at the end of the nineteenth century, one of their main goals was to co-opt these local intermediaries—one aspect of the military 'pacification' campaigns—and to take control of upland-lowland trade (Le Failler 2014; Poisson 2004).

The six (Lao: *hok*) principalities of Houaphan (Houaphan Tang Hok, according to old Lao chronicles; see Bourlet 1906) had established tributary relations with the Vietnamese court of Hué to balance Siamese pressure during the eighteenth and nineteenth centuries. The Sipsong Chau Tai (Twelve Tai Counties),[2] an upland Tai confederation, is a similar case. The White, Black, and Red Tai (sub-groups of the Tai-Kadai language family) enjoyed certain autonomy from lowland empires, even if they were considered tributary vassals. The Sipsong Chau Tai entertained tributary relations with Chinese, Vietnamese, Lao, Siamese, and Burmese centers, and constituted a regional power that was not fully integrated into the Vietnamese state until after the French defeat in 1954 (Lentz 2011). Both Houaphan and Sipsong Chau Tai are characterized by the scarcity of suitable land for wet rice cultivation. Livelihoods in the region consist of a mixture of wet rice and shifting or swidden cultivation, with the latter practiced by all non-Tai groups (Michaud and Forsyth 2011).

Considering the socio-political peculiarity of these upland confederations in comparison with the more unified lowland kingdoms, linguistic aspects are revealing. Houaphan means 'head of a thousand', which arguably refers to the population of each of the six principalities of this Lao upland confederation (Sam Neua, Sam Tai, Houamuang, Muang Son, Muang Soi, Xieng Kho). The Twelve Tai Counties of the Sipsong Chau Tai clearly reflect the loose structure of the alliance with its independent local rulers, who were related through kinship, trade relations, and occasional conflict. In the nineteenth century, the six *muang* of Houaphan constituted a field of tension between different civilizational influences.

They entertained direct tributary relations with the pre-colonial Lao and Vietnamese kingdoms and indirect relations with the Siamese and Chinese. Siam, which had subjugated the Lao principalities at the beginning of the eighteenth century, competed with Vietnam for political control of the frontier regions.

The six principalities of Houaphan were different from neighboring Sipsong Chau Tai because they had been dominated since the sixteenth century by a small Buddhist Lao elite who considered themselves to be 'civilized' lowlanders.[3] In contrast, before World War II, the Vietnamese never bothered to assume direct control in any upland areas, which were considered 'unhealthy', preferring instead the indirect cooperation of local elites (Hardy 2003; Poisson 2009). Yet the Lao principalities in the upland valleys resembled the upland Tai principalities of the Sipsong Chau Tai more than the lowland Lao kingdoms, not least because of geographic and demographic constraints (Boutin 1937). Sipsong Chau Tai and Houaphan—together with their southern neighbor, Xieng Khouang, the former kingdom of the Tai-speaking Phuan—constituted a contested space between the expanding Vietnamese and Siamese kingdoms until the French established their colonial administration in the region at the end of the nineteenth century (Goscha 2012; Ivarsson 2008).

Placed under pressure in this way, the socio-political configurations of the northern frontier regions were further disrupted by invasions of the Ho Chinese, in fact the ethnically heterogeneous remnants of various rebellions that had unsettled the Qing Empire from the mid-nineteenth century. In 1867, the first Vietnamese reports about so-called Qing rebels informed the Vietnamese emperor at Hué about the increasing political chaos in the northwestern mountains (Davis 2009: 26; 2017). Local Tai rulers of the Sipsong Chu Tai either fought against the intruders or sided with them against the increased Vietnamese military presence. Early French explorers deplored the sad state of affairs in the devastated uplands (see, e.g., Cupet [1900] 2000) and took this state of exception as their main argument for the French *mission civilisatrice* (civilizing mission) and pacification of the upland frontier (Fourniau 2002).

Certainly, with the arrival of the French, the general political situation and local power configurations changed considerably. The French intervened both militarily and by co-opting outstanding local powerbrokers. In doing so, the French administration implied a certain continuity with the indirect 'hybrid rule' (Poisson 2004) of imperial Vietnam. As Philippe Le Failler (2011: 44) points out: "It was generally decided to let the inhabitants govern themselves and to uphold the Vietnamese imperial system of delegating power to aristocratic clans." We see here a deliberate selection of allegedly 'traditional' leaders who then self-consciously took advantage of these new power configurations. Before I turn to the specific mimetic faculty of such 'traditional rulers', I will discuss the vector of French mimetic strategies and tactics as part of colonial governance in the mountainous hinterland.

French Colonial Mimesis

In the case of French Indochina, the strategy of colonization was twofold. First, it involved the *mise en valeur* (enhancement) of the colony for the economic benefit of the metropole, that is, extracting resources and countering Chinese economic influence to protect imports from the motherland (see Brocheux and Hémery 2009; Sarraut 1923). The second strategy was aimed at 'civilizing' the colonial subjects, in particular the dominant Lao, Vietnamese, and Khmer populations. This *mission civilisatrice* included the spread of Western culture, education, language, and science in the colonies (Conklin 1997). Yet the idea of assimilation was soon abandoned in Indochina, as the principle of association—co-opting local elites while preserving 'traditional' forms of governance—prevailed (Betts [1961] 2005; Lanessan 1889). The association policy, similar to British indirect rule, provided numerous examples of mimetic interaction between the French colonizers and different indigenous political actors.

When the French came to the mountains of Southeast Asia, the ethnically heterogeneous region was characterized by overlapping spheres of Chinese, Vietnamese, and Siamese political and cultural influence. For the French established in lowland imperial cities such as Hué, the upland margins constituted "zones of unpredictability at the edges of discursive stability, where contradictory discourses overlap[ped], or where discrepant kinds of meaning-making converge[d]" (Tsing 1994: 279). Houaphan and Sipsong Chau Tai were considered rebellious hinterlands and challenges to the French strategy of pacification. Houaphan—being claimed by the kings of both Luang Prabang and Annam, and notorious as an arena of local conflict—became a particular space of contestation also within the French administration (Gay 1989).

The French responded to cases of local unrest in Houaphan with two solutions: either increasing the Vietnamese military presence and integrating Houaphan into Annam proper, or assisting the local Lao notables in solving the conflict and preserving the status of Houaphan as an upland confederation dependent on the Lao kingdom of Luang Prabang (Tappe 2015a). After having seized authority over the Lao territories east of the Mekong from Bangkok in 1893, the French replaced the Siamese as protector of the Lao king in Luang Prabang. However, the question remained as to whether this kingdom should be a semi-autonomous part of French Indochina or annexed to Annam (Goscha 2012). The people of the Lao-Vietnamese upland frontier thus encountered various French actors and motivations instead of a monolithic colonial state.

In Luang Prabang, Commandant Supérieur Joseph Vacle[4] suggested following the previous Siamese model of upland governance in Houaphan. He argued that the authority of the king and viceroy of Luang Prabang was supported "by their presence in the Siamese realm" and by their ability to make the population believe that Bangkok operated on behalf of the Lao people.

Although factual authority was in the hands of the Siamese, the king of Luang Prabang still held considerable prestige and authority in his kingdom. Vacle concluded: "We have the same opportunity ... the King would be the first to accept our presence if we let him keep his face ... and time will peacefully complete our conquest of the country."[5] Co-opting the king of Luang Prabang and underpinning the Lao king's authority in the uplands constituted the key to efficient administration (see Pavie 1942).

Some French administrators in Thanh Hoa (in the province of Annam), however, disagreed with Vacle. They preferred the example of Vietnamese indirect rule in the mountainous hinterland as had been established under Minh Mang in the nineteenth century (Poisson 2004). Claiming to defend 'Annamite rights' in the uplands (Ivarsson 2008; Lemire [1894] 2008), the French had approached local elites to discuss the expense of Siamese political influence. The French authorities in Thanh Hoa looked on Houaphan as an unruly hinterland where a strong Vietnamese military presence should guarantee stability and thus fulfill a major precondition for the *mise en valeur* of the uplands.[6] Their stance in fact favored a more direct rule enforced by a Vietnamese militia under the direction of French officials.

The extent and manner of French colonial adoption of Siamese or Annamite ways differed considerably. Various French political actors considered different models of governance and mimetically adapted elements of indigenous forms of statecraft (Tappe 2015a). Their goal was to gain a thorough understanding of local political culture (Michaud 2013) so as to establish military control and efficient administration. The adaptation of French bureaucracy to local conditions and the appropriation of indigenous forms of governance, including ritual elements, created new political and socio-cultural configurations. This mimetic practice of state making can be considered a "production of a world with relation to another world" (Gebauer and Wulf 1995: 9).

With this policy, the French colonial administration forged political relations between France and the various 'races' of Indochina as state subjects. Unlike previous attempts to turn the colonialized into French citizens via a policy of assimilation, the Indochinese situation was characterized by a shift toward association. The French considered local political hierarchies and singled out strategic groups for co-optation—mainly the elites of the dominant lowland groups such as the Vietnamese, the Khmer, and the Lao, but sometimes also locally influential upland groups (called *montagnards* by the French). As Jean-Marie de Lanessan (1889) proposed, this divide-and-rule strategy would guarantee more efficient administration and economic development. However, the policy of association was implemented differently by different colonial actors and often entailed political tensions between privileged groups and those ignored by the French.

In his excellent analysis of French colonial politics toward the *montagnards*, Salemink (2003) introduces the administrator Léopold Sabatier as an example of successful co-optation of upland groups. Sabatier adopted and apparently mimicked the practice of annual oaths of allegiance, which were characteristic of the hierarchized societies in mainland Southeast Asia.[7] The *palabre du serment* (palaver of the oath) was a deliberate appropriation of a local traditional way of governance in order to harmonize French colonial claims for authority with political and ritual conventions in the highlands. This approach corresponded with former Gouverneur Général Albert Sarraut's "political paternalism, which adapted indigenous policies to the perceived needs of every 'race' according to its degree of evolution" (ibid.: 90; see also Sarraut 1923). Sabatier claimed the key position in the *palabre du serment* as paramount authority while affirming local autonomy—reminiscent of previous practices of indirect rule by lowland rulers.

In the *palabre du serment*, village chiefs and other influential men swore an oath of allegiance to the French. As Salemink's analysis indicates, Sabatier succeeded in institutionalizing this ceremony as a kind of interface between local socio-political configurations and the French colonial apparatus. Mimesis provides the key to this process. Sabatier identified the oath of allegiance as a key element of *montagnard* political ritual and appropriated it—albeit in a slightly transformed and fixed form—for the purpose of colonial administration. Acting like a powerful local ruler, he thus blended into indigenous socio-political logics. Sabatier replaced other potential rulers and epitomized the potential of efficient protection, a crucial aspect of political authority in pre-colonial Southeast Asia. While the French adapted to selected variants of indigenous governance, the ceremony provided a channel for peripheral groups to interact and negotiate directly with this powerful new political actor.

Sabatier was not the first to experiment with forms of local political ritual. In 1895, Jean Gustave Monpeyrat became head of the commissariat in Houaphan where he soon forged close alliances with Lao notables. Within the French administration, he was considered an expert on Tai-Lao culture and politics who was skilled at fostering good relations with the locals.[8] This included organizing an annual *fête du serment* (festival of the oath) or *ceremonie de l'eau du serment* (water-sprinkling ceremony of the oath) to foster the unity of the confederation and to underpin French authority.[9] In April 1897, on the occasion of the Lao New Year, Monpeyrat summoned notables from the six Houaphan for the oath of allegiance, ritually enacted by sprinkling water, as in many Buddhist purification rites (Archaimbault 1971). Most of them were Lao notables linked to the court of Luang Prabang, where the French had already established a loyal protectorate.

The ceremony was a bricolage of European and indigenous practices of political ritual. It started with a military parade of the *garde indigène* (local militia). After that, Monpeyrat handed over certificates of appointment and letters of honor to certain Lao *phaya* (lords), a common practice in upland Southeast Asia. This element implies official recognition of local authority by an external power, with the French commissar having replaced the Siamese and Lao kings. In a letter to Vacle, Monpeyrat regretted that the medals intended for this occasion did not arrive on time "because the handing-over of the medals in the presence of all mandarins and notables would have made an excellent effect."[10] The French commissar was aware of the efficacy of combining indigenous and foreign elements of political ritual.

While Monpeyrat invited the principal notables into the commissariat for lunch—a specific separate space representing the emergent French colonial state—the population of Muang Son and the surrounding villages gathered for 'amusements' including games, music, and dance. At 10:00 PM, the monks started to chant oaths and recitations *pour la prosperité du pays* (for the prosperity of the country), important ritual aspects of Buddhist statecraft. Meanwhile, the party continued all night. Unfortunately, Monpeyrat's account provides no ethnographic details about the music, dances, and costumes or the ethnic composition of the crowd. After the ceremony, the notables stayed another three days at Muang Son to discuss various issues. Monpeyrat took advantage of this meeting to give them instructions about tax collection, thus integrating aspects of modern governmentality into indigenous governance.

By organizing such a ceremony, Monpeyrat adhered to Vacle's strategic adaptation of Lao-Buddhist statecraft. As Iain Walker (2005: 189) points out, "pseudotraditions" like our examples of the *fêtes/palabres du serment* have to be grounded in a specific socio-cultural matrix to be efficacious and to acquire any legitimacy. Monpeyrat occupied the ritual position of the Lao king as a node within the socio-cosmological relations in the upland *muang*. As in the case of Sabatier discussed by Oscar Salemink, this partial mimesis also entailed considerable transformations and resulted in the routinization of French authority in the following years. Mimesis thus contributed to shifts in local socio-political configurations and power relations.

It is evident here that mimesis goes beyond mere copying or imitation. Inspired by Taussig's (1993) paired contrasting of mimesis with alterity, Walker (2005: 192) interprets mimetic practice as "appropriation of the Other, and the power of the Other, as part of a process of social change." In the context of colonial encounters that preceded the establishment of a pervasive colonial state apparatus, this process of mimesis was a reciprocal one characterized by mutual appropriation and adaptation. As Bronwen Douglas (1992: 98) indicates in the context of French colonization of New Caledonia, for the local people "the French had become a meaningful element in their present political realities." In the next section I will discuss examples of mimetic tactics adopted by local powerbrokers to engage with external sources of power.

Mimesis and Upland Agency

During pre-colonial and colonial times, it was a common practice among uplanders in Southeast Asia to imitate the 'civilized' Other in order to win him/ her as a trading partner or to attain local prestige. This kind of everyday practical ethnography implied "knowledge of their habits" (I. Walker 2005: 188), in particular with regard to gestures and material culture. Colonial photographs show upland Tai lords dressed in precious Chinese-style silk dresses that differed strongly from locally woven garments, mainly black cloth with colored embroidery. As my case studies will illustrate, local powerbrokers presented themselves to representatives of external powers such as China and France as prestigious 'mandarins' by appropriating dress codes and postures of allegedly 'civilized' Chinese nobles.

While such mimetic strategies might appear at first sight as mimicry intended to subvert specific power structures, I would prefer to analytically separate mimicry from mimesis. Criticizing Taussig's conflation of mimesis, mimicry, and imitation and his focus on subversion, Graham Huggan (1997: 94) suggests that mimetic processes should be considered as forms of representation and mediation between different worlds or symbolic systems (see also Gebauer and Wulf 1995; Ladwig and Roque, this volume). As E. R. Leach (1954, 1960) has indicated, the boundary between upland and lowland societies is fluid and permeable, a dynamic field of diverging processes of inclusion and exclusion, of interaction and difference.

In the ethnically heterogeneous upland polities characterized by shifting Tai-Kha hierarchies—with in-migrating Hmong and Yao groups a new factor in regional power configurations—frictions resulting from "interconnection across difference" (Tsing 2005: 4) were commonplace. Entitled intermediaries (Lao: *lam*), often of lowland origin but not necessarily so (see Évrard 2006; A. Walker 1999), represented communicative linkages that ensured trade and tax flows. Such powerbrokers distinguished themselves by their linguistic and strategic skills. Badenoch and Tomita (2013: 40–49) provide the fascinating case study of Lanten clan leaders who acted as an "interface between the non-Tai upland people and the Tai rulers in the *muang*." They received Lao titles and enjoyed administrative authority prior to and in the first years of French colonial rule. The frequent use of Lao titles, for example, *hua na* (headman), and Chinese ones, such as *quan* (mandarin), by upland leaders also epitomizes their appropriation of external sources of power for local authority.

One of the most prominent examples of an intermediary between uplands and lowlands was Đèo Văn Trị (1849–1909), the chief of the White Tai ethnic group of the Black River area (see Le Failler 2011, 2014).[11] Following Scott (2009), Đèo Văn Trị would be considered as head of a 'mimicry state', that is, a small upland principality that only superficially imitated lowland imperial structures so as to gain advantage in upland-lowland (economic) interactions and in order to be recognized as 'civilized'. However, the White Tai *muang* organization must not be confused with state mimicry since, as indicated above, it constituted a socio-political model of all Tai groups that existed before ideas of Buddhist kingship expanded to Southeast Asia (Condominas 1980).

Yet it is evident that Đèo Văn Trị, who was of Chinese ancestry, strategically adopted elements of Chinese civilization to qualify himself as a suitable intermediary between the Chinese empire and the 'raw' frontier. By mimetically appropriating Chinese mandarin panache—for example, wearing pompous silken clothing and honorary medals as documented by colonial photographs (Dion 2010: 111)—he made himself visible in a specific way. The French traveler Eugène Lefèvre (1898: 30) assigned him "a general appearance of ruse and finesse ... His clothes consisted of a Chinese coat, flowing trousers and a turban, all of bright colors. He talked sufficient French so that he needed an interpreter only in a pinch. He was fluent in Lao, Chinese from Yunnan, Chinese from Canton, and Vietnamese." Here, the White Tai leader appears as the intermediary par excellence, a local powerbroker capitalizing on his various external relations and communicative skills.

Mimetic appropriation of and adaptation to external sources of power were widespread practices among political actors in upland Southeast Asia. Leach (1954: 223) cites a travelogue from 1871 that mentions a similar case of efficient mimesis, here of a Kachin chief: "He wears his hair in Burmese fashion, but his dress is a mixture of Shan and Chinese." This practice probably contributed to his successful recognition by Burmese and British authorities, who gave him "gold umbrellas and honorific titles appropriate to the status of a *saopha*" (ibid.). The partial assimilation toward a Shan prince (*saopha*) was not without risk, though, and an ambitious Kachin chief risked enmity and isolation from local sources of power—a tendency that made him increasingly dependent on the aid of external authorities (ibid.: 224).[12]

In addition to the adoption of certain aesthetic aspects of the Chinese mandarin system, specific concepts also traveled into the upland Tai realm, most importantly the Chinese/Vietnamese word for mandarin as such: *quan*. While the Lao used the expression *nai ban* (head of village) to designate village headmen, the Red Tai in Vietnam used the expression *quan ban* instead (Robert 1941: 23). The appropriation of the title *quan* by Tai groups hints at an inclination to mimetically adapt to the Confucian bureaucratic system. Here again, the idea of mimesis refers to local processes of appropriation (see Jonsson 2010), which must be distinguished from systems imposed by a dominant civilization. When Đèo Văn Trị received the title Quan Dao (Uplands Patrol Commissioner) from the French colonial administration in 1893 (Le Failler 2011: 49), it served his self-empowerment through superficial incorporation into the French-Vietnamese colonial state.

When doing research in the French colonial archives on the local history of Sam Tai district (of Houaphan), I came across a certain *lasa quan*, a notable "of Kha origin,"[13] probably ethnic Khmu. His story illustrates the interstitial position of upland powerbrokers entangled in a complex network of socio-political hierarchies and shifting alliances. After the notorious Kha Cheuang rebellion (see Proschan 1998) against the domination of the Tai-Lao groups was quelled with the aid of Siamese troops, and when most Khmu "had taken on the yoke again" (Boutin 1937: 96), a Khmu headman was apparently incorporated into the feudal hierarchy of the Lao upland *muang* of Sam Tai. The title *lasa quan* is in fact a combination of the Tai-Lao word for king (*lasa* being derived from Sanskrit *rājā*) and the Chinese/Vietnamese term for mandarin (*quan*). This title, a rare example of the combination of Indianized and Sinicized politico-administrative terms, indicates two levels of mimesis—one toward a Lao aristocracy and one toward the Confucian world.

In 1894, the *lasa quan* of a Khmu village in Sam Tai district demanded the payment of a large sum of silver ingots from their Lao neighbors. That money, incurred when the Lao recruited the Khmu as mercenaries against attacking Ho bands, had been overdue for 10 ten years. Since the demand had been declined again and again, the *lasa quan* turned his allegiance away from the Lao and encouraged his fellow Khmu to adopt stronger measures against the debtors. Having recruited some Hmong fighters from the surrounding mountains, the *lasa quan* attacked the combined Lao and Vietnamese militia—the *garde indigène* installed by the French—in Sam Tai. When the headman of a Hmong village died in the skirmishes, his followers called for revenge and instigated a general revolt of the local Hmong clans.[14]

The French, who had only recently quelled a prolonged revolt in Houaphan and adjacent Thanh Hoa province in Annam, were alarmed (Fourniau 2002). Two strategies seemed viable as already indicated above. The first was to increase the military presence by dispatching more Vietnamese troops to Sam Tai, thus integrating these Lao upland *muang* more into Annam proper. Indeed, parts of eastern Houaphan were attached to Thanh Hoa in 1894 and occupied by a Vietnamese militia (Gay 1989). Second, some French administrators preferred to assist the locals in solving the conflict according to traditional Lao law and customs—"in a way a moral treatise"[15]—while preserving the status of Houaphan as an upland confederation within the Lao realm of Luang Prabang.

Therefore, in order to appease at least the Khmu population, the French commissar in Luang Prabang, Vacle, suggested that the French—besides strengthening the military presence in the upland region—take over the compensation of the Khmu as requested by the *lasa quan*.[16] Actually, the *lasa quan* accepted an advance payment, and the Khmu returned apparently peacefully to their fields. The *lasa quan* even provided the French with information about the rebel Cầm Bá Thước, a Tai leader associated with the Vietnamese anti-French

Can Vuong movement (Fourniau 2002), with whose partisans he had previously attempted to ally himself. Moreover, the *lasa quan* denounced some of the Lao responsible for violent retaliative assaults on the Hmong. Shortly after, references to the *lasa quan* disappear from the French sources.

In the case of the *lasa quan* and his shifting allegiances, the keyword is reciprocity. The Khmu had entered into a hierarchical relation with the Lao and questioned it only when the Lao refused to pay their Khmu mercenaries—or maybe this was the last straw in a context of aggravated tensions and socio-economic pressures. The *lasa quan* tried to renegotiate an adjustment within the Tai-Kha hierarchy—possibly as *lam kha* (Gunn 1985: 56), a local intermediary in charge of the organization of corvée labor—as he always at risk in case local rivals should turn against him. He was partially integrated into the Lao hierarchy, and a matrimonial alliance can be assumed (cf. Condominas 1990). Evans (2000: 279) argues that intermarriage between Tai and Kha commoners did not occur often, but concedes that integration into Tai society through marriage was one way for a Khmu chief to raise his status.

Obtaining a position in the Tai hierarchy and elevating himself above other chiefs, the *lasa quan* was probably under stronger pressure to fulfill his reciprocal obligations within the Khmu community. This is reminiscent of Leach's (1954: 220–224) aforementioned case studies dealing with the ambiguities of Kachin-Shan intermarriage and the tensions between the two social systems. Did the *lasa quan* face a crisis of authority within the Khmu community that forced him to put his newly established position within the Lao hierarchy at risk by attacking them? Or did the Lao rebut the mimetic approximation of the ambitious Kha and try to put him off with a title and some minor privileges, provoking him to engage in a show of power for both internal and external observers?

The sources reveal little about the motivations of the *lasa quan* and the internal dynamics of the Khmu in Houaphan. We also do not know to what extent specific items such as Lao regalia or mandarin dress were part of the *lasa quan*'s mimetic tool kit. Yet the fact that he entertained various risky relations with the outside world—with Lao notables, anti-colonial rebels from Vietnam, Hmong peasants, and French administrators—betrays a considerable mimetic faculty that made the *lasa quan* stand out from other Khmu leaders in the region. Like Đèo Văn Trị, he appears at least temporarily to have been a flexible networker and efficient powerbroker at the Lao-Vietnamese upland frontier.

Le Failler (2011: 61) argues that "if, from 1895 to 1945, a handful of French 'controlled the area' to use the expression of the time, it was because their activity presented no hindrance to incumbent power structures or, more likely, because some people had something to gain from it." I agree to the extent that at least some local actors, perceiving the French as potential allies and thus as an emergent part of local socio-political configurations, reckoned with this new external source of power and attempted to appropriate it for their own benefit.

Such local powerbrokers became the first targets for French co-optative strategies in the hinterlands in what Osterhammel (2009: 72) describes as a "conver-
gence of interests" to avoid the negatively connoted term 'collaboration'.

With the establishment of the colonial state and later the Lao and Vietnamese nation-states, upland rulers increasingly witnessed more constraints
to local modes of governance. A process of internal colonization (Evans 1992;
Hardy 2003) came to dominate relations between the state and minorities.
The emergence of the idea of national minorities entailed a growing tension
between mechanisms of belonging and marginalization (Lentz 2014). The dialectic of identity and alterity became more dramatic, as Hjorleifur Jonsson's
(2005, 2014) inspirational work on the relation between the Mien and the state
of Thailand demonstrates. Mimesis remained a (sometimes performative) tactic to gain recognition and negotiate relations with the outside world.

To conclude this focus on local elites, I would still like to hint at the contemporary role of upland village headmen as intermediaries between the socialist
state and local communities (see Lentz 2014; Schopohl 2011). Not unlike their
(pre-)colonial predecessors, they switch roles and appearances based on the
context, dressing either like communist functionaries or according to local
customs. As Lentz (2014: 5) puts it: "The village head embodies a multiply-
fractured, sometimes contradictory orientation: as an official, split between
high and low administrative units; as a communal leader, straddling inside and
outside relationships." The uplanders' mimetic faculty in the post-colonial,
socialist state context of the Lao-Vietnamese frontier deserves further analysis.

Conclusion

As Patrice Ladwig and Ricardo Roque suggest in their introduction, the chapters in this book assume a shared history of mimesis and colonialism. Mimetic
practices are indeed part and parcel of imperial and colonial encounters and
interaction. Historical processes of mutual appropriation characterize the relationship between imperial actors and local elites on the fringes of empire. Common political and economic interests initially motivated interaction in spite of
latent suspicion. The aim of my historio-anthropological analysis is to show
the significance of the mimetic process for a thorough understanding of upland
Southeast Asia under colonialism.

In the case of French Indochina, the relationship between colonial administrators and local powerbrokers in the uplands shows properties of mutual
parasitism, a relationship of interdependence across difference that involved
"reciprocal gains and reciprocal losses" (Roque 2010: 18). At the beginning of
the establishment of French administration in the uplands following the military
pacification campaigns, the French were perceived locally as a new power, not

unlike other external powers such as the Vietnamese and Chinese mandarins. In fact, from the outset French colonialization took up previous Vietnamese rationalizations of governance (Davis 2009). Control mainly remained indirect through the co-optation of local elites, such as the Đèo family or selected Lao *phanya*. To underpin their authority, French officials adopted the attributes of lowland mandarins or claimed to represent the interests of the king.

This policy corresponded with practices assumed by local rulers to increase their authority by tapping into external sources of power. Local powerbrokers appropriated elements of the lowland Other. Resembling the Other implied being recognizable and accepted as an intermediary. This tactic had the potential to aggravate local power hierarchies and inequalities and consequently to increase socio-political tensions. Self-empowerment through temporarily becoming the Other came at the risk of internal misrepresentation or provoking local rivals' resentment. Entertaining relations with the external Other thus implied power, potentiality, risk, and vulnerability. This became particularly acute when the French tightened their bureaucratic grasp in the first decades of the twentieth century, often leaving local elites with no choice but to collaborate or face deprivation.

The early colonial state provides ample evidence of mutual mimetic appropriation resembling upland-lowland relations in the mid-nineteenth century and the varying imperial frontier politics of Bangkok and Hué. Colonial administration of the northern frontier regions constituted less a radical break with pre-colonial governance or a sudden enclosure than a gradual process of socio-political transformation of the imperial upland fringes. James Scott (2009) correctly identifies a considerable state enclosure of *zomia* after World War II, but his insistence on the resistance paradigm for the preceding history leaves key aspects of upland-lowland entanglements aside.

The case studies presented in this chapter discuss different mimetic processes that characterized the intercultural encounters and interactions in the ethnically heterogeneous Lao-Vietnamese upland frontier region. Some shaped strategies of (internal) colonization as part of state-making processes; others implied responses to and local appropriation of external sources of power. The upland-lowland relation, from this perspective, appears both as a social continuum and as a contract that is permanently renegotiated. This relationship might be likewise interpreted as a kind of symbiosis, an intimate relation characterized by hospitality and hostility, by mutually parasitic relations, at least in the first decades of colonial administration.

The first case study aimed to illustrate how the emergent colonial state of French Indochina was in fact characterized by a fractured state-making process that was shaped by the mimetic faculty of different political actors. Colonial functionaries such as Sabatier and Monpeyrat experimented with indigenous forms of governance and appropriated specific local elements to include in colonial administrative practice. In the process, they blended into local socio-political configurations by playing roles similar to those of former powerholders. In particular, they participated in traditional political rituals that were eventually transformed by colonial reinvention.

In the next section, I presented some examples of mimetic appropriation of external sources of power by local powerbrokers. Outstanding individuals like Đèo Văn Trị, as well as lesser-known figures such as the Kha *lasa quan* of Sam Tai, forged strategic alliances with various Others to strengthen their own positions in local power structures. This practice called for making oneself recognizable and appealing as a potential partner. While Đèo Văn Trị played the role of an upland mandarin with elements of Chinese/Vietnamese aesthetic conventions, the general tendency was to adopt foreign titles, such as the Lao honorific title *phanya* or the Chinese *quan*, and to underpin the mimetic appropriation of the powerful Other by displaying prestigious items, like the medals that were identified by Monpeyrat as having an "excellent effect."

I have juxtaposed these two variants of mimesis in the colonial context to demonstrate how different mimetic practices create a dynamic interplay entailing cultural innovation and transformation. Competing mimeses—arguably mutually parasitic—stimulate and constrain each other. Here, I follow Jonsson's (2010: 125) convincing argument: "Mimesis calls attention to the practical impossibility of delimiting any identity as unique and uniform (bounded, homogeneous, having a fixed agenda)." Since it takes place in relations and negotiations across difference, mimesis is always linked to power contestation and social control.

The question remains as to whether mimetic practices that only partially and temporarily allow for a certain degree of assimilation—in the sense of selective resemblance—are at odds with or correspond to state-making mimesis projects. It can be argued that neither state nor minorities desire full mimicry, and that mimetic practices on both sides necessarily have to remain limited and flexible to be efficacious. Self-empowerment through mimesis must balance rapprochement and differentiation, not least when competing mimetic practices intersect in a culturally heterogeneous social space such as *zomia*. The entanglements of multi-layered mimetic interactions within emergent state formations highlight the significance of both collective and individual agency in historical and anthropological discussions of state-making projects on the upland frontier.

Acknowledgments

This chapter is the product of a fruitful research exchange between the Max Planck Institute for Social Anthropology (Halle/Germany) and the Instituto de Ciências Sociais (Lisbon/Portugal). The author would like to thank both institutions for their support of this project (funded by the German Academic Exchange Service). Special thanks go to Patrice Ladwig and Ricardo Roque for the initiative to organize this exchange, and to Cristiana Bastos and Christoph Kohl for the interesting discussions during our joint workshops. The Global South Studies Center at the University of Cologne provided an inspiring intellectual environment during the writing-up phase of this chapter.

Oliver Tappe is a Researcher at Hamburg University (CRISEA program). His research interests include the history of the Lao-Vietnamese upland frontier and the past and present dynamics of labor migration in Southeast Asia. He is co-editor, with Vatthana Pholsena, of the volume *Interactions with a Violent Past: Reading Post-Conflict: Landscapes in Cambodia, Laos, and Vietnam* (2013) and editor of the special issue "Frictions and Fictions: Intercultural Encounters and Frontier Imaginaries in Upland Southeast Asia" in the *Asia Pacific Journal of Anthropology* (2015). E-mail: oliver.tappe@uni-koeln.de

Notes

1. Case studies included in this chapter are based on secondary literature and archival research in the Archives nationales d'outre-mer (hereafter ANOM), the French colonial archives in Aix-en-Provence. For the purpose of this chapter, I consulted the inventories of the Gouvernement Général de l'Indochine (GGI) and the Résidence Supérieur du Laos (RSL).
2. According to Le Failler (2011: 65), the Vietnamese word *chau* (county) replaced the almost homonymous Tai word *chao* (lord). The Vietnamese administration conceived upland polities in territorial terms, unlike the Tai focus on manpower.
3. See Ladwig (2016) for a related case study from southern Laos.
4. A member of the Mission Pavie 1888–1891 (see Dion 2010; Pavie 1901), Joseph Vacle was an intimate expert on the Lao-Vietnamese upland frontier since the 1880s (Brébion 1935: 420). He was trusted with the command of Luang Prabang (Haut-Laos) by Gouverneur Général Jean-Marie de Lanessan, one of the most influential proponents of the policy of association.
5. Letter dated 22 November 1894, from Vacle to Gouverneur Général; ANOM, GGI 20871. All translations from French into English are my own if not otherwise indicated.

6. For a contemporaneous view on the Annamese province, see Robequain (1929).
7. See Archaimbault (1971) and Platenkamp (2008) for similar practices in Laos.
8. Dossier Monpeyrat, GGI 30571.
9. Letter from Monpeyrat to Commandant Supérieur Vacle; 5 May 1897; ANOM, RSL, E2.
10. Ibid.
11. Le Failler's (2014) insightful book *La rivière Noire* includes a meticulous historical analysis of Đèo Văn Trị and his relationship with the French colonial administration. It should be noted that Monpeyrat—by 1902 a commissary in Son La and still on good terms with the Lao and Black Tai (at that time dominated by the White Tai)—became a strong opponent of Đèo Văn Trị's local autonomy, which was granted to him by the French administration thanks to Pavie's patronage (ibid.: 201–205). Unlike the more submissive Lao notables in Houaphan, the White Tai leader was apparently a counterpart on an equal level.
12. Jonsson (2014) discusses similar cases of lowland rulers seeking strategic partnerships with upland powerbrokers, for example, the Lao king of Luang Prabang giving the title *phaya* to Yao and Hmong chiefs.
13. Telegram from the commissar in Houaphan to the Gouverneur Général; 3 April 1895; ANOM, GGI 20749.
14. Report from Vacle to the Gouverneur Général; 12 April 1895; ANOM, GGI 20749.
15. General report, 18 October 1894, administrative post of Muang Et (Houaphan); ANOM, GGI 20724.
16. Ibid. Vacle shared Pavie's good relationship with Đèo Văn Trị and thus knew about the specific mechanisms of socio-political configurations in the ethnically heterogeneous upland *muang* (see Le Failler 2014).

References

Archaimbault, Charles. 1971. *The New Year Ceremony at Basak (South Laos)*. Ithaca, NY: Cornell University Press.

Arnason, Johann P. 1997. "The Southeast Asian Labyrinth: Historical and Comparative Perspectives." *Thesis Eleven* 50 (1): 99–122.

Badenoch, Nathan, and Shinsuke Tomita. 2013. "Mountain People in the Muang: Creation and Governance of a Tai Polity in Northern Laos." *Southeast Asian Studies* 2 (1): 29–67.

Benjamin, Walter. (1933) 1986. "On the Mimetic Faculty." In *Reflections: Essays, Aphorisms, Autobiographical Writings*. Ed. Peter Demetz; trans. Edmund Jephcott, 333–336. New York: Schocken Books.

Betts, Raymond F. (1961) 2005. *Assimilation and Association in French Colonial Theory, 1890–1914*. Lincoln: University of Nebraska Press.

Bourlet, Antoine. 1906. "Socialisme dans les hua phan (Laos, Indo-Chine)" [Socialism in Houaphan (Laos, Indo-China)]. *Anthropos* 1 (3): 521–528.

Boutin, André. 1937. "Monographie de la province des Houa-Phan" [Monograph of the province of Houaphan]. *Bulletin des Amis de Laos* 1: 69–119.

Brébion, Antoine. 1935. *Dictionnaire de bio-bibliographie générale, ancienne et moderne de l'Indochine française* [Dictionary of general bio-bibliography, ancient and modern French Indochina]. Paris: Société des Éditions Géographiques, Maritimes et Coloniales.

Brocheux, Pierre, and Daniel Hémery. 2009. *Indochina: An Ambiguous Colonization, 1858–1954.* Trans. Ly Lan Dill-Klein. Berkeley: University of California Press.

Certeau, Michel de. 1984. *The Practice of Everyday Life.* Berkeley: University of California Press.

Coedès, George. 1968. *The Indianized States of Southeast Asia.* Ed. Walter F. Vella; trans. Susan B. Cowing. Honolulu: East-West Center Press.

Condominas, Georges. 1980. *L'espace social: A propos de l'Asie du Sud-Est* [The social space: About Southeast Asia]. Paris: Flammarion.

Condominas, Georges. 1990. *From Lawa to Mon, from Saa' to Thai: Historical and Anthropological Aspects of Southeast Asian Social Spaces.* Ed. and trans. Gehan Wijeyewardene. Canberra: Australian National University.

Conklin, Alice L. 1997. *A Mission to Civilize: The Republican Idea of Empire in France and West Africa, 1895–1930.* Stanford, CA: Stanford University Press.

Cooper, Frederick. 2005. *Colonialism in Question: Theory, Knowledge, History.* Berkeley: University of California Press.

Cupet, Pierre-Paul. (1900) 2000. *Travels in Laos and Among the Tribes of Southeast Indochina: The Pavie Mission Indochina Papers.* Vol. 6. Trans. Walter E. J. Tips. Bangkok: White Lotus.

Davis, Bradley C. 2009. "Post-Taiping Fallout: Nguyen-Qing Collaboration in the Pursuit of Bandits on the Border." In Gainsborough 2009, 25–34.

Davis, Bradley C. 2011. "Black Flag Rumors and the Black River Basin: Powerbrokers and the State in the Tonkin-China Borderlands." *Journal of Vietnamese Studies* 6 (2): 16–41.

Davis, Bradley C. 2015. "The Production of Peoples: Imperial Ethnography and the Changing Conception of Uplands Space in Nineteenth-Century Vietnam." *Asia Pacific Journal of Anthropology* 16 (4): 323–342.

Davis, Bradley C. 2017. *Imperial Bandits: Outlaws and Rebels in the China-Vietnam Borderlands.* Seattle, WA: Washington University Press.

Dion, Isabelle. 2010. *Auguste Pavie, l'explorateur aux pieds nus* [Auguste Pavie, the barefoot explorer]. Aix-en-Provence: Archives nationales d'outre-mer.

Douglas, Bronwen. 1992. "Doing Ethnographic History: The Case of Fighting in New Caledonia." In *History and Tradition in Melanesian Anthropology*, ed. James G. Carrier, 86–115. Berkeley: University of California Press.

Evans, Grant. 1992. "Internal Colonialism in the Central Highlands of Vietnam." *Sojourn* 7 (2): 274–304.

Evans, Grant. 2000. "Tai-Ization: Ethnic Change in Northern Indo-China." In *Civility and Savagery: Social Identity in Tai States*, ed. Andrew Turton, 263–290. Richmond: Curzon Press.

Évrard, Olivier. 2006. *Chroniques des cendres: Anthropologie des sociétés khmou et dynamiques interethniques du Nord-Laos* [Chronicles of ashes: Anthropology of Khmu societies and inter-ethnic dynamics of North Laos]. Paris: IRD.

Fourniau, Charles. 2002. *Vietnam: Domination coloniale et résistance nationale, 1858–1914* [Vietnam: Colonial domination and national resistance, 1858–1914]. Paris: Les Indes Savantes.

Gainsborough, Martin, ed. 2009. *On the Borders of State Power: Frontiers in the Greater Mekong Sub-Region*. London: Routledge.

Gay, Bernard. 1989. "La frontière Vietnamo-Lao de 1893 à nos jours" [The Vietnam-Lao border from 1893 to the present day]. In *Les frontières du Vietnam: Histoire des frontières de la péninsule indochinoise* [Frontiers of Vietnam: History of the borders of the Indochinese peninsula], ed. Pierre-Bernard Lafont, 204–232. Paris: l'Harmattan.

Gebauer, Gunter, and Christoph Wulf. 1995. *Mimesis: Culture, Art, Society*. Trans. Don Reneau. Berkeley: University of California Press.

Giersch, C. Patterson. 2006. *Asian Borderlands: The Transformation of Qing China's Yunnan Frontier*. Cambridge, MA: Harvard University Press.

Goscha, Christopher E. 2012. *Going Indochinese: Contesting Concepts of Space and Place in French Indochina*. Rev. ed. Copenhagen: NIAS Press.

Grabowsky, Volker. 2003. "Chiang Khaeng 1893/96: A Lü Principality in the Upper Mekong Valley in the Focus of British-French Rivalry." In *Contesting Visions of the Lao Past: Lao Historiography at the Crossroads*, ed. Christopher E. Goscha und Søren Ivarsson, 37–70. Copenhagen: NIAS Press.

Gunn, Geoffrey. 1985. "A Scandal in Colonial Laos: The Death of Bac My and the Wounding of Kommadan Revisited." *Journal of the Siam Society* 75 (1–2): 42–59.

Hardy, Andrew. 2003. *Red Hills: Migrants and the State in the Highlands of Vietnam*. Honolulu: University of Hawai'i Press.

Harrison, Simon. 2006. *Fracturing Resemblances: Identity and Mimetic Conflict in Melanesia and the West*. New York: Berghahn Books.

Huggan, Graham. 1997. "(Post)Colonialism, Anthropology, and the Magic of Mimesis." *Cultural Critique* 38: 91–106.

Imamura, Masao. 2015. "Rethinking Frontier and Frontier Studies." *Political Geography* 45: 96–97.

Ivarsson, Søren. 2008. *Creating Laos: The Making of a Lao Space between Indochina and Siam, 1860–1945*. Copenhagen: NIAS Press.

Izikowitz, Karl G. 1969. "Neighbours in Laos." In *Ethnic Groups and Boundaries: The Social Organization of Culture Difference*, ed. Fredrik Barth, 135–148. Bergen: Universitetsforlaget; London: Allen & Unwin.

Jonsson, Hjorleifur. 2005. *Mien Relations: Mountain People and State Control in Thailand*. Ithaca, NY: Cornell University Press.

Jonsson, Hjorleifur. 2010. "Mimetic Minorities: National Identity and Desire on Thailand's Fringe." *Identities* 17 (2–3): 108–130.

Jonsson, Hjorleifur. 2012. "Paths to Freedom: Political Prospecting in the Ethnographic Record." *Critique of Anthropology* 32 (2): 158–172.

Jonsson, Hjorleifur. 2014. *Slow Anthropology: Negotiating Difference with the Iu Mien*. Ithaca, NY: Cornell University Press.

Kramer, Fritz. 1993. *The Red Fez: Art and Spirit Possession in Africa*. Trans. Malcolm R. Green. New York: Verso.

Ladwig, Patrice. 2016. "Religious Place Making: Civilized Modernity and the Spread of Buddhism among the Cheng, a Mon-Khmer Minority in Southern Laos." In *Religion, Place and Modernity: Spatial Articulations in Southeast Asia and East Asia*, ed. Michael Dickhardt and Andrea Lauser, 95–124. Leiden: Brill.

Lanessan, Jean-Marie de. 1889. *L'Indo-Chine Francaise* [French Indo-China]. Paris: Alcan.

Le Failler, Philippe. 2011. "The Đèo Family of Lai Châu: Traditional Power and Unconventional Practices." *Journal of Vietnamese Studies* 6 (2): 42–67.

Le Failler, Philippe. 2014. *La rivière Noire: L'intégration d'une marche frontière au Vietnam* [The Black River: The integration of a border march in Vietnam]. Paris: CNRS Editions.

Leach, E. R. 1954. *Political Systems of Highland Burma: A Study of Kachin Social Structure*. London: Athlone.

Leach, E. R. 1960. "The Frontiers of Burma." *Comparative Studies in Society and History* 3 (1): 49–68.

Lefèvre, Eugène. 1898. *Un voyage au Laos* [A trip to Laos]. Paris: Plon.

Lemire, Charles. (1894) 2008. *Laos in 1893*. Bangkok: White Lotus.

Lentz, Christian C. 2011. "Making the Northwest Vietnamese." *Journal of Vietnamese Studies* 6 (2): 68–105.

Lentz, Christian C. 2014. "The King Yields to the Village? A Micropolitics of State-making in Northwest Vietnam." *Political Geography* 39: 1–10.

Lorrillard, Michel. 2008. "Pour une géographie historique du bouddhisme au Laos" [For a historical geography of Buddhism in Laos]. In *Recherches nouvelles sur le Laos* [New research on Laos], ed. Yves Goudineau and Michel Lorrillard, 113–181. Paris: EFEO.

Melberg, Arne. 1995. *Theories of Mimesis*. Cambridge: Cambridge University Press.

Michaud, Jean. 2006. *Historical Dictionary of the Peoples of the Southeast Asian Massif*. Lanham, MD: Scarecrow Press.

Michaud, Jean. 2013. "French Military Ethnography in Colonial Upper Tonkin (Northern Vietnam), 1897–1904." *Journal of Vietnamese Studies* 8 (4): 1–46.

Michaud, Jean, and Tim Forsyth, eds. 2011. *Moving Mountains: Ethnicity and Livelihoods in Highland China, Vietnam, and Laos*. Vancouver: University of British Columbia Press.

Osterhammel, Jürgen. 2009. *Kolonialismus: Geschichte, Formen, Folgen* [Colonialism: History, forms, consequences]. Munich: C. H. Beck.

Pavie, Auguste. 1901. *Mission Pavie Indo-Chine, 1879–1895: Géographie et voyages* [Pavie's Indo-China mission, 1879–1895: Geography and travel]. Paris: Leroux.

Pavie, Auguste. 1942. *A la conquête des coeurs: Le pays des millions d'éléphants* [A conquest of hearts: The country of millions of elephants]. Paris: Presses universitaires de France.

Pels, Peter. 1997. "The Anthropology of Colonialism: Culture, History, and the Emergence of Western Governmentality." *Annual Review of Anthropology* 26: 163–183.

Pels, Peter, and Oscar Salemink, eds. 1999. *Colonial Subjects: Essays on the Practical History of Anthropology*. Ann Arbor: University of Michigan Press.

Platenkamp, Jos D. M. 2008. "The Canoe Racing Ritual of Luang Prabang." *Social Analysis* 52 (3): 1–32.

Poisson, Emmanuel. 2004. *Mandarins et subalternes au nord du Viêt Nam: Une bureaucratie à l'épreuve (1820–1918)* [Mandarins and subalterns in northern Vietnam: A bureaucracy to the test]. Paris: Maisonneuve & Larose.

Poisson, Emmanuel. 2009. "Unhealthy Air of the Mountains: *Kinh* and Ethnic Minority Rule on the Sino-Vietnamese Frontier from the Fifteenth to the Twentieth Century." In Gainsborough 2009, 12–24.

Proschan, Frank. 1998. "Cheuang in Kmhmu Folklore, History, and Memory." In *Tamnan keokap thao hung thao chuang: Miti thang prawattisat lae wattanatham* [Proceedings of the First International Conference on the Literary, Historical, and Cultural Aspects of Thao Hung Thao Cheuang], ed. Sumitr Pitiphat, 174–209. Bangkok: Thammasat University.

Robequain, Charles. 1929. *Le Thanh-Hoá: Étude géographique d'une province annamite* [Thanh-Hoá: Geographical study of an Annamese province]. Paris: G. Van Oest.

Robert, René. 1941. *Notes sur les Tay Dèng de Lang Chánh (Thanh-hoá—Annam)* [Notes on the *Tay Dèng de Lang Chánh (Thanh-hoá—Annam)*]. Hanoi: Imprimerie d'Extrême-Orient.

Roque, Ricardo. 2010. *Headhunting and Colonialism: Anthropology and the Circulation of Human Skulls in the Portuguese Empire, 1870–1930*. Basingstoke: Palgrave Macmillan.

Roque, Ricardo. 2015a. "Mimesis and Colonialism: Emerging Perspectives on a Shared History." *History Compass* 13 (4): 201–211.

Roque, Ricardo. 2015b. "Mimetic Governmentality and the Administration of Colonial Justice in East Timor, ca. 1860–1910." *Comparative Studies in Society and History* 57 (1): 67–97.

Salemink, Oscar. 2003. *The Ethnography of Vietnam's Central Highlanders: A Historical Contextualization, 1850–1990*. London: RoutledgeCurzon; Honolulu: University of Hawai'i Press.

Salemink, Oscar. 2015. "Revolutionary and Christian Ecumenes and Desire for Modernity in the Vietnamese Highlands." *Asia Pacific Journal of Anthropology* 16 (4): 388–409.

Sarraut, Albert. 1923. *La mise en valeur des colonies françaises* [Enhancement of the French colonies]. Paris: Payot.

Schendel, Willem van. 2002. "Geographies of Knowing, Geographies of Ignorance: Jumping Scale in Southeast Asia." *Environment and Planning D: Society and Space* 20 (6): 647–668.

Schopohl, Andrea. 2011. "Processes of Social Differentiation and (Re-)Integration in Northern Laos." *Sojourn* 26 (2): 248–276.

Scott, James C. 2009. *The Art of Not Being Governed: An Anarchist History of Upland Southeast Asia*. New Haven, CT: Yale University Press.

Tappe, Oliver. 2015a. "A Frontier in the Frontier: Sociopolitical Dynamics and Colonial Administration in the Lao-Vietnamese Borderlands." *Asia Pacific Journal of Anthropology* 16 (4): 368–387.

Tappe, Oliver. 2015b. "Introduction: Frictions and Fictions—Intercultural Encounters and Frontier Imaginaries in Upland Southeast Asia." *Asia Pacific Journal of Anthropology* 16 (4): 317–322.

Taussig, Michael. 1993. *Mimesis and Alterity: A Particular History of the Senses*. London: Routledge.

Tsing, Anna L. 1994. "From the Margins." *Cultural Anthropology* 9 (3): 279–297.

Tsing, Anna L. 2005. *Friction: An Ethnography of Global Connection*. Princeton, NJ: Princeton University Press.

Turner, Frederick J. 1921. *The Frontier in American History*. New York: Henry Holt.

Walker, Andrew. 1999. *The Legend of the Golden Boat: Regulation, Trade and Traders in the Borderlands of Laos, Thailand, China and Burma*. Richmond: Curzon Press.

Walker, Iain. 2005. "Mimetic Structuration: Or, Easy Steps to Building an Acceptable Identity." *History and Anthropology* 16 (2): 187–210.

Winichakul, Thongchai. 1995. *Siam Mapped: A History of the Geo-Body of a Nation*. Chiang Mai: Silkworm Books.

Chapter 3

THE HUT-HOSPITAL AS PROJECT AND AS PRACTICE
Mimeses, Alterities, and Colonial Hierarchies

Cristiana Bastos

Subject to philosophical reflection since at least the time of Plato and Aristotle, imitation was ultimately theorized by French sociologist Gabriel Tarde (1890), whose *Laws of Imitation* became a standard reference in the years to follow. There were no major conceptual changes in the study of imitation in society in the following century, except for the surrealist, psychological, and psychoanalytic explorations into the realm of the sacred and its connections with violence, as epitomized in the work on the mimesis-sacrifice dyad by Roger Caillois ([1935] 1984, 1939) and René Girard (1972). Recently, critical theorist Rey Chow (2006) speculates that mimesis and sacrifice may have fallen victim to the current politics of representation. Much of the cognitive potential of these twin concepts thus remains unexplored, suggests Chow in her review of the complex interrelations of mimesis, sacrifice, biopolitics, and the multiple hierarchies that structure human interaction—from which emerge, among others, Agamben's (1998) understanding of 'bare life' and Fanon's (1952, 1961) 'ambivalent subjectivities'. Sacrifice and mimesis should be salvaged for the better understanding of the "formidable—and terrifying—questions of freedom, violence, moral constraints, community, and boundary-setting" (Chow 2006: 147), and, we may add, colonial domination. In order to address this further application, I will make use of the concept of mimesis and, for the moment, leave aside sacrifice with its too literal, visceral, even graphic associations with colonialism.

It is not that mimesis, or imitation, has been absent from reflections about colonialism and colonial subjectivities. On the contrary, many works have made good use of it—from V. S. Naipaul's (1967) *The Mimic Men* to Homi Bhabha's (1984) *Of Mimicry and Man*; from Jean Rouch's (1955) film *Les maîtres fous* to the scholarship that engaged with it (Lim 2002; Stoller 1992), including Paul Stoller's (1995) explorations into the embodiment of colonial memories; from Frantz Fanon's (1952) *Black Skin, White Masks* to Michael Taussig's (1993) *Mimesis and Alterity* and the multiple works it inspired from different empirical and theoretical groundings (e.g., Anderson 2002; Ferguson 2002; Huggan 1997). These works sift through the connections between colonialism and imitation, be it as the incomplete, faux-copy mode of masquerade, or in the playful, ironic, and resistance-loaded mode of mimicry—to use the insightful distinction of Fuss (1994)—or yet, to use Huggan's (1997) distinction, as the mischievous imitation that stands as mimicry, or as the mediation between different worlds that stands as mimesis.

Diverse as they are, those authors are consistent in exploring colonial imitation as almost exclusively enacted by the colonized subjects: the copy emerges from below, while the original stands on the dominating side of the colonial or post-colonial asymmetrical dyads. A similar framework is used for the exploration of contemporary cultural issues involving imitation, as in Rosemary Coombe's (1996) discussion of patents and borders or Jean Langford's (1999) approach to composite medical practices in India.

To this day, less has been written about mimicking from above (see Ladwig and Roque, this volume; Roque 2014, 2015a). There is only a little interrogation of situations in which the colonizers imitate the colonized subjects, and these are concerned with turning native, as depicted in variations of the embarrassing category of *kaffrealization* (Africanization), or in the romanticized freedom of Paul Gaugin in the southern seas, or again in the Orientalist enchantment of Europeans who adopted Eastern philosophies and lifestyles.[1] Finally, some authors have developed idiosyncratic theories about porous modes of colonialism based on cases in which colonial powers borrowed native themes and motives as a way to legitimate domination.[2]

This chapter focuses on a particular mode of colonial 'imitation from above', as epitomized by the hut-hospital. Created between the 1920s and the 1950s for the purpose of providing medical assistance to the indigenous populations of Angola, Mozambique, and other Portuguese-administered African regions, hut-hospitals were designed as fenced compounds with a main building and a variable number of smaller, hut-like constructions. The sponsors of the project believed that this was an affordable and locally sensitive type of construction and that it had the potential to attract the local populations in ways that conventional European hospitals would not. Africans tended to avoid European medicine on most occasions. If the colonial medical facilities looked more African, the planners thought, people would be less reluctant to go there.

Behind this rationale was the assumption that visual similarity had the power to erase differences and reduce distances, whether physical, social, cultural, or political. Imitation was adopted for the mitigation of dissension, as a process of 'de-othering' the neighbor, the enemy, the colonial subject, and, in this case, as a masquerade of one's own self in order to please, attract, and capture someone else. The huts in the hospitals would have the power, or at least the potential, to minimize the Otherness and potential hostility of the hospital as perceived by Africans. Or at least that was what the planners thought.

I will approach the hut-hospital as a materialization of mimesis that became a technique of colonial governance. Rather than evidence of an imagined cultural propensity toward blending in, as later theorized for other aspects of material culture by Lusotropicalist authors (Freyre 1961), imitation and borrowing instanced de-othering as an exercise of power in the governance of life, or, in other words, as a technique of colonial biopower. My analysis of the ways in which colonial rulers imitated, simulated, and borrowed aspects of the indigenous cultures they ruled follows trends shared by Roque (2010, 2014, 2015b, this volume) for East Timor, Ladwig (this volume) and Tappe (this volume) for Laos, Bastos (2011, 2014) for Angola and Mozambique, Saraiva (2014) for Angola, and Xavier (2014) and Chakravarti (2014) for Goa.

The Huts in the Hospital

Evoking the trope of imitation (or mimesis) as a means to overcome (or camouflage) difference (or alterity), hut-hospitals were developed as a tool for colonial politics. Given the scarcity of analytical and primary sources on the topic, one may ask whether they were a programmatic procedure, identifiable as a mark of a certain type of colonial governance, or just an idiosyncratic project that existed in potential but was never effectively implemented in the field.

Evidence about hut-hospitals and their role in the larger spectrum of Portuguese colonial health policies is elusive. Data are scattered through rare primary sources, defying the efforts of researchers on the topic (Bastos 2007, 2012, 2014; Coghe 2014, 2015; Duarte and Dória 2014; Duarte et al. 2012; Havik 2013, 2014; Milheiro et al. 2013). Much is still to be known about these structures: how many of them were actually built, both when and where; how long did they last; what was their impact; how were they perceived by the population and by the patients, health workers, and administrators; what was their place and role in colonial policies; what critical interpretations of colonialism can they substantiate.

Recent academic works on Portuguese colonial architecture (Fernandes 2009; Ferreira 2006; Fonte 2007; Milheiro 2012a, 2012b; Tostões and Gonçalves 2009) report extensively and in detail on the construction of large and iconic buildings, including hospitals, in Angola, Mozambique, and other colonial sites. The authors develop interesting arguments about modernism, brutalism, and tropicalism, yet they rarely mention the existence of the typology of hut-hospitals and infirmaries. In a 2013 exhibit on Portuguese colonial architecture held in a major venue in Lisbon, there was a discrete appearance of the hut structures as *sanzala* (native headquarters) in one of the plants (Milheiro et al. 2013), with no further commentary.

Approaches to ascertaining the actual existence of hut-hospitals can be frustrating: little is left of them on the sites where they were once erected, and written or oral sources are scarce. There is no complete survey about how many of them were made, where exactly they were located, and what happened to them. My own excursions to find ruins or remains in Angola and Mozambique had limited results (Bastos 2014).

However, as the study of Portuguese colonial architecture is moving from an exclusive focus on monumental works to forms that are vernacular, hybrid, and less monumental, recent findings provide good support for our quest. Meticulous research conducted by João Couto Duarte shows that some of those structures still exist, although they are hard to identify in the field as they were often subject to adaptation (Duarte and Dória 2014; Duarte et al. 2012). The exhaustive research on Angolan colonial medical sources conducted by Samuël Coghe (2014) reveals that there may have been a large number of these structures in the 1920s, but little trace is left of them now (Coghe, pers. comm.).

As for documentary sources, they include the few legal documents that mention hut-hospitals and infirmaries (e.g., *Diário do Governo*, 6 February 1944, 21 February 1945), occasional booklets published for international colonial exhibits (such as *Portugal–Colonie de Moçambique–L'Assistance Médicale*, prepared in 1931), and above all the medical articles about indigenous outreach health care presented at a pioneering international conference on colonial medicine held in Luanda in the 1920s (Blanchard 1923; Correia 1923; Sant'Anna 1923; Santos 1923).[3] From these sources we can gather formal, idealized descriptions of the structure and functions of the hospitals in question, some visual sketches of them, and a few rare photographs, as analyzed further in this chapter. So far, no field photography of people actively using these hospitals has been identified, nor have real-life narrative accounts of the hospitals' services.

While direct testimonies about lived experience in these compounds have yet to be found, evocative objects and documents related to their conception and implementation will provide the empirical basis for the discussion in this chapter. Among those objects there is a collection of three-dimensional plaster models representing different health care constructions (Duarte et al. 2012). After some years inhabiting obscure locations, the collection is currently on exhibit to the public in the top hall of the Tropical Medicine Institute in Lisbon (Duarte and Dória 2014). These objects will, for the moment, move to the center of our analysis.

The Social Lives of Plaster Models

The three-dimensional plaster models representing hut-hospitals will hold the spotlight in this section of the chapter. They will be addressed along the lines suggested by anthropologists engaged in the study of objects as sources for understanding social relations and wider politics (e.g., Appadurai 1986; Kopytoff 1986; Miller 2008; Porto 2007, 2009). What was the history and social life of these plaster models? What does their 'biography of objects' tell us about the uses of imitation in colonial policies and about colonialism in general? The next paragraphs will be dedicated to exploring further the biographies of these second-degree objects of imitation. I will discuss what they are, when they were made, as well as why, where, and by whom, and their afterlife since being manufactured.

What

When we think about these models as architectural maquettes that for some reason outlived the stone-and-concrete life-size buildings they heralded, a tone of dissonance emerges from the fact that the fragile plaster models have survived to the present day so remarkably clean and well-finished while the constructions they ought to have inspired are very hard to find. The dissonance dissipates when we get to know a little more about their object biographies. Rather than anticipatory models, they were modeled after constructions that already existed, even if embellished or made to look more regular and geometrical than they might have been in the field. The intent behind their production was to showcase the constructions of the Gabinete de Urbanização Colonial (Office of Colonial Urbanization) (Duarte and Dória 2014; Duarte et al. 2012).

ILLUSTration 3.1: Maquette of a health center in southern Mozambique. Collection of the Institute of Hygiene and Tropical Medicine, Lisbon, Portugal. Photograph © Cristiana Bastos, 2014

When

Thanks to recent research (Duarte and Dória 2014; Duarte et al. 2012), we now know that those models were produced for an exhibition that took place in Lisbon in 1952: the "Exposição Documental das Actividades Sanitárias do Ultramar" (Documentary Exhibition of Overseas Health Activities). The exhibit coincided with the jubilee of the Tropical Medicine Institute and the Colonial Hospital, both founded in 1902 and later renamed the Overseas Hospital (Hospital do Ultramar). This was a moment when Portugal drifted away from what was becoming the shared trend for European imperial powers after World War II. While most prepared for decolonization and anticipated new modalities of engagement with the emerging Asian and African countries that replaced former colonies, the Portuguese government invested like never before in the colonial project in Africa (Castelo 2007). A whole new vocabulary for colonial governance was put forward. What had once been the colonies were now the overseas provinces. What had formerly been the empire was now a transcontinental, multi-local imagined community of organic Portugueseness, theatrically exhibited in two previous major fairs in 1934 in Porto and 1940 in Lisbon as "O Mundo Português" (The Portuguese World) (Serén 2001; Thomaz 2002). What had previously been relatively disjointed colonial policies, left to the agency and judgment of those in the field, were now a priority for the central government (Alexandre and Dias 1998; Castelo 2007).

Why

At that juncture, narratives had to be brought together to support the claims of the originality, value, and goodness of the 'humanitarian civilization' that in the Portuguese official vocabulary replaced empire. Stories, tales, images, symbols, and objects that could be displayed as evidence of a long-term engagement of the Portuguese with overseas peoples were now used for showcasing the reinvented empire. At that exact moment, Gilberto Freyre had been invited by the Ministry of the Colonies to go to different places in Africa and Asia under Portuguese administration, to take notes, and to write about the unique Portuguese mode of benign colonization. Freyre (1953) would later come up with the theory of Lusotropicalism (see also Bastos 1998; Castelo 1999). But the term had not yet been coined at the time of the exhibit. Nor was there a complete transition from an ideology of imperial glory and conquest to the later claims of humanitarian, interactive civilization in the tropics. Both in law and in life, the colonial regime in Portuguese Africa in the early 1950s was about separation and segregation, with ideologies of white supremacy and economies based on indigenous labor. In a sense, the inclusion of models of segregated infirmaries—of hut-hospitals that looked so clearly like native headquarters—fulfilled the purpose of promoting medical care for all, while making it look different for different groups.

Where

The 1952 "Exposição Documental das Actividades Sanitárias do Ultramar" was held in the Burnay Palace, Rua da Junqueira. The plaster models of hut-hospitals were part of a larger set of models representing health buildings in the colonies, from smaller infirmaries with half a dozen huts to large-scale, monumental central hospitals, to the Tropical Medicine Institute, which was soon to move into the large modernist headquarters it now inhabits, also in Rua da Junqueira. From the catalogue and the pictures, we can see that the exhibit was a grand and solemn event. While the previous exhibits of 1934 and 1940 had been massive occasions that attracted thousands of people (Serén 2001; Thomaz 2002), this was a selective showcase, prepared for the eyes of health professionals and politicians. Together with the models, there were plenty of tables and images reporting on medical missions in Africa. There was one room for the Tropical Medicine Institute, one for the Colonial/Overseas Hospital, two for Angola, one for Mozambique, one for Guinea, Cape Verde, and São Tomé and another for India (Goa-Daman-Diu), Macao, and Timor, plus one for tropical plants and yet another for corporations in Angola, with a highlight on Diamang. It was predominantly in the room dedicated to Mozambique that the hut-hospital models were shown.

ILLUSTration 3.2: Aspect of the overseas health activities exhibit, Burnay Palace, Rua da Junqueira, 1952. Collection of the Institute of Hygiene and Tropical Medicine, Museum Photographic Album IHMT.000535, photograph # 35, permission kindly granted by the Institute of Hygiene and Tropical Medicine, Lisbon, Portugal

By Whom

A study of the documents related to the exhibition, including letters, memos, and references to shipments of boxes and packages, along with other elements, enabled authors João Couto Duarte and José Luís Dória (2014: 4, 29–30) to establish that the models were made in Mozambique from 1951 to 1952 and shipped to Portugal in the vessel *Quanza* for the purpose of being exhibited during the Tropical Medicine Conference, itself scheduled to coincide with the jubilees of the Tropical Medicine Institute and the Colonial/Overseas Hospital. Although there is no official record of the artists who produced the models, they took the initiative of inscribing their signatures and playful comments on the bottom of one of the box cases—the one that supports the model of the Marraquene maternity facility. The text reads: "These maquettes and all of the graphs were made by the competent worker-artists." The signatures read: "Master-general João Aires, picasso artist" "Francisco Matos Lopes, Horácio Alves dos Santos Portugal, Joaquim Portugal dos Santos, all great guys." Individual signatures of "João Aires, competent painting artist," "Serafim Rebelo, officer on duty," "Francisco Matos Lopes, carpenter," "Horácio Alves dos Santos Portugal," "Joaquim Portugal Santos," "Seturate-painter," and "Ramalho-painter" complete the entangled inscriptions transcribed by Duarte and Dória (ibid.: 29).

Afterlife

Once the exhibit was over, the plaster models turned into something other than what they had been commissioned for. Their existence became detached from the web of intentions and agencies that had brought them into being. They lost their original meaning and achieved new ones. No longer objects of public visibility, they were now 'has-beens' with no assigned role or place—too good to discard and trash, yet not valued enough to be worth the cost of shipping them back or keeping them visible. They remained in Lisbon, semi-abandoned in warehouses (Duarte and Dória 2014: 5) until they were rescued from further decay by artist and restorer Luis Marto from the Tropical Medicine Institute (ibid.: 7). Throughout the 1990s and early 2000s, the models occupied different places in the corridors and back alleys of that Institute, eventually to be fully restored and exhibited in great dignity in its main hall with a dedicated institutional catalogue (ibid.).

As suggested elsewhere, the travels of those objects between the gray areas of shade and the lights of the exhibit hall go hand in hand with a shift in attitude of the Tropical Medicine Institute about its colonial past (Bastos 2014). The Institute was originally fashioned as a central pin in a system of medical research and assistance related to the colonies. After the 1975 period of decolonization and the birth of new African nations, it maintained ties with the same places in Africa, now providing assistance in development. References to past colonial ties were suspended from systematic reflection for a few decades, and the relationship to the material objects related to that past was also suspended, leaving the collections in oblivion. Recently, they have received new attention as objects of heritage and are now the subject of prestigious exhibits.

Imitation Exponential: Models That Mimic Mimetic Hospitals

If the miniature hospital models may be depicted as a product of mimicry, a conscious exercise of imitation (not without the playful component of the artists' hidden inscriptions), they also work as multipliers of imitation procedures, as they endeavor to replicate—for purposes of a celebratory exhibition—what had started as an imitation, or mimesis, in a colonial setting. The models aimed to show how hospitals sought to duplicate indigenous housing. It is now time to investigate the projects and programs that generated these hospitals and the actual practices to which they corresponded.

The most comprehensive description of the hut-hospital as a project was presented at the 1923 Tropical Medicine Conference held in Luanda. The conference was a scientific landmark, hardly ever replicated. It was graced by the presence of various international medical celebrities of the time and was organized thanks in large part to the efforts of António Damas Mora, whose role in Portuguese Tropical Medicine has yet to be fully acknowledged (Coghe 2014). The proceedings were published in the coming years in the journal *Revista Médica de Angola*, which was created for that purpose. They include a complete transcription of the papers presented in the sessions, of the discussions that followed, and of the complete articles written by the authors. Several of them discuss modes of better promoting health outreach for the indigenous populations (Blanchard 1923; Correia 1923; Sant'Anna 1923; Santos 1923). Their commitment to the mission of keeping more people alive and healthy in places of empire reveals that the colonial biopolitics of that moment corresponded to a mandate for life in the classical Foucauldian sense, but also that this same mandate rested upon an understanding of difference, separation, and hierarchization of groups.

It is worth noting that there was no consensus at this conference on what were the most efficient ways of promoting the health of indigenous groups. While Ferreira dos Santos and others were committed to the creation of special hospitals, or infirmaries, in the rural outpost serving indigenous populations, with constructions "like the common huts, with conical roof, a little higher, with a glass window and a door ... and a cemented floor" (transcript of the second session, 17 July 1923, 12), not everyone in the audience agreed on the fact that different construction types should be made for different groups. Dr. Santos Jr., for example, commented that providing medical assistance to the indigenous populations should be "just like providing assistance to the white people, forgetting color, not separating the white patient and the black patient" (transcript of the second session, 17 July 1923, 24). But the idea of making constructions that mimicked indigenous housing was the most prominent of the day.

J. Firmino Sant'Anna, a prominent professor of Tropical Medicine in Lisbon who had much experience serving in the colonies, provided an extensive memorandum about every possible dimension of assistance to the African indigenous populations, including how to compromise with African practices while still providing good care (e.g., the doctors should act like African healers and minister the prescribed drugs to themselves), how to select locally sensitive approaches, and why not to insist on prescribing things that might be incompatible with local traditions (e.g., baby bottles). When it came to the hospitalization systems, Sant'Anna (1923) was firm in suggesting that the races should be separated. He made clear that he did not mean to separate black from white, but to separate those who kept their traditions (*indígenas*) from those who were under the sphere of European society (ibid.: 153). As for the equipping of indigenous hospitals and infirmaries, he suggested that instead of multiple permanent buildings, the structures should be fewer and more transient, "whether canvas tents, pavilions, or huts in the *kaffreal* style, or portable rooms, etc." (ibid.: 154).[5]

The most articulate arguments supporting hut-hospitals came from Ferreira dos Santos (1923: 65–69), who conceived a complex system with major health centers and a full hierarchy of larger and smaller outposts. He argued that the hut-like constructions would cost less, would be easier to maintain, and, above all, would be more attractive to the indigenous populations, who, he claimed to know based on his own experiences, were traditionally reluctant to accept European health care (ibid.: 66). In other words, Santos argued for imitation as a means to reduce differences and as a device to create proximity via resemblance.

Other authors added their arguments defending the construction of separate infirmaries that looked like indigenous housing. Germano Correia, a physician from Goa who had also served in Angola and whose racialized views of the world have been analyzed previously (Bastos 2005), suggested that indigenous patients should not face abrupt transitions when receiving medical care: moving from their dark huts into bright infirmaries might make them dizzy (Correia 1923: 187). Also, the construction should have internal and external features that are able to "attract, agreeably, the attention and interest of the inpatients, through the similitude of architectonic particularities, which can remind them of the huts" (ibid.: 187–188). For those reasons, he supported the construction of *enfermarias sanzalas* (native-settlement infirmaries).

Regardless of what they might have thought about African imitations of Europeanness, they were pleading for European imitations of Africanness, putting this forward as a practicable and desirable tool of empire at no less a forum than a prestigious international conference on tropical medicine. And as if anticipating the colonial and post-colonial theorizations, Santos and Correia displayed a

Vue générale d'une infirmerie régionale

ILLUSTration 3.3: Photograph of a hut-hospital compound. Included in *Portugal–Colonie de Moçambique–L'Assistance Médicale,* a booklet prepared for the International Colonial Exhibit in France, 1931

note of further originality in an almost-but-not-quite mode. While the huts were supposed to look like those of the natives, round with straw conic roofs, they ought also to adopt all the modern materials of construction: cemented walls, pavements, doors, glass windows, and whitewash finishing.

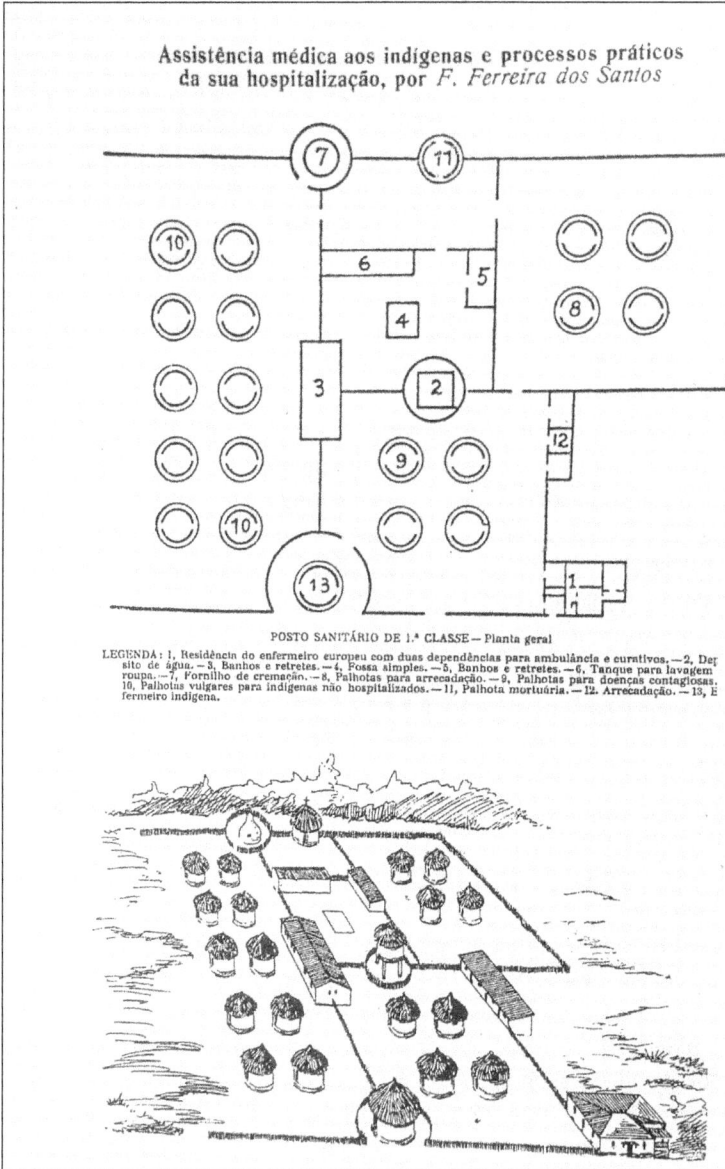

ILLUSTRATION 3.4: Sketch of a first-class health outpost. Included in Santos (1923)

Projects and Practices of Colonial Domination

The hut-hospitals sketched by Ferreira dos Santos (1923) seem to represent the exact same thing as those represented in the plaster models analyzed earlier in this chapter. Yet they stem from different moments in the long and scattered history of Portuguese colonial biopolitics. When Santos and his colleagues gathered in Luanda to discuss modes of outreach for the indigenous populations, they seemed truly to be engaged in finding better solutions to keep Africans alive and healthy. Whether the main purpose behind their efforts related to the need for cheap, docile, and abundant labor or was rooted in more humanitarian principles and the mandate to protect life—or perhaps was an equal measure of both—is a matter for further discussion, as noted by Coghe (2014) in his analysis of demographic anxieties in colonial Angola.

The 1920s were a time when there was room to explore new ideas, models, and projects. Portugal was under what came to be known later as the First Republic (1910–1926), that is, the first wave of republican, democratic governments. Aspirations to make up for lost time and to overcome the backwardness attributed to monarchic rule were now in the air. The colonies should also make up for the backwardness they were presumed to be left in, and the most modern techniques of governance should be implemented. The atmosphere would change in the coming decades, and a very long authoritarian regime was about to begin. The cosmopolitan open-mindedness of the 1920s gave way to the gloom of the 1930s, followed by a political cycle with a self-contained ideology of exceptionalism that peaked in the 1950s and 1960s and lasted until the mid-1970s.

In the transition decade of the 1930s, there was conceptual and political space for the implementation of some hut-hospitals in precise locations. There is evidence regarding support for *tabancas enfermarias* (infirmary villages) in Guinea (now the country Guinea-Bissau). The booklet *Assistência aos indígenas da Colónia da Guiné* (Imprensa Nacional da Guiné 1933) argues in favor of those compounds, which had been established, together with the Fundo de Assistência Médica Indígena, by Legal Decree #728 (dated 18 December 1932). The text noted that Africans dreaded the Portuguese system of assistance and would rather hide and die than seek out Portuguese health care. The *tabancas* thus attempted to recreate a friendly environment, made to be similar to the patients' own hamlets and allowing for the presence of relatives—while at the same time attempting to keep invalids under such a close watch that they were unable to escape (ibid.: 6). The *tabanca* was thus a mock native village, used consciously as a tool of colonial biopolitics in the more remote regions of Guinea.

At precisely this time, Portuguese politics were about to shift into what became the basis for the long-lasting regime of António Salazar. The year 1933 was also the year of legitimation for the Estado Novo or New State (the Second Republic) and for the Colonial Act, which separated the population into two groups: whites and *assimilados*, on the one hand, versus natives (*indígenas*), on the other.[6] In the 1940s, a wave of legislation regulated the colonial health services. The Gabinete de Urbanização Colonial (GUC) was created in 1944 with the purpose of improving the quality of construction in the African colonies (Legal Decree #34173, 6 December 1944). It was inspired by an exhibit held at the engineering institute in Lisbon that promoted cooperation between engineers and architects. From then on, African hospitals, like other constructions, were to be supervised by the GUC.

In 1945, a complete program for the colonial health services was defined in the extensive Legal Decree #34417 (21 February), which marked the biopolitical agenda for the coming decades. The purpose of the program was to "support, defend, and expand the indigenous population" (the labor providers) and also to help white settlers adjust to the tropical regions. The program provided for the creation of a central hospital for each colony, plus regional hospitals and health outposts in varying numbers. It explicitly promoted a veiled apartheid, segregating the health care facilities made for whites and 'assimilated natives' from those made for the 'non-assimilated natives'. The principles stated by Ferreira dos Santos 20 years earlier were now adopted as a programmatic law:

> In the colonial hospitals it is required to separate the headquarters for Europeans and *assimilados* from those destined to the natives (*indígenas*). Not because of racial prejudice (as shown by the fact that assimilated natives have a place together with Europeans), but to accommodate the differences in mentality and habits. The indigenous peoples only feel at ease, even morally comforted, when they do not miss the atmosphere they are used to. Is it better, or worse than ours? If it ought to be changed, that will be a matter of slow persuasion and adaptation; not by the imposition in exceptional periods of life.
>
> For that reason it is admissible that on certain occasions the indigenous person can live, not in an infirmary, but within the circumscription of the hospital, in an independent home, part of a village, eventually accompanied by the family, that came along from afar. The housing should be built in the indigenous style, however improved in the use of materials, capacity, orientation, protection against solar rays, comfort, and hygiene, etc., so that they provide a model for their own evolution. (*Diário de Governo* 21 February 1945: 96–97)

The hut-hospital was thus adopted not just as a means to attract more of the indigenous population into the hospital, but also as an educational device. The 'almost' in its 'not-quite' mode—looking African, but made of supposedly more advanced construction materials—worked as an asset in the promotion of a taste for what Europeans considered better housing. Efforts to attract the local population into the hospital were expanded and included the possibility of setting up entire villages around the health compounds, so that some patients could be lodged in the vicinity while receiving medical care as outpatients (*Diário de Governo* 21/2/1945: 103).

Almost-but-Not-Quite: Partial Imitation as a Colonial Tool

In this chapter I have presented a case of imitation as a colonial device: the conception, the practice, and later the programmatic adoption of hospitals with hut-like housing as a means to attract indigenous populations into colonial health care. I have addressed the hospitals as imitations and the plaster models of the hospitals as second-degree imitations. At once unusual yet familiar to their targeted African patients, the models embody the colonial program, configure colonial and para-colonial encounters, and evoke missions to rural colonies and settlements. They contain within them the tensions of colonialism, in its hybridisms, pastiche, collage—the private tensions of a particular utopia inscribed in a device that combines the aesthetics of futurist design, on the one hand, and of a certain rural, colonial nostalgia, on the other. Like self-aware simulacra, the models seem to idealize local constructions and reinvent them by adopting original materials and using a regular, geometric layout.

A discussion on whether this sort of imitation and its outcomes should better be considered mimesis (Taussig 1993), mimicry (Bhabha 1984), mockery, masquerade (Fuss 1994), pantomime, or simulacra (Baudillard 1981) would in my view be a relatively sterile exercise in the academic vertigo of shifting signification and representation politics (e.g., Chow 2006; Trajano Filho 2011). I find it more productive to analyze the ways in which colonial powers have used imitation as a means to simulate the erasure of distance under an agenda of domination, while creating enhanced possibilities of fashioning their narratives of collective selves, along the lines suggested in the studies of imperial tensions (Bastos et al. 2002; Cooper and Stoler 1997; Stoler 1995, 2002).

In the case examined in this chapter, imitation took the 'not-quite' mode of looking indigenous while using modern European sanitary devices. From the beginning, this was an appealing display of colonial apparatus: sympathetic, via imitation, but 'not-quite'. And while in the 1920s the rationale behind the display of similitudes might have been guided by humanistic principles of life promotion, when the seed project gave way to a programmatic law, it became clear that the almost-but-not-quite mode now corresponded to a regime of segregation, veiled apartheid, and a masquerade of inclusiveness that would have its higher ideological formation in the myths of Lusotropicalism (Freyre 1953, 1961). In other words, the imitation analyzed in this chapter appears to be less about inclusiveness than about keeping clear and visible the principle that each individual and type must be assigned one specific place in a divided, hierarchical, and racialized order.

Acknowledgments

This chapter is based on research that began under the projects "Tropical Medicine and Colonial Administration" (FCT PLUS/15157/1999) and "Colonial Medicine, Imperial Structures and Postcolonial Lives" (FCT POCTI/ANT/41075/2001), which I coordinated at the Institute of Social Sciences, University of Lisbon (ICS). The analysis matured while collaborating in the project "Colonial Mimesis in Lusophone Asia and Africa" (PTDC/CS-ANT/101064/2008), coordinated by Ricardo Roque, and achieved its current form in the context of the DAAD/ CRUP Exchange Grant A-07/2011 led by Ricardo Roque (ICS) and Patrice Ladwig (Max Plank Institute of Social Anthropology). I extend my warmest thanks to all the participants in the workshops in Lisbon and Halle—Patrice Ladwig, Ricardo Roque, Oliver Tappe, Christoph Koll, Carmo Daun, Wilson Trajano Filho, and Tiago Saraiva—and to the anonymous reviewers for *Social Analysis*. Special thanks go to architect João Couto Duarte, who generously shared with me the results of his then unfinished PhD research on architectural models (Duarte 2016). Finally, the time taken to revise the final proof was borrowed from my current project, "The Colour of Labour" (ERC 2015 AdG 695573), which brings the biopolitics of labor into a further level of analysis.

Cristiana Bastos is an anthropologist at the Institute of Social Sciences, University of Lisbon. She has conducted research in medical anthropology, the social history of medicine, and migration and colonialism. She is currently leading a large-scale European Research Council project, "The Colour of Labour: The Racialized Lives of Migrants." Her publications include *Global Responses to AIDS* (1999), *Trânsitos Coloniais* (2002), *Clínica, Arte e Sociedade* (2011), *A Circulação do Conhecimento* (2013), *Healing Holidays* (2015), and articles in the *Journal of Southern African Studies, International Migration, Bulletin of the History of Medicine, Anthropology and Medicine, Medical Anthropology,* and *History and Anthropology,* among others. E-mail: cristiana.bastos@ics.ulisboa.pt

Notes

1. The enchantment and awe with Eastern philosophies, a form of Orientalism in the broad sense, differs from what is theorized by Said (1978) and is closer to Vicente's (2012) depiction in *Other Orientalisms*. It corresponds to the use of imitation by eighteenth- and nineteenth-century European men and women who experienced existential transformations in places like Turkey, Egypt, or India and merged with those cultures by borrowing the local looks and customs.
2. Although borrowing local elements occurred frequently in many places and times, no author argued so consistently on the matter as Brazilian sociologist-anthropologist Gilberto Freyre (1952, 1961). Freyre claimed that the Portuguese colonizers had a special vocation to mix, mingle, and adopt the ways of the natives they encountered throughout the world, thus creating what he described as an original form of civilization—Lusotropicalism. Regardless of the value of Freyre's occasional insights about historical details, his theories have been dismissed as ideologically loaded. Particularly after 1961 they were conveniently useful to, and used by, the dictatorial regimes of António Salazar and Marcelo Caetano in Portugal (roughly from 1933 to 1974), as they provided a doctrine and pseudo-theoretical basis for a supposedly more benign, supposedly less racist, long-lasting colonial regime in Africa. See Bastos (1998), Bastos et al. (2002), Castelo (1999), and Castelo and Cardão (2015), among others.
3. For further analyses of these articles on indigenous outreach health care, see Bastos (2014) and Coghe (2014).
4. Unless otherwise indicated, all translations are my own.
5. *Assimilados* were Africans who adopted European lifestyles, including language, religion, clothing, housing, diet, and so forth. Their status allowed for some rights of citizenship that were denied to *indígenas*, who were subject to harsh labor demands.
6. The sources about this exhibit are very scarce. I thank architect João Couto Duarte and my colleague Jorge Freitas Branco for their assistance on the topic.

References

Agamben, Giorgio. 1998. *Homo Sacer: Sovereign Power and Bare Life*. Trans. Daniel Heller-Roazen. Stanford, CA: Stanford University Press.
Alexandre, Valentim, and Jill Dias, eds. 1998. *O Império Africano, 1825–1890* [The African empire]. Lisbon: Estampa.
Anderson, Warwick. 2002. "Going through the Motions: American Public Health and Colonial 'Mimicry.'" *American Literary History* 14 (4): 686–719.
Appadurai, Arjun, ed. 1986. *The Social Life of Things: Commodities in Cultural Perspective*. Cambridge: Cambridge University Press.
Bastos, Cristiana. 1998. "Tristes trópicos e alegres luso-tropicalismos: Das notas de viagem em Lévi-Strauss e Gilberto Freyre" [Sad tropics and joyful

Luso-tropicalisms: Travel notes in Lévi-Strauss and Gilberto Freyre]. *Análise Social* 33 (146–147): 415–432.

Bastos, Cristiana. 2005. "Race, Medicine and the Late Portuguese Empire: The Role of Goan Colonial Physicians." *Journal of Romance Studies* 5 (1): 23–35.

Bastos, Cristiana. 2007. "Medical Hybridisms and Social Boundaries: Aspects of Portuguese Colonialism in Africa and India in the Nineteenth Century." *Journal of Southern African Studies* 33 (4): 767–782.

Bastos, Cristiana. 2011. "My Medicines, Your Medicines, Our Medicines: Substances, Commodities and Healthcare Facilities in Colonial Settings." Paper presented at the "Colonialism and Theories of Imitation" workshop of the joint ICS-MPI program Colonial Crisis and Mimetic Encounters in Historical and Anthropological Perspectives, Institute of Social Sciences, Lisbon, 12–13 April.

Bastos, Cristiana. 2012. "Palácios, palhotas e pedras recicladas: Materialidades da assistência médica colonial" [Palaces, huts, and recycled stones: Materialities of colonial health care]. In *A Outra Face do Colonialismo Português* [The other face of Portuguese colonialism], ed. Maria Paula Diogo and Isabel Maria Amaral, 163–182. Lisbon: Colibri.

Bastos, Cristiana. 2014. "'No género de construções cafreais': O hospital-palhota como projecto colonial" [The hut-hospital as a colonial project]. *Etnográfica* 18 (1): 185–208.

Bastos, Cristiana, Miguel Vale de Almeida, and Bela Feldman-Bianco, eds. 2002. *Trânsitos Coloniais: Diálogos Críticos Luso-Brasileiros* [Colonial transits: Luso-Brazilian critical dialogues]. Lisbon: Imprensa de Ciências Sociais.

Baudrillard, Jean. 1981. *Simulacres et simulation* [Simulacra and simulation]. Paris: Galilée.

Bhabha, Homi. 1984. "Of Mimicry and Man: The Ambivalence of Colonial Discourse." *October* 28: 125–133.

Blanchard, Maurice. 1923. "Sur quelques facteurs moraux et matériels d'attraction des indigènes dans les centres de consultation" [On some moral and material factors of attraction of the natives in consultation centers]. *Revista Médica de Angola* 2 (4): 201–207.

Caillois, Roger. (1935) 1984. "Mimicry and Legendary Psychastenia." *October* 31: 16–32.

Caillois, Roger. 1939. *L'homme et le sacré* [Man and the sacred]. Paris: Gallimard.

Castelo, Cláudia. 1999. *'O Modo Português de Estar no Mundo': O Luso-Tropicalismo e a Ideologia Colonial Portuguesa (1933–1961)* ['The Portuguese way to be in the world': Luso-Tropicalism and the Portuguese colonial ideology]. Porto: Edições Afrontamento.

Castelo, Cláudia. 2007. *Passagens para África: O Povoamento de Angola e Moçambique com Naturais da Metrópole (1920–1974)* [Passages to Africa: The settlement of Angola and Mozambique with mainlanders]. Porto: Afrontamento.

Castelo, Cláudia, and Marcos Cardão, eds. 2015. *Identidades, Hibridismos, Tropicalismos: Leituras Pós-Coloniais de Gilberto Freyre* [Identities, hybridisms, tropicalisms: Post-colonial readings of Gilberto Freyre]. São Paulo: EDUSP.

Chakravarti, Ananya. 2014. "The Many Faces of Baltasar da Costa: *Imitatio* and *Accommodatio* in the Seventeenth Century Madurai Mission." *Etnográfica* 18 (1): 135–158.

Chow, Rey. 2006. "Sacrifice, Mimesis, and the Theorizing of Victimhood (A Speculative Essay)." *Representations* 94 (1): 131–149.

Coghe, Samuël. 2014. "Population Politics in the Tropics: Demography, Health and Colonial Rule in Portuguese Angola, 1890s–1940s." PhD diss., European University Institute.

Coghe, Samuël. 2015. "Inter-imperial Learning and African Health Care in Portuguese Angola in the Interwar Period." *Social History of Medicine* 28 (1): 134–154.

Coombe, Rosemary. 1996. "Embodied Trademarks: Mimesis and Alterity on American Commercial Frontiers." *Cultural Anthropology* 11 (2): 202–224.

Cooper, Frederick, and Ann L. Stoler, eds. 1997. *Tensions of Empire: Colonial Cultures in a Bourgeois World*. Berkeley: University of California Press.

Correia, A. C. Germano. 1923. "Processos práticos de hospitalização dos indígenas e o problema da sua assistência médica" [Practical procedures for hospitalization of indigenous people and the problem of their medical care]. *Revista Médica de Angola* 2 (4): 179–200.

Duarte, João Miguel Couto. 2016. "Para uma Definição de Maqueta: Representação e Projecto de Objectos Arquitectónicos" [For a Definition of Maquette: Representation and Project of Architectural Objects]. PhD dissertation, University of Lisbon, Faculty of Architecture. https://www.repository.utl.pt/handle/10400.5/13708.

Duarte, João Miguel Couto, and José Luis Dória. 2014. *Maquetas de Edificações de Saúde* [Models of health buildings]. Lisbon: Instituto de Higiene e Medicina Tropical.

Duarte, João Miguel Couto, José Luis Dória, and Luís Marto. 2012. "Maquetas de estruturas de serviços de saúde no antigo Ultramar português: Ciência, arquitectura e política (colecção do Museu do IHMT)" [Models of health service structures in the former Portuguese overseas: Science architecture and politics (collection of the IHMT Museum). Paper presented at the conference "Congresso Internacional Saber Tropical em Moçambique: História, Memória e Ciência," IICT-JBT, Palácio dos Condes de Calheta, Lisbon, 24–26 October.

Fanon, Frantz. 1952. *Peau noire, masques blancs* [Black skin, white masks]. Paris: Seuil.

Fanon, Frantz. 1961. *Les damnés de la terre* [The wretched of the earth]. Paris: Maspero.

Ferguson, James. 2002. "Of Mimicry and Membership: Africans and the 'New World Society.'" *Cultural Anthropology* 17 (4): 551–569.

Fernandes, José Manuel. 2009. *Geração Africana: Arquitectura e Cidades em Angola e Moçambique, 1925–1975* [African generation: Architecture and cities in Angola and Mozambique]. Lisbon: Livros Horizonte.

Ferreira, André Faria. 2006. "Obras Públicas em Moçambique: Inventário da produção arquitectónica executada entre 1933 e 1961" [Public works in

Mozambique: Inventory of architectural production executed between 1933 and 1961]. MA thesis, University of Coimbra.

Fonte, Maria Manuela. 2007. "Urbanismo e Arquitectura em Angola: De Norton de Matos à Revolução" [Urbanism and architecture in Angola: From Norton de Matos to the revolution]. PhD diss., University of Lisbon.

Freyre, Gilberto. 1953. *Aventura e Rotina: Sugestões de Uma Viagem à Procura das Constantes Portuguesas de Carácter e Ação* [Adventure and routine: Suggestions for a journey in search of Portuguese constants of character and action]. Rio de Janeiro: José Olympio.

Freyre, Gilberto. 1961. *The Portuguese and the Tropics: Suggestions Inspired by the Portuguese Methods of Integrating Autocthonous Peoples and Cultures Differing from the European in a New, or Luso-tropical, Complex of Civilisation.* Trans. Helen M. D'O. Matthew and F. de Mello Moser. Lisbon: Executive Committee for the Commemoration of the Vth Centenary of the Death of Prince Henry the Navigator.

Fuss, Diana. 1994. "Interior Colonies: Frantz Fanon and the Politics of Identification." *Diacritics* 24 (2-3): 19-42.

Girard, René. 1972. *La violence et le sacré* [Violence and the sacred]. Paris: Grasset.

Havik, Philip J. 2013. "Reconsidering Indigenous Health, Medical Services and Colonial Rule in Portuguese West Africa." In *O Colonialismo Português: A nova historiografia dos PALOP* [Portuguese colonialism: The new historiography of the PALOP], ed. Ana Roque et al., 233-265. Porto: CEAUP-Humus.

Havik, Philip J. 2014. "Public Health and Tropical Modernity: The Combat against Sleeping Sickness in Portuguese Guinea, 1945-1974." *História, Ciência, Saúde–Manguinhos* 21 (2): 641-666.

Huggan, Graham. 1997. "(Post)Colonialism, Anthropology, and the Magic of Mimesis." *Cultural Critique* 38: 91-106.

Imprensa Nacional da Guiné. 1933. *Assistência aos indígenas da Colónia da Guiné: Instrução e beneficiência.* Botoma: Imprensa Nacional da Guiné.

Kopytoff, Igor. 1986. "The Cultural Biography of Things: Commoditization as Process." In Appadurai 1986, 64-91.

Langford, Jean M. 1999. "Medical Mimesis: Healing Signs of a Cosmopolitan 'Quack.'" *American Ethnologist* 26 (1): 24-46.

Lim, Kien Ket. 2002. "Of Mimicry and White Man: A Psychoanalysis of Jean Rouch's *Les maîtres fous.*" *Cultural Critique* 51: 40-73.

Milheiro, Ana Vaz. 2012a. "A arquitectura dos Gabinetes de Urbanização Colonial em Moçambique (1944-1974)" [The architecture of the colonial urbanization offices in Mozambique]. Paper presented at the conference "Congresso Internacional Saber Tropical em Moçambique: História, Memória e Ciência," IICT-JBT, Palácio dos Condes de Calheta, Lisbon, 24-26 October.

Milheiro, Ana Vaz. 2012b. *Nos Trópicos sem Le Corbusier: Arquitectura Luso-Africana no Estado Novo* [In the tropics without Le Corbusier: Luso-African architecture in the new state]. Lisbon: Relógio d'Água.

Milheiro, Ana Vaz, with Ana Cannas and João Vieira. 2013. "África: Visões do Gabinete de Urbanização Colonial" [Africa: Visions of the colonial urbanization office]. Exhibition at the Centro Cultural de Belém, Lisbon.

Miller, Daniel. 2008. *The Comfort of Things*. Cambridge: Polity.

Naipaul, V. S. 1967. *The Mimic Men*. London: Andre Deutsch.

Porto, Nuno. 2007. "From Exhibiting to Installing Ethnography: Experiments at the Museum of Anthropology of the University of Coimbra (Portugal), 1999–2005." In *Exhibition Experiments*, ed. Sharon Macdonald and Paul Basu, 175–196. Oxford: Blackwell.

Porto, Nuno. 2009. *Modos de Objectificação da Dominação Colonial: O Caso do Museu do Dundo, 1940–1970* [Modes of objectivation of colonial domination: The case of the Dundo Museum]. Lisbon: Fundação Calouste Gulbenkian.

Roque, Ricardo. 2010. *Headhunting and Colonialism: Anthropology and the Circulation of Human Skulls in the Portuguese Empire*. New York: Palgrave Macmillan.

Roque, Ricardo. 2014. "Mimetismos coloniais no império português" [Colonial mimesis in the Portuguese empire]. *Etnográfica* 18 (1): 101–109.

Roque, Ricardo. 2015a. "Mimesis and Colonialism: Emerging Perspectives on a Shared History." *History Compass* 13 (4): 201–211.

Roque, Ricardo. 2015b. "Mimetic Governmentality and the Administration of Colonial Justice in East Timor, ca. 1860–1910." *Comparative Studies in Society and History* 57 (1): 67–97.

Rouch, Jean, dir. 1955. *Les maîtres fous*. Documentary film, 36 min. Produced by Les Films de la Pléiade.

Said, Edward W. 1978. *Orientalism: Western Representations of the Orient*. London: Routledge & Kegan Paul.

Sant'Anna, J. Firmino. 1923. "O problema da assistência médico-sanitária ao indígena em África" [The problem of health care for indigenous people in Africa]. *Revista Médica de Angola* 2 (4): 73–178.

Santos, F. Ferreira dos. 1923. "Assistência médica aos Indígenas e processos práticos da sua hospitalização" [Medical assistance to indigenous people and practical processes of their hospitalization]. *Revista Médica de Angola* 2 (4): 51–71.

Saraiva, Tiago. 2014. "Mimetismo colonial e reprodução animal: Carneiros caracul no Sudoeste angolano" [Colonial mimesis and animal reproduction: Karakul sheep in Southwestern Angola]. *Etnográfica* 18 (1): 209–227.

Serén, M. Carmo. 2001. *A Porta do Meio: A Exposição Colonial de 1934* [The middle door: The colonial exposition of 1934]. Porto: Centro Português de Fotografia.

Stoler, Ann L. 1995. *Race and the Education of Desire: Foucault's History of Sexuality and the Colonial Order of Things*. Durham, NC: Duke University Press.

Stoler, Ann L. 2002. *Carnal Knowledge and Imperial Power: Race and the Intimate in Colonial Rule*. Berkeley: University of California Press.

Stoller, Paul. 1992. *The Cinematic Griot: The Ethnography of Jean Rouch*. Chicago: University of Chicago Press.

Stoller, Paul. 1995. *Embodying Colonial Memories: Spirit Possession, Power, and the Hauka in West Africa*. New York: Routledge.

Tarde, Gabriel. 1890. *Les lois de l'imitation* [The laws of imitation]. Paris: Félix Alcan.

Taussig, Michael. 1993. *Mimesis and Alterity: A Particular History of the Senses.* New York: Routledge.

Thomaz, Omar Ribeiro. 2002. *Ecos do Atlântico Sul* [Echoes of the South Atlantic]. Rio de Janeiro: Editora FRJ.

Tostões, Ana, and Inês Gonçalves. 2009. *Moderno Tropical: Arquitectura em Angola e Moçambique 1948–1975* [Modern tropical: Architecture in Angola and Mozambique 1948–1975]. Lisbon: Tinta-da-China.

Trajano Filho, Wilson. 2011. "A mimese e a obesidade conceitual: Uma crítica etnográfica" [Mimesis and conceptual obesity: An ethnographic critique]. Paper presented at the symposium "Mimetismos Coloniais no Império Português," Instituto de Ciências Sociais, Lisbon, 24 March.

Vicente, Filipa L. 2012. *Other Orientalisms: India between Florence and Bombay, 1860–1900.* Hyderabad: Orient Blackswan.

Xavier, Ângela Barreto. 2014. "'Parecem indianos na cor e na feição': A 'lenda negra' e indianização dos portugueses" ['They look like Indians in color and feature': The 'black legend' and Indianization of the Portuguese]. *Etnográfica* 18 (1): 111–133.

Chapter 4

IMITATIONS OF BUDDHIST STATECRAFT
The Patronage of Lao Buddhism and the Reconstruction
of Relic Shrines and Temples in Colonial French Indochina

Patrice Ladwig

When in 2004 I carried out fieldwork in the Lao capital of Vientiane, the temple
to which I was assigned for my research and ordination as a monk was one that
is located close to the That Luang, the largest and most important Buddhist
relic shrine (*stūpa*) of Laos. None of the 60 monks and novices knew that this
stūpa, and many other temples, had been rebuilt by the French colonial regime
between 1893 and 1940. When I mentioned this one evening while we were
having a chat on the balcony of the temple, some of the monks were utterly
astonished. How could the That Luang, today the most sacred national symbol
of the Lao People's Democratic Republic, and some of the major temples of
Vientiane be a 'product' of colonialism? What some of my friends and fellow
monks knew was the fact that when Laos became a French colony in 1893, it

was the last country to be added to an entity to be called Indochina. Functioning as a buffer state between the expanding British Empire and the Kingdom of Siam, it remained the most underdeveloped colony—a 'colonial backwater', as Geoffrey Gunn (1990) called it.[1] However, the Communist Revolution of 1975 and the socialist writing of history had already eradicated or rewritten other histories. Most Lao did not know that after the almost complete demolition of Vientiane in 1827 by the Siamese, many temples and Buddhist monuments were reconstructed under the supervision of colonial officials.

Although studies of colonialism have emphasized the heterogeneous, localized nature of colonialism (N. Thomas 1994: 51) and its fractured and at times rather limited impact on the colonized (Stoler 1989: 135), French colonial politics in Indochina did have a coherent agenda that produced clear effects, especially in the domains of architecture and religion. Cambodia and Laos were subject to quite similar colonial politics rooted, for example, in the fact that both had Theravāda Buddhist kingship and statecraft as forms of indigenous political organization. For French colonialism, indirect rule was considered a "unique form of rule far superior to the colonial regimes of Britain and other Western powers because of its supported basis in spirituality, and its supposed responsiveness to the culture and worldview of native peoples" (Bayly 2000: 595). By 1896, the French had succeeded in establishing regimes of indirect rule in both countries and started to sponsor and partially revive Buddhist kingship by restructuring and revitalizing monastic education and by renovating Buddhist temples and monuments. Creating knowledge about the Buddhist cultures of the dominant ethnic groups, the ethnic Lao and the Khmer,[2] was of crucial importance in this context, and the French School of the Far East—the École française d'Extrême-Orient (EFEO)—had an important role in this field. Over several decades, its members collected, classified, and analyzed the histories, artistic productions, religions, literature, and architecture of Laos and Cambodia. From early on, the EFEO put a special emphasis on architecture and archaeology. Ideas about the built environment in general, especially in the form of Buddhist temples and monuments, remained a crucial focus of French colonial rule (Cooper 2001: 29). This was of primary importance for Vientiane—the colonial capital of Laos—because the city was rebuilt almost from the ground up after the 1827 attack by Siam.

This chapter examines the colonial politics of 'rebuilding' Buddhism in Laos in the period between 1893 and 1940. I will here explore the larger project of the colonial patronage of religion—visible in the textual, institutional, and educational aspects of Buddhism—by examining the material rebuilding of Buddhism and the revival and transformation of state rituals in these reconstructed places. Focusing on the reconstruction of major temples and that of the important Buddhist relic shrine of Laos—the That Luang in Vientiane—the chapter explores the motivations and strategies for this endeavor. I propose that in the context of French colonialism, indirect rule lends itself to political strategies that are essentially of a mimetic and imitative nature. By employing (among others) Michael Taussig's (1993: xiii) account of mimesis, in which the "wonder of mimesis lies in the copy drawing on the character and power of the original," I propose that the French colonial system and its ideology of 'association' based its concepts of rule and power on imitative processes, or a variant of what in the introduction of this book is described as "mimetic governmentality" (see also Ladwig 2011; Roque 2015).[3] In contrast to some of the works on mimesis outlined in the introduction to this collection that emphasize the resistance aspects of mimesis, I suggest that French efforts to 're-materialize' Lao Buddhism, act as its protector, and revitalize its rites can be understood as a governmental strategy to stabilize rule. This established an "order of ceremonial government" (Roque 2010: 40), which in Foucault's (2009: 108) various approaches to governmentality is absent due to a stronger focus on modern techniques of governing through apparatuses of security, population management, and so forth. Finally, by discussing the fragmentary and partial nature of imitative processes (Lempert 2014), I want to argue that the 'magic' effects of mimetic procedures in colonial rule also become visible in what Ann Stoler (2004: 5) has called "fashioning techniques of affective control." By linking this to Danilyn Rutherford's (2009) discussion about sympathy and empire building, I argue that imitation can produce affective communities that—despite inequalities with regard to power relations—at least temporarily stabilize colonial rule.

The EFEO, French Colonialism, and the Built Environment

When Lao King Setthathilat officially established Vientiane as the capital of the Kingdom of Lan Xang in 1563, the city quickly became a regional center of religious learning, with a multitude of temples and Buddhist educational facilities (Askew 2007: 48–50). The Dutch merchant Gerrit van Wuysthoff, one of the first European visitors to Vientiane, included an impressive description of the city in his travel records of 1641 and 1642 (see Wuysthoff 1987). Vientiane became an independent kingdom in 1707, but in 1779 it was conquered by the Siamese and became a vassal state, paying tribute to Siam. A few decades later, in 1827, the Siamese completely devastated Vientiane in order to crush the uprising of the Lao vassal King Anouvong, who was to be the last king of Vientiane. Therefore, the first French missions between 1866 and 1868 found Vientiane in ruins (Garnier 1885: 286). Sophie Clément-Charpentier (2008: 288) states that "its political and administrative structures had in large part disappeared ... Hence, the city of Vientiane was nothing but a field of ruins in 1828."[4] As a result of the Franco-Siamese treatise of 1893, the city and the territory on the left bank side of the Mekong were put under the control of France, and due to strategic and commercial reasons, Vientiane was chosen as the capital of the Lao part of French Indochina. As opposed to Saigon, where in the 1860s spatial planning was driven by fears of uprisings and the old city was largely destroyed (Cooper 2001: 44), in Laos a 'new' city was built that was modern yet also 'traditional'.

Colonial authorities clearly articulated the political implications of this decision to rebuild Vientiane. The résident supérieur, Colonel Tourinier, stated in 1899: "I do not hesitate to affirm that the day Vientiane will become the new capital of Laos, we can count on the absolute fidelity of the Lao people" (cited in Clément-Charpentier 2008: 294). Rebuilding Vientiane and its monuments was therefore considered of prime importance. Ernst Outray, résident supérieur in Laos in 1911, informed Louis Finot, then the EFEO president, of a letter he had written to the gouverneur général of Indochina about "the unfortunate condition in which the most beautiful historical monuments are currently to be found."[5] Henri Parmentier, one of the first architects to work in Laos for the EFEO, created several reports on the general situation of the built environment of Vientiane. Parmentier (1912: 188) stated that, according to oral history accounts, the city had a multiplicity of monasteries (*vat*) before its destruction, but now only the ruins of about 20 to 25 temples could be discovered. Most of the work of the EFEO concentrated on Cambodia and the Angkor Wat temple complex. Replicas of the latter also featured prominently in various French colonial exhibitions and were thereby regarded as a part of French heritage (*patrimoine*).[6] Nevertheless, the interest in Angkor also fueled research on Laos, and the EFEO's missions led to a mapping of the architectural heritage of Lao Buddhist civilization. In 1912, Parmentier sent a report to the EFEO director, listing monuments to be renovated (see Lorrillard 2001: 2).[7]

The emphasis on the ruins of temples and other Buddhist architectural monuments is a recurrent theme of the reports and exchanges between colonial administrators and the staff of the EFEO. In order to pursue their active program of remaking the cultural heritage of Laos, the EFEO employed architects alongside Indologists and archaeologists. The Public Buildings Department and the EFEO primarily hired architects from the Ecole des Beaux-Arts, where 15 of the 16 architects who worked for the EFEO had been trained (Singaravélou 1999: 115). Why this emphasis on the built environment in French colonialism, and why such an expertise of architectural knowledge combined with studies of history and culture? Wright (1987: 299) has argued that in French colonial governmentality "political problems were defined in cultural terms that gave urban planning and architectural design a central importance in consolidating political power." Metcalf (2002) has suggested something very similar for British colonialism in India, perhaps hinting at a pan-European desire to restore Oriental architecture in the context of colonial rule.[8] With this emphasis on culture and architecture in the French colonial project, the EFEO became a key instrument in the pursuit of knowledge about the civilizations of Indochina.

Although members of the EFEO certainly had their own diverse agendas, and some—like Paul Mus—later revealed a strong engagement with anti-colonial sentiments (Bayly 2009; Chandler 2009), on an institutional level the EFEO closely cooperated with other units of the colonial administration,[9] paying employee salaries out of the colonial budget of French Indochina. Louis Finot's (1908) opening speech at the Collège de France exemplified this ambivalence. The long-time chief of EFEO Indochina lectured on 'native policy': "It is on the observation of those different facts, not on abstract principles, sentimental effusions, and humanitarian sentences, that a real native policy can be shaped, which must be firm, wise, and methodical, and can ensure the future of our colonies" (ibid.: 222). However, Finot also critiqued a colonial policy that was based on earlier ideas of 'assimilation' and demanded a shift to the doctrine of 'association'.

Imitating Buddhist Kings: The Revival and Patronage of Buddhism

This 'regeneration' and 'protection' of Indochinese civilization had not only a strong focus on archaeology and the reconstruction of religious monuments. In the context of the colonial politics of association, architecture was rarely seen in an isolated manner; more importantly, it was linked to the recreation and reinvention of institutions and rites that sustained traditional concepts of rule. French colonial politics were based on "the realization that a strong type of cooperation between colonial and native was imperative. This would be achieved … through the retention of native institutions" (Betts 1961: 107). Although the shift in colonial policy was rather tentative and linked to complex power games in the metropolis (M. Thomas 2005: 54–60), the move from assimilation to association in colonial rule "called for the preservation of distinctive local cultures. Including tribal councils and historic monuments, and they [colonial officials] believed that this respect, when combined with social services like schools and hospitals, could counter resistance far more effectively than military strength" (Wright 1987: 299).

Therefore, the colonial project to sponsor, sustain, and protect indigenous concepts of rule was also embedded in imitating and adapting rites of rule and statehood in Indochina. A good example is the renovation of Wat Si Saket, constructed from 1818 to 1824 under the reign of King Anouvong, where rites of statehood were performed before the city's destruction. In cooperation with Lao Prince Phetsarath, EFEO architects Charles Batteur and Léon Fombertaux oversaw the reconstruction of the temple and the impressive building of the Buddhist library (Lorrillard 2001: 4). The oath of allegiance to the Lao king,

ILLUSTration 4.1: Wat Si Saket during its renovation in 1929. Photograph by EFEO architect Charles Batteur. EFEO LAO22434, © École française d'Extrême-Orient

performed twice annually by Lao notables in a ceremony held at Wat Si Saket, was revived by the French, but now local rulers pledged alliance to France via the Buddhist King Sisavangvong (Evans 2002: 69).[10] The latter was a life-long supporter of French rule, first as a king of Luang Prabang (1904–1946) and later as king of Laos (1946–1959). French indirect rule strongly relied on indigenous intermediaries for maintaining authority (M. Thomas 2005: 54), and what developed was a ceremonial form of governing that David Cannadine (2002: 122) describes for the British Empire: "Chivalry and ceremony, monarchy and majesty, were the means by which this vast world was brought together, interconnected, unified and sacralized."

This was by no means a unique phenomenon of colonialism in Indochina, but part and parcel of the colonial politics of association in most parts of the French Empire. Concerning the forms of political organization and colonial architecture in Morocco, the French résident supérieur in 1912 remarked that one of the tasks of the colonial regime was "reviving around the sultan the ancient traditions and old ceremonies of the court … as well as building and maintaining opulent palaces for the ruler" (see Wright 1987: 292). Exactly the same strategy was taken up in colonial Indochina. In addition to the oath of loyalty, the Khmer monarchy benefited from having a palace built in Phnom Penh (Chandler 1993: 150), and Lao King Sisavangvong moved into a new palace in Luang Prabang that mixed French Beaux-Art and Lao-style elements.

Some of the architects and archaeologists responsible for redesigning Vientiane and its religious monuments also worked in North Africa and were therefore acquainted with these policies in other parts of the French Empire.[11] In Laos, the colonial politics of association even tapped into the economy of Buddhist donations. Due to a shortage of resources, the Lao Buddhist believers were successfully animated to get involved in the renovation of Wat Si Saket: "The credit given for this restoration from the local budget was found to be insufficient; the religious community ... was kindly contributing 1000 piastres" (Chronique 1930: 583).

Knowing that the *saṅgha* (monastic order) had a crucial role in legitimizing the power of Buddhist rulers, EFEO scholars more oriented toward historical and textual studies of Buddhism also got heavily involved in reviving Buddhism beyond the narrow field of architecture and restoration. In order to build an Indochinese Buddhism and counter Siamese dominance, these measures primarily focused on the educational facilities of the Lao and Khmer Buddhist *saṅgha*. In order to put the colonial politics of association into practice and contribute to a retention of native institutions, it was deemed necessary to set up new institutions of training for Buddhist monks in both Cambodia and Laos, a process that has been well documented by recent research.[12] On 24 November 1914, the Ecole de Pali was founded by royal decree in Phnom Penh and renamed Ecole Supérieure de Pali in 1922. Its aim was to develop "the theological studies of Buddhism through a rational teaching of the sacred languages Pali and Sanskrit" (Anon. 1922: 424). This language training was given to the monks personally by none other than Louis Finot (ibid.: 440). Lao branches of this institute were to be officially founded in 1931, reflecting the peripheral position of Laos in the colonial project. The French introduced new curricula based on the study of selected and appropriate texts, awarded certificates to monks, and printed Buddhist books.[13] Moreover, future Lao intellectuals and nationalists like Maha Sila Viravong got part of their training in these institutes and worked there under the auspices of important figures such as Prince Phetsarath.[14] These efforts were directed at a general revitalization of Buddhism, mixing the local rulers' traditional patronage of Buddhism with practical considerations deriving from colonial governmentality. An anonymous note from 1928 concerning the resurgence of Buddhism in Laos states that "this regulation has the aim of revitalizing the cults that have fallen out of use, to control monks and novices, to conserve temples, and to develop temple schools that are the basis of primary education for the natives."[15] The control of persons and the recreation of rites, architectural conservation, schooling, and teaching were thereby integrated into a larger project of reviving Buddhist culture and local patterns of rule under the auspices of the French colonial regime.

The French were also acutely aware of the fact that Buddhism had anti-colonial and radical potential. Although the cooperation between the EFEO, local elites, and Buddhist monks in the implementation of these new religious policies was generally successful, the Buddhist Institute, opened in 1931 in Phnom Penh, nevertheless became the site of anti-colonial activities. Lao monks such as Maha Buakham Voraphet (1909–1996) and Maha Khamphan Virachit (1914–1995) participated in those activities, but their influence in the Lao monastic order became stronger only after the end of the colonial regime. Perhaps more importantly, in the south of Laos, messianic Buddhist movements led by charismatic 'men of merit' troubled the French for almost 30 years (Ladwig 2014).[16]

I think what we are encountering here is essentially a modern, colonial version of two interrelated processes that have been of prime importance throughout the history of Theravāda Buddhism in South and Southeast Asia. First, in Theravāda theories of statecraft, rulers are always dependent on the monastic order and vice versa. The power of Buddhist kings is in need of legitimation, and worldly power is sanctified or sanctioned by the *saṅgha*. Ideal kings therefore sponsor the *saṅgha* (or certain sections of it), for instance, by promoting monastic education or by building and renovating monastic properties. Studies of Theravāda Buddhism have extensively discussed this theme.[17] Suksamran (1993: 103) neatly summarizes this interdependence between ruler and *saṅgha*:

> The state, represented by the ruler, upholds Buddhism by providing support and protection for the sangha, in effect acts as a law enforcement officer with regard to the monastic code of discipline, the vinaya. The sangha, in co-operation with the ruler and sometimes advising him, provides a symbol of morality, integrity and legitimacy for the state. In their relationship with the people, sangha members act as teachers, religious guides, and mentors, and provide the model of moral conduct which the people regard as an ideal to be striven for.

Secondly, Buddhist rulers are often involved in what has been called the 'purification of the *saṅgha*'. This usually entails a variety of measures that are meant to secure the purity of Buddhist teachings, including redacting and copying manuscripts and more strictly enforcing the code of conduct for monks (Pali: *vinaya*), activities that are inextricably linked to each other. The goal of these purifications is also to secure the *saṅgha*'s loyalty toward the ruler.[18] One could say that the Buddhist Institute engaged in the simultaneous sponsorship and control of Buddhism by taking over most of the tasks described above, and that in this process EFEO specialists of Buddhism, like Louis Finot, directly supervised Lao and Khmer monks.

What becomes apparent here is the fact that concepts of indirect rule lend themselves to processes of mimesis. Mimesis is viewed by Iain Walker (2005: 195) as "the appropriation of the power of the other and as a mechanism for social change"; in this sense, it is a mediating process that involves "innovative social adaptation at its most efficient." However, appropriating the power to support and purify Buddhism without completely eliminating the role of Buddhist kings can only ever be a selective and partial process. Although the selection of what is to be imitated has to resonate with local understandings of power, it is not necessary to imitate an object or process in full in order to make it efficacious: pieces and fragments can be sufficient "to get hold of something by means of its likeness" (Taussig 1993: 21).[19] While Western theorizations of mimesis often represent it as a mere act of imitation,[20] some recent anthropological (Walker 2005: 192) and older sociological (Tarde 1903) approaches stress the incorporation of new influences through processes of imitation.[21] Consequently, the French not only copied the patronage of Buddhist rulers, but also introduced new elements: the subjects taught in monasteries were to be changed, monks were to receive passports, and a 'scientific' study of Buddhism was supposed to be advanced.

The Power of Buddhist Relics: The Renovation of the That Luang

Throughout the history of Buddhism, Buddhist kings have exemplified their power through acts of construction. Large relic shrines, often said to contain relics of the Buddha himself, were among the most important monuments that kings either built or enlarged during their reigns. The That Luang in Vientiane is just such a relic shrine, and it was also the object of extensive French renovations during the same phase in which the Buddhist Institute was opened in Laos. What Louis Finot and many other EFEO researchers did for the history, textual traditions, and monastic instruction of Lao Buddhism[22] was also applied to a specific part of the architectural heritage of Laos, namely, Buddhist relic shrines. As mentioned before, in French Orientalist discourse, the architectural monuments of Buddhism were intricately linked to the civilizational traditions and forms of social life. For scholars such as Paul Mus and many other EFEO employees, "everything in the built environment, from the most rudimentary stone altar-shrines to the region's great stone-built monuments, was to be understood as a living and accessible materialization of the social" (Bayly 2000: 607). Paul Mus, who published the first in-depth analysis of Borobudur, a large *stūpa* in Indonesia, actually took indigenous concepts seriously. Accordingly, Mus (1935: 248) described the Borobudur *stūpa* as "a materialization of the cosmic law" and as an architectural monument that "makes the *dhamma* visible." Ahead of his time, Mus understood that according to emic conceptions throughout the Buddhist world, relics emanate the teachings of the Buddha (*dhamma*): they have magical properties (*saksit* in Thai and Lao) and are considered to be 'living beings' that are essential for governing through ritual.[23]

While Mus was writing his massive study on Borobudur, the EFEO in Vientiane made plans to renovate the most important *stūpa* of Laos, the That Luang.

Parmentier (1912: 190) recalled its similitude to Borobudur, the *stūpa* studied later by Mus in Indonesia: "About five kilometers from the city center there is the That Luang, a building with real character, which, through its layout and concentric galleries, bears some resemblance to Borobudur." After a number of surveys had been conducted in the late 1920s, it was "found to be the only important monument of this type in the region of Vientiane."[24] The large relic shrine, surrounded by a number of temples and having a square base about 70 meters wide, is labeled *lokacūḷāmaṇi stūpa* in chronicles and epigraphic sources, which signifies 'the *stūpa* of the diadem'. Although epigraphic sources analyzed by Michel Lorrillard (2003: 316–317) describe it as a *jinaguyhadhātu* (hidden or secret relic), it is widely believed that it is a relic of the Buddha himself. Moreover, the mythical history of the relic—traveling from Sri Lanka to the Lao kingdom—builds a bridge to King Asoka, the ideal Buddhist king who used relics to spread the *dhamma*.[25]

Partial restorations of the tower of the *stūpa* had been carried out earlier, but they were later criticized by several EFEO scholars.[26] As the monument was a ruin, there was actually no 'original' that could be faithfully restored and thereby copied. The EFEO relied largely on the rather fantastic images of a landscape painter, Louis Delaporte (1842–1925), who made a sketch of a more complete That Luang during the first Mekong expedition from 1866 to 1868.[27] Before the new restorations were started, Parmentier made a visit to the That Luang in 1928 in order to examine the situation and the possible renovation of the cloister. Beyond the technical details, the revitalization of cults around the monument was also being considered. As Parmentier put it: "This undertaking perhaps goes beyond the limits of the capacities of the institute, but could be justified by local necessities. The monument is the center of important festivals and pilgrimages … Undertaking this work would be a good move in indigenous politics [*bonne politique indigène*] and presents no archaeological difficulties."[28]

Like his colleague Paul Mus, Parmentier was certainly aware of the significance that this *stūpa* held for the Lao. But what did Parmentier really mean by the phrase *bonne politique indigène*? *Stūpas* have been at the center of Buddhist kingdoms, presenting an *axis mundi* and a cosmology in stone essential for claiming political power. Describing the cult of relics in South and Southeast Asia, Anne Blackburn (2010: 318–319) argues that "relic monuments were at the heart of local moves to employ centers of rituals and remembrance within a highly charged cosmic and regional map … In the formation of new polities and/or new dynasties, relics were drawn into the physical landscape." It thus comes as no surprise that quite quickly after the decision to make Vientiane the capital of the Lao protectorate, the aforementioned renovation of the That Luang was first begun. The old and new capital needed a ritual relic center.

Progress was slow until more concerted renovation work on the That Luang was undertaken. This finally started on 1 June 1930, five days after the arrival of Léon Fombertaux (1871–1936), who supervised the restoration of the *stūpa* until 1935. The extensive archaeological documentation exemplifies how the That Luang was systematically taken apart, photographed, and analyzed. During this process, Fombertaux discovered a 'primitive *stūpa*' inside the construction, revealing the original form of the pagoda hidden under the present one.[29]

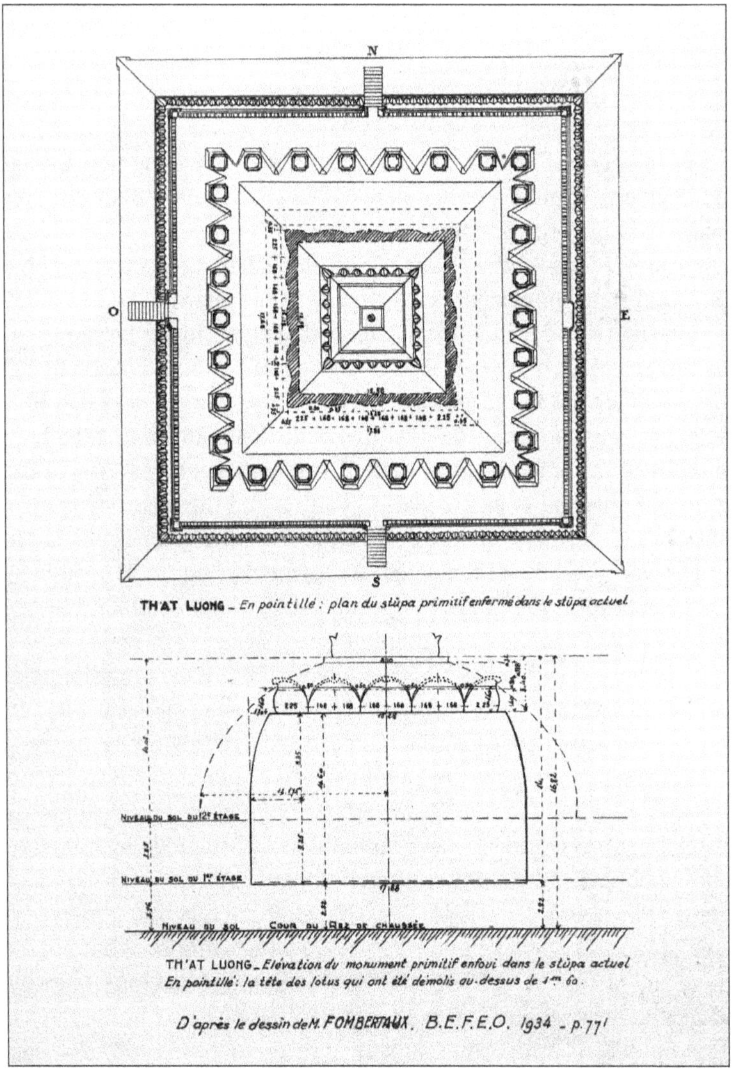

THAT LUONG _ *En pointillé : plan du stūpa primitif enfermé dans le stūpa actuel*

TH'AT LUONG _ *Elévation du monument primitif enfoui dans le stūpa actuel*
En pointillé : la tête des lotus qui ont été demolis au-dessus de 1.m 60.

D'après le dessin de M. FOMBERTAUX . B.E.F.E.O. 1934 _ p.77¹

ILLUSTration 4.2: Plan of the That Luang *stūpa* originally drawn by Léon Fombertaux. The image shows the smaller, 'hidden' *stūpa* that was discovered during excavation work, but also reveals the 'cosmological layout' typical for many *stūpas*. EFEO LAO21998 © École française d'Extrême-Orient

In historical terms, the aim was to archaeologically approach the original as closely as possible. Although the renovation projects seemed to have run smoothly, the ruin presented some challenges, judging from the available archival material: the vegetation had already sunk its roots into some of the walls of the *stūpa*, and the temples that are close to the That Luang were also in ruins. The résident supérieur, Prince Phetsarath, and the highest monk of Vientiane agreed that a partial demolition was necessary in order to rescue them.[30] Nevertheless, most of the work in progress satisfied the officials, and when the résident supérieur of Laos, Yves Chatel, made an official visit to the site on 22 May 1931, his comments were noted: "He is very interested in the already undertaken works and on this occasion also gave expression to his wish that the other archaeological works of the EFEO continue."[31]

EFEO employees and colonial administrators not only cared about the aesthetics of the monument, but also sought to recreate its religious character in order to enhance its attractiveness as a site of ritual worship.[32] In a 1935 report by the chief of the archaeological service, we find a positive review of the work that had been accomplished, but the overall design of the area was yet to be finished, as the *stūpa* now stood among the ruins of the temples close by: "We have to bring the ensemble [of temples and ruins] into order for creating a religious character around the *that* in order to avoid the newly renovated monument looking disparate and almost like an anomaly in the

ILLUSTRATION 4.3: Workers employed for the renovation of the That Luang relic shrine, 1931. EFEO LAO22743 © École française d'Extrême-Orient

milieu of the pagodas, which are more or less abandoned and covered by the vegetation around them."[33] In 1935, the governor of Vientiane ordered that another 1,000 piastres should go toward "the consolidation and restoration of the *that*."[34] Restoration work was nearly complete. The That Luang was not the only shrine to be renovated. A number of other carefully chosen monuments that once housed other important libraries or statues became building sites. After the completion of the That Luang project, Henri Marchal, who had previously worked at Angkor, took over the restoration of Wat Phra Kaew. Before being destroyed by the Siamese in 1828, this particular temple had housed the Emerald Buddha, the palladium of the kingdom of Vientiane, which was taken to Bangkok as the spoils of war, never to return to Laos.[35]

As in the case of monastic education and the renewal of kingly rites, I think what we are dealing with here is another layer of mimetic processes that imitate and re-enact activities usually performed by Buddhist rulers. Apart from the fact that renovating and extending already existing *stūpas* was a very common means for rulers to add to their prestige, the cosmological underpinnings inherent in the construction and worship of *stūpas* such as the That Luang are also of interest. The beginnings of Buddhist kingship are linked to relics,[36] and in general Buddhist rulers try to recall Asoka's policy toward Buddhism, reflected in the sponsorship and building of temples and *stūpas*. As outlined in the previous section, this also includes efforts to purify Buddhism and regulate the life of monks through patronage and control. Donald Swearer (2010: 82) neatly traces these measures back to the rule of a renowned ancient Buddhist king: "According to the Theravada chronicles of Southeast Asia, successful rulers … were those who emulated King Asoka. This suggests that the Asokan model had a mimetic potency: to imitate King Asoka legitimated a ruler as a *dhammaraja*. In particular, Buddhist monarchs built edifices, especially stupas, and purified the dhamma and the sangha in self-conscious imitation of King Asoka. By such mimetic repetition, peace and prosperity would be guaranteed in the realm and enable the king to rule as a universal monarch."

Hence, in yearly rites Lao kings also meditated close to the *stūpa*, identifying with King Asoka in order to fill themselves with Buddhist *dhamma* and bring about fertility and prosperity (Reynolds 1969: 82). From this perspective, Buddhist kings have long been engaged in a sort of mimetic repetition of Asoka's pious acts. In the Lao case, one must add another level of repetition, namely, the colonial project of rebuilding and enlarging a relic shrine. To explore this level of interpretation, let us once again return to Swearer's (2010) presentation of *stūpa* worship. He elaborates: "Sponsoring stupa construction was a major activity of these Buddhist monarchs … the cult of relics became a primary expression of Buddhist piety as well as part of Asoka's policy of *using Buddhism as a unifying instrument of imperial power*" (ibid.: 77; emphasis added). The patronage of Buddhism and the restoration of the That Luang can in this light also be seen as a French colonial strategy to cement imperial rule through Buddhism via the indirect rule of Buddhist kings and rites of statecraft.

In this interpretation, Vientiane was the new capital of Laos as a protectorate, and the French had renovated the *stūpa* and the temples surrounding it in order to create a religious atmosphere, which essentially is another element of Buddhist statecraft and a way of sanctifying a new center of power. Blackburn (2010: 336) maintains that "the installation of such potent traces in a new space, and the construction of royal monastic centers near existing relic or burial sites, drew blessings and magical power into human lives." Renovating the That Luang was a way to rematerialize a small 'Buddhist empire', or a "galactic polity" as Tambiah (1976: 102) has called it. In local cosmology, the rites taking place there produced fertility and prosperity (or 'life') and thereby integrated smaller peripheral polities. Yet at the same time, these polities were integrated into the French Empire. Although French colonial governmentality became much more scientific in the inter-war period by focusing on typical Foucauldian topics such as population, health, and schooling (Dimier 2002), this ritual governing of life through relics is reminiscent of Arthur Hocart's work. Hocart (1970: 35) proposed that ritual is a primordial form of government without offices that aims at the revitalization of life, and that kingship and ritual already constitute "a governing body before there is any governing to do."[37] One could say that in Laos, the poorest and most understaffed colony in Indochina, "colonial government was ... the government of ceremonial," as Roque (2010: 68) has said of Timor Leste, another peripheral colony.

However, these interventions also implied changes. Although French colonial rule created an 'overlap' that allowed for mimetic processes to take place and to mediate between different orders, it is evident that differences and modifications (as in the measures discussed above) had to be integrated into these mimetic procedures. The French could not entirely emulate the relic patronage of kings. They introduced their own forms of mimesis, for example, through scientific archaeological studies. The 'raw material' of mimetic processes (buildings, symbols, rites, institutions) undergo transformations since "in passing from one ethnical environment to another the radiation of imitation is refracted ... this refraction may be enormous without it leading to any consequence" (Tarde 1903: xxi). One important refraction was the introduction of nationalism and nation building with regard to monuments such as That Luang (Tappe 2008). Søren Ivarsson (2008) has rightly remarked that these renovations played an important role in the formation of Lao nationalism, cutting Lao Buddhism off from Siam and 'nationalizing' in terms of style and history, thereby shaping a novel state imaginary.[38] The question of the original versus the copy might be too restrictive to account for the creativity of imitative acts, as these processes do not "come from just two things called original and copy, but rather from a highly distributed assemblage of signs" (Lempert 2014: 386).

Mimesis, Sympathy, and Colonial Rule

According to the reports and communications, the revitalization of Buddhist cults that was supposed to be brought about by the reconstruction of the That Luang was indeed accomplished. In December 1934, it was reported that "the That Luang festival took place with success from 20–22 November. One particularly had to notice the crowds of monks who came from the bordering provinces and from Siam."[39] The *bonne politique indigène*—mentioned by Henri Parmentier before the building works began—was in this case successful and was ritually enacted. But what were the effects of these colonial building politics and the patronage of Lao Buddhism on a broader level, and what do they reveal about the nature of mimetic processes in the context of colonial rule?

I have already alluded to the ideas and agendas that stood behind this *politique indigène*. The EFEO enacted architectural and cultural projects that were in line with the politics of association. Joseph Marrast (1935: 24) commented on the role of indigenous Indochinese arts in the construction of buildings: "The sympathies of the natives [*indigènes*] are affirmed in our respect for their works and their association with our works. Hence, step by step, one wins the heart of the natives and conquers their sympathy. It is the role of the colonizers to achieve this." How should we understand 'winning hearts' and 'sympathy' in the colonial politics of mimesis?

ILLUSTration 4.4: The That Luang festival in 2011. After the colonial period, the top was covered with golden paint. The festival linked to the Buddha's relic has remained the most important Buddhist rite in Laos. Photograph © Patrice Ladwig

Approaches to the anthropology of colonialism and empire have empha-sized not only the 'rational' agendas of colonial governmentality à la Foucault, such as population screenings, schooling, and the economy, but also the role played by sentiments and emotions. In this 'anthropology of affect', senti-ments are conceptualized as the very "substance" of governing projects (Stoler 2004: 5). Rutherford (2009: 4–5) has recently advanced that empire building also has to be based in a "materialist concept of sympathy" that "tracks the intricate pathways through which encounters with objects and others gives rise to feelings and thoughts." The rematerialization ('objects') and the patron-age of Buddhism in the encounter with the French ('others') indeed gave rise to feelings and thoughts, at least on the level of ritual enactment and public discourse. It does not seem unreasonable to speculate that the French scholars and architects of EFEO deliberately played on the link between 'sacredness', the built environment (or what Rutherford calls 'objects'), and sympathy. In archival documents, one often finds estimations of the 'emotional impact' that certain construction projects might have on the Lao, along with an outline of the strategic value of these measures.

The construction of the residence of the résident supérieur on the old grounds of the Chao Anouvong palace of Vientiane in 1902 was already under-stood to be taking place on 'sacred terrain'. A French colonial officer reported that when talking to Lao officials, they "assured me that the *feelings of the population are with us*" (cited in Clément-Charpentier 2008: 304; emphasis added). After the renovation of the That Luang and of Wat Si Saket and the creation of the Buddhist Institute, these politics of sympathy and empire build-ing became even clearer with respect to the 'emotional impact' they could make on the population. When planning the renovations, Henri Marchal wrote that "the Phra Kaew pagoda is actually connected to the glorious past of the Vientiane kingdom and its period of prosperity. Its reconstruction will make a *profound impression* on the Lao people, and the prestige of France can only be enhanced by this."[40] Concerning the opening of the Buddhist Institute and the library of Wat Si Saket in February 1931, the résident supérieur of Laos reported to the gouverneur généneral of Indochina and the director of political affairs that the rite was attended by several hundred monks, Prince Phetsarath, and a delegate of the king of Luang Prabang, Sisavangvong. He continued: "This ceremony was a considerable event that will *make history in the spirit of the population* of this country ... The creation of the Buddhist Institute cannot help but have positive effects for our authority and moral influence in this part of Indochina."[41] The most open statement was made in the same letter by another observer:

The inauguration of the new Buddhist Institute has drawn a lot of atten-tion among the Lao on both sides of the Mekong river. They have been visibly satisfied to participate in these rites, which are for them something new; they were quite surprised that we take such great interest in the free practice of Buddhist cults, in the intellectual education of monks, and in the restoration of old temples ruined by time or the hands of man … It is beyond doubt that these actions have really touched the spirit of the population … On the other hand, we will also draw benefits from this for our authority and our prestige among religious groups. This will also ensure the impact of our political and moral actions. It is in the Buddhist clergy that we find our best allies in the fight against Soviet propaganda and the threats posed by the Communists.[42]

This is probably a very good example of Ann Stoler's notion of 'fashioning techniques of affective control'. Rational colonial governmentality can indeed be based in the emotional effects of rule. In this perspective, "sympathy with the native was more than a symptom or a means of coping with the contradictions of colonial identity; rather, it was an indispensable component of colonial rule" (Rutherford 2009: 21). Moreover, the reference to security questions demonstrates that the politics of association were also driven by the "underlying need to limit popular dissent while keeping administrative costs down" (M. Thomas 2005: 82).

Conclusion

Nicholas Thomas (1994: 195) has critiqued homogenizing accounts of colonialism and has explored the "multiplicity of colonizing projects and the plurality of potential subversions of them." In direct line with this emphasis on subversion and partiality under colonial rule are interpretations of mimesis or mimicry that stress their resistance aspects. Taussig (1993) and Bhabha (1997), among others, have emphasized the potential of mimesis to subvert colonial rule by becoming a means of native empowerment against colonial violence and oppression. Due to the scarcity of Lao historical sources in the cases I have described, I cannot say to what extent the mimesis of colonial rule was subject to critique among the Lao.[43] I do not wish to suggest that all Lao were content with these policies of imitation. Buddhism, its institutions, and its actors were not simply passive recipients in these imitative exchanges, as is clear in the example of the monks who became involved in rebellions and anti-colonial activities, to which I briefly alluded above. Yet seen from a broad perspective, resistance appears to have been the exception rather than the rule.

From a theoretical standpoint, Huggan (1997) has questioned the subversive potential of mimetic processes, and Sherry Ortner (1995: 181) has critically examined the notion of "religiosity as an authentic dimension of subaltern culture," advanced in the resistance studies boom of the 1990s. With regard to colonialism, I think that there is indeed a multiplicity of projects of varying impacts, as Nicholas Thomas suggests, but I have argued that some of these projects involving imitation are not necessarily subversive, but can actually enhance colonial rule. By simple inversion, I have argued that the colonizers could draw on the power of native conceptions of rule in their institutional, architectural, and cosmological dimensions. Colonial rule could be enhanced through the construction of buildings, monastic schooling, and practices of ceremonial government and mimetic governmentality. The emotional dimension of colonialism, the "strange forms of sympathy that these actions entail" between colonizers and colonized (Rutherford 2009: 4–5), played an important role in creating the mimetic processes I have outlined in this chapter.

Gebauer and Wulf (1995: 315) have suggested that mimesis opens up a communication between different symbolic orders: mimetic processes are not closed systems, but a priori have to make reference to another world. Buddhist patronage and the imitation of Buddhist kings possessed an emotional appeal for the Lao, opening up the possibility of shared systems of signification, especially with regard to concepts of Buddhist statecraft. Winning the sympathy of the colonized through mimetic processes was a means of entering a relationship that demands—to use the words of Robert Foster (2001: 66)—an "imaginary identification." In the cases I have discussed, this identification was produced through acts of imitation and mimesis. Mimetic processes can, when following a similar aim, create what Rosenwein (2002: 844) has called "emotional communities." Colonial knowledge and the capacity to achieve an imaginary identification are preconditions for the success of such a community.

Mimesis can generate new capacities to shape and be shaped within the colonial encounter. Drawing on the powers associated with Buddhist kingship, its patronage of Buddhism and the power of relic shrines, imitation creates an 'overlap' in symbolic reference: a common horizon, a common point on which emotions can crystallize. However, these imitations create only temporary, fragile, and partial common horizons that are subject to continuous change. Mimesis always works on itself by employing its own central principle—by partially imitating what has already been subject to partial imitation.

Acknowledgments

This chapter is based on research that began at the Max Planck Institute for Social Anthropology. Thanks go to Oliver Tappe, Dittmar Schorkowitz, Chris Hann, and many other colleagues there for fruitful discussions and inspiration. Further research and meetings took place in the context of the DAAD/CRUP Exchange Grant A-07/2011, whose support is gratefully acknowledged. Draft versions of this chapter were presented at conferences in Hamburg, Lisbon, Paris, and Chicago. I thank all colleagues who participated for their feedback and ideas, and especially Yves Goudineau for his spirited defense of the École française d'Extrême-Orient during our heated discussions on French colonialism in Wisconsin. I also extend thanks to the editors of *Social Analysis* and the anonymous reviewers and to the staff at the Archives l'École française d'Extrême-Orient (Cristina Cramerotti and Christophe Caudron) and at the Archives Nationales d'Outre-Mer. I want to express my gratitude to Oliver, Christoph, Ricardo, and Cristiana for having marvelous times and exchanges in Lisbon, Berlin, and Halle. Finally, thanks to Michel Lorrillard and all others at EFEO Vientiane for hosting me over many years while working in Laos.

Patrice Ladwig studied social anthropology and sociology and obtained his PhD from the University of Cambridge. He has worked at the University of Bristol, the Max Planck Institute for Social Anthropology, and the University of Zurich. His work focuses on the anthropology of Buddhism (Laos and Thailand), death and funeral cultures, colonialism, the link of religion to communist movements, and general social theory. He currently works at the Max Planck Institute for the Study of Religious and Ethnic Diversity and carries out research on economic modernization, religion, and ethics in the context of the Max Planck Cambridge Centre for the Study of Ethics, Human Economy and Social Change. E-mail: ladwig@mmg.mpg.de

Notes

1. For studies of colonialism in Laos, see Stuart-Fox (1995) and the relevant sections in the general histories of Laos by Evans (1998, 2002). For a larger overview of the position of Laos in Indochina, see Brocheux and Hémery's (2009) seminal study.
2. The 'savage' and 'tribal' populations were subject to a different kind of politics, especially in Laos. In this chapter I will focus only on colonialism at large in Vientiane and other urban areas, mostly occupied by ethnic Lao adhering to Buddhism. For the highlands of Vietnam and French colonial rule of minorities, see, for example, Salemink (2003). See also Pels (1997) and Scott (1995) on the ethnography and genealogy of Western and colonial governmentality.
3. See the introduction of this issue for an explication of the concept of (mimetic) governmentality and further details on various theories of mimesis and imitation. I partially focus on Taussig's (1993) use of the concept and his idea of the powers that can be drawn from such processes. For more on Taussig's theory, see Stoller (1994); for a critical view, see Jay (1993). Tarde's (1903) theory of imitation has usually not been subsumed under the field of mimesis, but I think it offers interesting angles that I will explore in some parts of the chapter.

4. Unless otherwise indicated, all translations are my own.
5. Ernst Outray, Résident Supérieur au Laos à Monsieur le Directeur d l'École française d'Extrême-Orient. A.S. de la restauration des monuments historiques de Vientiane, 3 Février 1911. Archives l'École française d'Extrême-Orient (hereafter AEFEO).
6. EFEO member Victor Goloubew undertook major travels and works for getting the data needed to produce a replica for the exhibition in Paris in 1931. According to Kostova (2011: 187) "this was a major investment on behalf of the Exposition." See also Norindr (1996: 25–28) on Angkor Wat as architectural patrimony in the context of colonial exhibitions.
7. However, it was not until 1926 that the first official list of historical monuments of Laos was compiled (Lorrillard 2001: 4), representing a kind of archaeological heritage mapping.
8. Metcalf (2002: xv) suggests that in British India "political authority took shape in stone" and concludes that "to study colonial architecture is therefore to study the allocation of power, and the relationships of knowledge and power, that made up the colonial order."
9. See Singaravélou (1999) on the EFEO's general colonial entanglements. This is also visible in the cooperation between various branches of the Indochinese administration. A good example of the integration of the EFEO into wider fields are the works in Angkor that were effective "due to the harmonious cooperation between EFEO, public works, and the Forestry Department" (Anon. 1922: 426).
10. For Laos, see Marcel Zago's (1972: 332–338) very good overview of this rite, which took place not only in Vientiane but also in smaller provincial capitals. During my research in the French colonial archives, the numerous references to the rite over several decades confirm the central position this imitation ritual held in French indirect rule. Commenting on the same rite under the Buddhist king in Siam, Quaritch-Wales (1931: 193) attests that it was "one of the most important State Ceremonies from the point of view of the upkeep of the established form of government."
11. Henri Parmentier (1871–1949) worked for a brief spell in Tunisia and arrived in Indochina in 1900. After several decades of research, he produced a monumental work on art and architecture in Laos (see Parmentier 1954). Léon Fomberteaux (1871–1936) had gathered work experience in Morocco where he was responsible for the renovation of the palace of the sultan of Rabat. He arrived in Indochina in 1925 and worked at Angkor, but later also in Laos where he led the restoration of several Buddhist temples in Vientiane.
12. See Penny Edwards (2007: chap. 8) and Anne Hansen (2007) on the Cambodian case, and Gregory Kourilsky (2006) and Søren Ivarsson (2008: 93–95) on the creation and restructuring of Buddhist education under French colonialism in Laos.
13. For a discussion about the Lao curricula and certificates at the Buddhist Institute, see Kourilsky's (2006: 30–63) excellent analysis. For a broader elaboration of monastic learning in Lao Buddhism, see McDaniel (2008).

14. Maha Sila Viravong probably had the largest impact on Buddhism in Laos in the twentieth century. He compiled many books, taught, and was the personal secretary of Prince Phetsarath. For the career of Viravong and his ideas about Buddhism, see Kourilsky (2008). For Phetsarath's influential career as an engineer, a nationalist, and the Lao head of the Buddhist Institute, see Ivarsson and Goscha (2007).

15. Le Résident Supérieur aus Laos à Messieurs les Commissaires du Gouvernement au Laos et le Commandant du 5e Territoire Militaire, Phongsali. Vientiane, le 12 mars 1928. AEFEO.

16. These rebellions, which also integrated various ethnic minorities, had their first peak in 1900–1901, but outbreaks lasted until the 1930s. See Ladwig and Shields (2014) for a general overview of the research on Buddhist-inspired rebellions and millenarian movements in Buddhism.

17. For Thailand, often cited studies in this field are Ishii (1986) and Tambiah (1976). For Burma, see Mendelson (1975).

18. See Tambiah (1976: 84, 170) for further elaborations on *saṅgha* purifications in Thailand and their link to (aspiring) political power-holders.

19. See also Lempert (2014: 386–387) for an illuminating analysis of partiality across a range of examples. See also the extensive discussion about the fragmentary nature of mimetic processes in the introduction of this volume.

20. See our introduction and Ladwig (2017) regarding the shifts of meaning of mimesis that occurred during the Renaissance and the Enlightenment.

21. This more dynamic and processual view also resonates with Gabriel Tarde's (1903: vii) complex theory of imitation, in which the repetition of imitation exists "for the sake of variation," leading not to a one-to-one scale of imitation, but to a transformation in the very act of appropriation.

22. Finot's (1917) extensive study of Lao literature and Buddhist manuscripts remains one of the best works on this topic.

23. For the living qualities of relics in early Indian Buddhism, see Schopen (1987). The concept of relics as living beings that bring the Buddha and the *dhamma* to life again has remained remarkably stable in the Theravāda world (Trainor 1997). For Laos and the qualities of relics as being *saksit*, see Ladwig (2015)

24. L'inspecteur du service archéologique de l'École française d'Extrême-Orient en mission à Vientiane, Laos. Rapport sur le That Luong—monument classé de la region Vientiane, Vientiane le 16 septembre 1929. AEFEO.

25. King Asoka did this by erecting 84,000 *stūpas* with relics of the Buddha. On Asoka as a paradigmatic Buddhist ruler, see Tambiah (1976: 54–72). Ladwig (2000) gives a sketch of the historical background of the That Luang and other Lao *stūpas*. For a wider contextualization of the link between Asoka, relics, and political centralization, see the excellent study by John Strong (2004: 127–144).

26. See L'inspecteur du service archéologique de l'École française d'Extrême-Orient en mission à Vientiane, Laos. Rapport sur le That Luong—monument classé de la region Vientiane, Vientiane le 16 septembre 1929. Signed Parmentier. AEFEO. See also the comments on the That Luang by Lajonquiere (1901: 112).

27. Delaporte's depictions, which were not aiming at realistic reproduction, included a number of imaginative features that actually influenced the rebuilding of the That Luang (Lorrillard 2010: 52).

28. Le chef de service archéologique de l'École française d'Extrême-Orient à Monsieur le Directeur d l'Ecole, Phnom Penh le 5 Janvier 1928. AEFEO.

29. On 18 January 1932, Parmentier visited the construction site and examined the primitive *stūpa*. It was extensively documented before being overbuilt again. See L'inspecteur du service archéologique de l'École française d'Extrême-Orient. Rapport sur le travaux de restoration du That-Luang à Vientiane en 1932. Vientiane 10 Avril 1932. AEFEO.

30. See L'inspecteur archéologique à Monsieur le Directeur d l'Ecole française d'Extrême-Orient. Rapport sur le travaux éxecutes à Vientiane (Laos) pendant le mois de juillet 1930. Vientiane le 7 Aout 1930. AEFEO.

31. L'inspecteur archéologique à Monsieur le Directeur de l'Ecole française d'Extrême-Orient en mission au Laos. Rapport sur le travaux de restauration du That Luong à Vientiane, Laos. 1. Juin 1931. AEFEO.

32. It is also mentioned that this work could be done with the free help of Lao Buddhist believers, but it seems to be preferable for the EFEO to direct it "in order to avoid the horrors that will befall the monks whose numbers will increase there." Extrait d'un rapport de M. le Chef du Service archéologique de l'Ecole française d'Extrême-Orient sur sa tournée aus Laos (février 1935). No date. AEFEO.

33. Extrait d'un rapport de M. le Chef du Service archéologique de l'Ecole française d'Extrême-Orient sur sa tournée aus Laos (février 1935). No date. AEFEO.

34. L'inspecteur archéologique à Monsieur le Directeur de l'Ecole française d'Extrême-Orient, Vientiane 7 Janvier 1935. AEFEO.

35. On the significance of palladia in Lao Buddhism and their continuing significance under socialist rule, see Ladwig (2014).

36. As reported in the Mahāparinibbāna Sutta, after the Buddha's cremation at Kusinārā, the king of Magadha, five aristocratic clans, and the Malla tribe claimed the relics. It was only through the intervention of a Brahmin that a war could be prevented.

37. See Needham's (1970) excellent introduction to Hocart's *Kings and Councillors* and Schnepel's (1988) insightful discussion about ritual and government with respect to Hocart's notion of 'life'. Marshall Sahlins (2016) recently presented the Inaugural Hocart Lecture, titled "The Original Political Society," in which he highlighted Hocart's original approach by connecting it, for example, to Foucauldian notions of governmentality—concepts that relate well to the notion of mimetic governmentality proposed in the introduction to this issue.

38. See the introduction to this issue for more details on state imaginaries and their role in colonial orders.

39. L'inspecteur archéologique à Monsieur le Directeur de l'Ecole française d'Extrême-Orient. Rapport sur le travaux de restauration du That Luong à Vientiane. Exercise 1934, mois de Novembre, Vientiane le 6 Décembre 1934.

40. Extrait d'un rapport de M. le Chef du Service archéologique de l'Ecole française d'Extrême-Orient sur sa tournée aus Laos (février 1935). No date. AEFEO.
41. Le Résident Supérieur au Laos à Monsieur le Gouverneur Généneral de l'Indochine (Direction des affaires politiques), Hanoi. Object: Inauguration de l'Institut Bouddique, Vientiane, le 23 février 1931. AEFEO (emphasis added).
42. Le Résident Supérieur au Laos à Monsieur le Gouverneur Généneral de l'Indochine (Direction des affaires politiques), Hanoi. Object: Inauguration de l'Institut Bouddique, Vientiane, le 23 février 1931. AEFEO
43. Lao voices are unfortunately mostly absent in the archives. Only the highest monk of Vientiane, who gave a speech on 19 February 1931 at the opening of the Buddhist Institute, is quoted in a letter. He emphasized that a "new era of renovation and conservation has begun for Buddhism" and thanked the French for the renovation of the library, a "heritage of the last sovereign of Laos, which has been rescued from falling into ruins." He concluded: "Please accept, Monsieur Résident Supérieur, the thanks and gratitude of our Lao for the restoration of this library, and also for the high interest you have always taken in the remains of our past, as for example Wat Si Saket and the That Luang." Le Résident Supérieur au Laos à Monsieur le Gouverneur Généneral de l'Indochine (Direction des affaires politiques), Hanoi. Object: Inauguration de l'Institut Bouddique, Vientiane, le 23 février 1931. AEFEO.

References

Anonymous. 1922. "Documents administratifs." *Bulletin de l'École française d'Extrême-Orient* 22: 419–444.
Askew, Marc. 2007. "From Glory to Ruins." In *Vientiane: Transformations of a Lao Landscape*, Marc Askew, William S. Logan, and Colin Long, 43–72. London: Routledge.
Bayly, Susan. 2000. "French Anthropology and the Durkheimians in Colonial Indochina." *Modern Asian Studies* 34 (3): 581–622.
Bayly, Susan. 2009. "Conceptualizing Resistance and Revolution in Vietnam: Paul Mus' Understanding of Colonialism in Crisis." *Journal of Vietnamese Studies* 4 (1): 192–205.
Betts, Raymond F. 1961. *Assimilation and Association in French Colonial Theory, 1890–1914*. New York: Columbia University Press.
Bhabha, Homi. 1997. "Of Mimicry and Man: The Ambivalence of Colonial Discourse." In *Tensions of Empire: Colonial Cultures in a Bourgeois World*, ed. Frederick Cooper and Ann L. Stoler, 152–160. Berkeley: University of California Press.
Blackburn, Anne M. 2010. "Buddha-Relics in the Lives of Southern Asian Polities." *Numen* 57 (3–4): 317–340.
Brocheux, Pierre, and Daniel Hémery. 2009. *Indochina: An Ambiguous Colonization, 1858–1954*. Trans. Ly Lan Dill-Klein. Berkeley: University of California Press.
Cannadine, David. 2002. *Ornamentalism: How the British Saw Their Empire*. Oxford: Oxford University Press.

Chandler, David. 1993. *A History of Cambodia.* Wales: Allen & Unwin.

Chandler, David. 2009. "Paul Mus (1902–1969): A Biographical Sketch." *Journal of Vietnamese Studies* 4 (1): 149–191.

Chronique. 1930. "Les travaux dirigés par M. Fombertaux on porté sur le Vat Sisaket et le That Luong de Vieng Chan" [The works directed by Mr. Fombertaux focused on Vientiane's Wat Si Saket and the That Luang]. *Bulletin de l'École française d'Extrême-Orient* 30: 487–647.

Clément-Charpentier, Sophie. 2008. "Les débuts de Vientiane, capitale coloniale" [The beginnings of Vientiane, colonial capital]. In *Recherches nouvelles sur le Laos* [New research on Laos], ed. Yves Goudineau and Michel Lorrillard, 287–337. Paris: EFEO.

Cooper, Nicola. 2001. *France in Indochina: Colonial Encounters.* Oxford: Berg.

Dimier, Véronique. 2002. "Direct or Indirect Rule: Propaganda around a Scientific Controversy." In *Promoting the Colonial Ideal: Propaganda and Visions of Empire in France,* ed. Tony Chafer and Amanda Sackur, 168–183. London: Palgrave.

Edwards, Penny. 2007. *Cambodge: The Cultivation of a Nation, 1860–1945.* Honolulu: University of Hawai'i Press.

Evans, Grant. 1998. *The Politics of Ritual and Remembrance: Laos since 1975.* Honolulu: University of Hawai'i Press.

Evans, Grant. 2002. *A Short History of Laos: The Land In Between.* London: Allen & Unwin.

Finot, Louis. 1908. "Les études indochinoises" [Indochinese studies]. *Bulletin de l'École française d'Extrême-Orient* 8 (1–2): 221–233.

Finot, Louis. 1917. "Recherches sur la littérature laotienne" [Research on Laotian literature]. *Bulletin de l'École française d'Extrême-Orient* 17 (5): 1–219.

Foster, Robert. 2001. "Unvarnished Truths: Masyln Williams and Australian Government Film in Papua and New Guinea." In *Colonial New Guinea,* ed. Naomi M. McPherson, 64-81. Pittsburgh, PA: University of Pittsburgh Press.

Foucault, Michel. 2009. *Security, Territory, Population: Lectures at the Collège de France, 1977–1978.* Trans. Graham Burchell. New York: Palgrave Macmillan.

Garnier, Francis. 1885. *Voyage d'exploration en Indochine* [Exploration trip to Indochina] Paris: Hachette.

Gebauer, Gunter, and Christoph Wulf. 1995. *Mimesis: Culture, Art, Society.* Trans. Don Reneau. Berkeley: University of California Press.

Gunn, Geoffrey C. 1990. *Rebellion in Laos: Peasant and Politics in a Colonial Backwater.* Boulder, CO: Westview Press.

Hansen, Anne R. 2007. *How to Behave: Buddhism and Modernity in Colonial Cambodia, 1860–1930.* Honolulu: University of Hawai'i Press.

Hocart, Arthur M. 1970. *Kings and Councillors: An Essay in the Comparative Anatomy of Human Society.* Ed. Rodney Needham. Chicago: University of Chicago Press.

Huggan, Graham. 1997. "(Post)Colonialism, Anthropology, and the Magic of Mimesis." *Cultural Critique* 38: 91–106.

Ishii, Yoneo. 1986. *Sangha, State and Society: Thai Buddhism in History.* Trans. Peter Hawkes. Honolulu: University of Hawai'i Press.

Ivarsson, Søren. 2008. *Creating Laos: The Making of a Lao Space between Indochina and Siam, 1860–1945.* Copenhagen: NIAS Press.

Ivarsson, Søren, and Christopher E. Goscha. 2007. "Prince Phetsarath (1890–1959): Nationalism and Royalty in the Making of Modern Laos." *Journal of Southeast Asian Studies* 38 (1): 55–81.

Jay, Martin. 1993. "Unsympathetic Magic." *Visual Anthropology Review* 9 (2): 79–82.

Kostova, Julia. 2011. "Spectacles of Modernity: Anxiety and Contradiction at the Interwar Paris Fairs of 1925, 1931 and 1937." PhD diss., Rutgers University.

Kourilsky, Gregory. 2006. "Recherches sur l'institut bouddhique au Laos (1930–1949): Les circonstances de sa création, son action, son échec" [Research on the Buddhist Institute in Laos (1930–1949): The circumstances of its creation, its action, its failure]. Master's thesis, École Pratique des Hautes Études.

Kourilsky, Gregory. 2008. "De part et d'autre du Mékong: Le bouddhisme du Maha Sila." *Péninsule* 56: 107–144.

Ladwig, Patrice. 2000. "Relics, 'Representation' and Power: Some Remarks on Stupas Containing Relics of the Buddha in Laos." *Tai Culture* 5 (1): 70–84.

Ladwig, Patrice. 2011. "Buddhist Relics and Mimetic Colonial Governmentality in French Laos." Paper presented at the workshop "Colonialism and Theories of Imitation," Lisbon, ICS-University Lisboa, 12–13 April.

Ladwig, Patrice. 2014. "Millennialism, Charisma and Utopia: Revolutionary Potentialities in Pre-modern Lao and Thai Theravāda Buddhism." *Politics, Religion and Ideology* 15 (2): 308–329.

Ladwig, Patrice. 2015. "Worshipping Relics and Animating Statues: Transformations of Buddhist Statecraft in Contemporary Laos." *Modern Asian Studies* 49 (6): 1875–1902.

Ladwig, Patrice. 2017. "Mimetic Theories, Representation, and 'Savages': Critiques of the Enlightenment and Modernity through the Lens of Primitive Mimesis." In *The Transformative Power of the Copy: A Transcultural and Interdisciplinary Approach*, ed. Corinna Forberg and Philipp W. Stockhammer, 37–77. Heidelberg: Heidelberg University Publishing.

Ladwig, Patrice, and James Shields. 2014. "Against Harmony: Radical Buddhism in Thought and Practice." *Politics, Religion & Ideology* 15 (2): 187–204.

Lajonquiere, Lunet de. 1901. "Vieng-Chan: La ville et les pagodes" [Vientiane: The city and its pagodas]. *Bulletin de l'École française d'Extrême-Orient* 1: 99–118.

Lempert, Michael. 2014. "Imitation." *Annual Review of Anthropology* 43: 379–395.

Lorrillard, Michel. 2001. "100 ans de recherche de l'EFEO au Laos" [100 years of EFEO research in Laos]. Report presented at the French Embassy, Vientiane, Laos, 15 June.

Lorrillard, Michel. 2003. "Les inscriptions du That Luang de Vientiane: Données nouvelles sur l'histoire d'un stūpa lao" [The inscriptions of That Luang of Vientiane: New facts on the history of a Lao *stūpa*]. *Bulletin de l'École française d'Extrême-Orient* 90–91: 289–348.

Lorrillard, Michel. 2010. "Vientiane, au regard de l'archéologie" [Vientiane, with regard to archaeology]. In *Vientiane, architectures d'une capitale: Traces, formes, structures, projets* [Vientiane, architectures of a capital: Traces, forms, structures, projets], ed. Sophie Clément-Charpentier, Pierre Clément, Charles Goldblum, Bouluean Sisoulath, and Christian Taillard, 51–76. Paris: Cahiers de l'Ipraus.

Marrast, Joseph. 1935. "Dans quelle mesure faut-il faire appel aux arts indigenes dans la construction des edifices?" [To what extent should aboriginal art be used in building construction?] In *L'Urbanisme aux colonies et dans les pays tropicaux* [Urbanism in the colonies and in the tropical countries], vol. 2, ed. Jean Royer. Paris: Éditions d'Urbanisme.

McDaniel, Justin T. 2008. *Gathering Leaves and Lifting Words: Histories of Buddhist Monastic Education in Laos and Thailand.* Seattle: University of Washington Press.

Mendelson, E. Michael. 1975. *Sangha and State in Burma: A Study of Monastic Sectarianism and Leadership.* Ed. John P. Ferguson. Ithaca NY: Cornell University Press.

Metcalf, Thomas R. 2002. *An Imperial Vision: Indian Architecture and Britain's Raj.* Oxford: Oxford University Press.

Mus, Paul. 1935. *Barabudur: Esquisse d'une histoire du bouddhisme fondée sur la critique archéologique des textes* [Barabudur: Outline of a history of Buddhism based on archaeological criticism of the texts]. Hanoi: Imprimerie d'Extrême-Orient.

Needham, Rodney. 1970. "Editor's Introduction." In Hocart 1970, xiii–xcix.

Norindr, Panivong. 1996. *Phantasmatic Indochina: French Colonial Ideology in Architecture, Film, and Literature.* Durham, NC: Duke University Press.

Ortner, Sherry B. 1995. "Resistance and the Problem of Ethnographic Refusal." *Comparative Studies in Society and History* 37 (1): 173–193.

Parmentier, Henri. 1912. "Chronique" [Chronic]. *Bulletin de l'École française d'Extrême-Orient* 12 (1): 163–216.

Parmentier, Henri. 1954. *L'art du Laos* [The art of Laos]. Paris: EFEO.

Pels, Peter. 1997. "The Anthropology of Colonialism: Culture, History, and the Emergence of Western Governmentality." *Annual Review of Anthropology* 26: 163–183.

Quaritch-Wales, H. G. 1931. *Siamese State Ceremonies: Their History and Function.* London: B. Quaritch.

Reynolds, Frank. 1969. "Ritual and Social Hierarchy: An Aspect of Traditional Religion in Buddhist Laos." *History of Religions* 9 (1): 78–89.

Roque, Ricardo. 2010. *Headhunting and Colonialism: Anthropology and the Circulation of Human Skulls in the Portuguese Empire, 1870–1930.* New York: Palgrave.

Roque, Ricardo. 2015. "Mimetic Governmentality and the Administration of Colonial Justice in East Timor, ca. 1860–1910." *Comparative Studies in Society and History* 57 (1): 67–97.

Rosenwein, Barbara H. 2002. "Worrying about Emotions in History." *American Historical Review* 107 (3): 821–845.

Rutherford, Danilyn. 2009. "Sympathy, State Building, and the Experience of Empire." *Cultural Anthropology* 24 (1): 1–32.

Sahlins, Marshall. 2016. "The Original Political Society." Inaugural Hocart Lecture presented at SOAS, University of London. YouTube video, 1:57:17, 29 April. https://www.youtube.com/watch?v = 34VEL9KzcLA.

Salemink, Oscar. 2003. *The Ethnography of Vietnam's Central Highlanders: A Historical Contextualization, 1850–1900*. Honolulu: University of Hawai'i Press.

Schnepel, Burkhard. 1988. "In Quest of Life: Hocart's Scheme of Evolution from Ritual Organization to Government." *European Journal of Sociology/Archives Européennes de Sociologie* 29 (1): 165–187.

Schopen, Gregory. 1987. "Burial '*ad sanctos*' and the Physical Presence of the Buddha in Early Indian Buddhism: A Study in the Archaeology of Religions." *Religion* 17 (3): 193–225.

Scott, David. 1995. "Colonial Governmentality." *Social Text* 43: 191–220.

Singaravélou, Pierre. 1999. *L'École française d'Extrême-Orient ou l'institution des marges (1856–1956): Essai d'histoire sociale et politique de la science colonial* [The French School of the Far East or the institution of the margins (1856–1956): Essay on the social and political history of colonial science]. Paris: L'Harmattan.

Stoler, Ann L. 1989. "Rethinking Colonial Categories: European Communities and the Boundaries of Rule." *Comparative Studies in Society and History* 31 (1): 134–161.

Stoler, Anne L. 2004. "Affective States." In *A Companion to the Anthropology of Politics*, ed. Daniel Nugent and Joan Vincent, 4–20. Oxford: Blackwell.

Stoller, Paul. 1994. "Double Takes: Paul Stoller on Jay on Taussig." *Visual Anthropology Review* 10 (1): 155–162.

Strong, John S. 2004. *Relics of the Buddha*. Princeton, NJ: Princeton University Press.

Stuart-Fox, Martin. 1995. "The French in Laos, 1887–1945." *Modern Asian Studies* 29 (1): 111–139.

Suksamran, Somboon. 1993. "Buddhism, Political Authority, and Legitimacy in Thailand and Cambodia." In *Buddhist Trends in Southeast Asia*, ed. Trevor Ling, 101–153. Singapore: ISEAS.

Swearer, Donald K. 2010. *The Buddhist World of Southeast Asia*. 2nd ed. New York: State University of New York Press.

Tambiah, S. J. 1976. *World Conqueror and World Renouncer: A Study of Buddhism and Polity in Thailand against a Historical Background*. Cambridge: Cambridge University Press.

Tappe, Oliver. 2008. *Geschichte, Nationsbildung und Legitimationspolitik in Laos: Untersuchungen zur laotischen nationalen Historiographie und Ikonographie* [History, nationhood, and legitimacy policy in Laos: Studies on Lao national historiography and iconography]. Münster: LIT Verlag.

Tarde, Gabriel. 1903. *The Laws of Imitation*. Trans. Elsie C. Parsons. New York: Henry Holt.

Taussig, Michael. 1993. *Mimesis and Alterity: A Particular History of the Senses*. New York: Routledge.

Thomas, Martin. 2005. *The French Empire between the Wars: Imperialism, Politics and Society*. Manchester: Manchester University Press.

Thomas, Nicholas. 1994. *Colonialism's Culture: Anthropology, Travel, and Government*. Princeton, NJ: Princeton University Press.

Trainor, Kevin. 1997. *Relics, Ritual, and Representation in Buddhism: Rematerializing the Sri Lankan Theravāda Tradition*. Cambridge: Cambridge University Press.

Walker, Iain. 2005. "Mimetic Structuration: Or, Easy Steps to Building an Acceptable Identity." *History and Anthropology* 16 (2): 187–210.

Wright, Gwendolyn. 1987. "Tradition in the Service of Modernity: Architecture and Urbanism in French Colonial Policy, 1900–1930." *Journal of Modern History* 59 (2): 291–316.

Wuysthoff, Gerrit van. 1987. *Le journal de voyage de G. van Wuysthoff et de ses assistants au Laos (1641–1642)* [The travel diary of G. van Wuysthoff and his assistants in Laos (1641–1642)]. Metz: Centre de Documentation et d'Information sur le Laos.

Zago, Marcel. 1972. *Rites et cérémonies en milieu bouddhiste lao* [Rites and ceremonies in Lao Buddhist milieu]. Rome: Università Gregoriana.

Chapter 5

COLONIAL MIMESIS AND ANIMAL BREEDING
Karakul Sheep in Southwestern Angola

Tiago Saraiva

South West Angola occupies a key role in narratives of the third Portuguese Empire. The region is commonly described as a privileged setting for the confrontation between African nomadism and the sedentary impulses of white settlers—both in chronicles that denounce the violent nature of the Portuguese presence in Africa and in the imperial, rose-tinted memories that extend the myth of Mozamedes and Sá da Bandeira (now Namibe and Lubango, respectively) as model cities of white colonization.[1] Since the mid-nineteenth century, many descriptions identified the Huila plateau as the natural destination for Portuguese settlers in Angola, and reiterated its environmental similarities with Portugal's temperate climate. The plateau conditions certainly spared Europeans from feared tropical diseases, but they also prevented the area from taking part in the colonial bonanza of the rubber or coffee cycles of northern regions of the territory. Colonial authorities thus envisioned Portuguese presence in South West Angola taking the form of small and medium-sized farms operated by white settlers, a very different colonial society from the plantations of the north relying on African forced labor (Almeida 1912; Bastos 2011; R. Carvalho 1997, 1999; Castelo 2007; Clarence-Smith 1979; Medeiros 1976; Pélissier 1997).

The alleged attachment to the land of Portuguese settlers, and the contrast with the nomadism of African populations, was particularly well suited to the ideological folklorizing of popular culture promoted by Portugal's Estado Novo (New State), the fascist regime institutionalized in 1933 that lasted until 1974 (Melo 2001). New State propaganda obsessed over a mythical rural Portugal as constitutive of the organic nation to be reproduced in the colonies through white settlement of regions like Southwestern Angola (Castelo 2007; Saraiva 2016). Settlers asserted their Portuguese identity by cultivating potatoes, cabbages, or tomatoes in small plots of land, keeping them apart from the Nyaneka-nkhumbi, Ambó, and Kuvale—people constantly on the move throughout the region, following transhumance routes of their cattle herds (Feio 1998; Vieira 1967). In other words, the colonization of South West Angola meant the overtaking of the African cattle complex (Evans-Pritchard [1940] 1965) by the Portuguese horticultural complex.

The actual historical dynamics were far more complicated and interesting. As many colonial officers acknowledged, there was no replacement of one complex by another, from African shepherding to European agriculture. The most successful settlers in Sá da Bandeira built their fortunes by trading with local shepherds, and often received cattle as a means of payment (E. Carvalho 1974; Medeiros 1976). Throughout the first half of the twentieth century, Portuguese settlers' livestock continued to be integrated within the large African herds for the purposes of subsequent sale, or simply as a way to accumulate capital. Such practices suggest the inadequacy of a colonial history built around notions of difference and materialized through simple dichotomies such as native/settler or nomad/sedentary.[2] This chapter also challenges these dichotomies by emphasizing the notion of colonial mimesis and its production, whereby white settlers incorporated features of the people they colonized.

While anthropologists, following in the footsteps of Evans-Pritchard, exhaustively studied the forms of organization of indigenous societies around oxen—famously known as the 'cattle complex', or, as Ruy Duarte de Carvalho (1997) preferred to call it, the 'social ox' (*boi social*)—historians have not been sufficiently symmetrical and have remained mostly oblivious to the importance of animals in building colonial sociability. It is perhaps in the field of science studies that we discover the most interesting and daring proposals about the role of non-humans in contemporary societies, as summed up by

Donna Haraway (2008: 1) with the provocation "we have never been human." Inspired by the methodology suggested by Sarah Franklin (2007) of simply following sheep's itineraries, this chapter also focuses on animals—in this case Karakul sheep—to suggest the power of mimesis to shed light on the nature of colonial relations in Southwestern Angola. It was through the (re)production of this specific breed of sheep used for luxurious fur coats that a new Portuguese settlement was envisioned for the arid areas of South West Angola.

One of the main merits of the attention placed on mimesis in post-colonial studies, in the wake of Homi Bhabha (1984), is that it introduced greater complexity into colonial relations that were once solely perceived in terms of 'difference' or the 'other'. In addition, Bhabha importantly pointed at the emancipatory potential of indigenous subjects that exaggeratedly mimicked the habits of white people. Mimicry disturbed clear white/black distinctions and exposed the fragility and inconsistency of colonial power. In this chapter, rather than recognizing mimetic forms of emancipation, I follow the darker paths explored by Michael Taussig (1987, 1993) and his recourse to mimesis to make sense of the practices of terror associated with rubber extraction activities in the rainforests of Southwest Colombia and the Belgian Congo.[3] In Taussig's version, in contrast to Bhabha's approach, colonial terror is a mimetic operation performed by the colonizer: nervous colonizers reproduce images of indigenous people as savages who will not hesitate to behead or cut off the hands of their enemies. However crude and unreliable the produced image may be, it guides the colonizer's mimetic action—beheading and cutting off the hands of the colonized—derived from the (mis)perception of indigenous savagery. It is fairly irrelevant whether the indigenous natives really act in the way described by the colonizers, who through mimesis become as wild and uncivilized as the images affirm that the indigenous people are.

For Taussig, mimesis reveals the power of images, the way images act in the world. In this chapter, the colonial Karakul Experimental Post (Posto Experimental do Caraculo, PEC), founded in 1948 in the Mozamedes desert of South West Angola, serves as a testing site for the power of the concept of mimesis. This scientific outpost dedicated to the breeding of Karakul sheep is approached as materializing the type of colonial mimesis conceptualized by Taussig. The physical constitution of the Post was largely the result of crude images of indigenous societies produced by the scientist in charge of the research facility. More importantly, the scientific practices carried out at the Post—namely, the artificial insemination of Karakul sheep—suggest the historical relevance of science in enabling colonial mimesis. Mimesis and its dangerous 'impoverishment of the world' that simplifies reality into crude images that lead to the violent colonial actions described by Taussig are treated here as the result of specific scientific reproduction practices.[4] The text details three distinct mimetic operations undertaken at the PEC: mimesis of other European empires; mimesis of indigenous sociability; and mimesis of Portuguese sociability. Engaging the physical space of the experimental Post will reveal its role as a laboratory for mimetic practices (re)producing colonial relations.

Transnational Colonial Violence

The historian René Pélissier (1997: 267–275) has already detailed for us the violent nature of Portuguese colonialism in South West Angola and its relation to cattle. In 1940, a Portuguese *funante* (bush trader)[5] from Mozamedes, after getting three Kuvale tribesmen drunk, ordered their oxen to be branded as a way to recover alleged previous debts.[6] After waking, the Kuvale tribesmen pursued their animals, killed two servants of the Portuguese trader, and kept the entire herd. As a result of this episode, two Portuguese army detachments were sent to Mozamedes with about 1,000 soldiers and as many African auxiliaries, as well as two aircraft equipped with machine guns. Between September 1940 and February 1941, a 'Kuvale hunt' was conducted throughout the semi-desert zone of South West Angola, between the ocean and the Chela mountains. A total of 3,500 prisoners were taken from a total Kuvale population of under 5,000. Military reports refer to scenes of abject violence during the captivity, including indiscriminate killings. Six hundred tribesmen were reportedly sent to the São Tomé cocoa plantations, an equal number to Diamang and the Damba prison colony, and 70 were assigned to the Mozamedes City Council. As for the oxen, most of the approximately 46,000 head of cattle were seized, with many added to the herds of the white settlers of the city of Sá da Bandeira in the plateau. The Kuvales were accused of being inveterate cattle thieves, only to have their oxen confiscated by colonial authorities. As in Taussig stories, colonizers justified their violent actions by reference to the violence of the colonized.

Such stories are common in many other experiences of white settlement. It would not be hard to establish comparisons between South West Angola and tales of frontier violence in the United States, Argentina, Australia, or South Africa (Griffiths and Robin 1997; Netz 2004: 39–55). However, instead of insisting on the comparative history of the different empires, it is perhaps more interesting and pertinent to follow the concrete historical relations that link the decimation of the Kuvale tribe to the extermination of the Herero tribe by German Imperial troops, commanded by General von Trotha between 1904 and 1907 in the German colony of South West Africa, now present-day Namibia (Gerwarth and Malinowski 2009; Zimmerer 2005, 2011). The continuity with the case of Angola, besides the obvious geographical proximity, results from the fact that the Kuvale are also Herero[7] and, furthermore, that the arguments advanced by the Portuguese justifying the suppression of the Kuvale seem to be rooted in those put forward by Germans for the annihilation of the Herero.

As early as 1900, the German missionary Peter Heinrich Brincker in South West Africa described the Herero tribe as "a nation submerged in the filth of cattle, a nation that lives only for its cattle, whose thought and desires only flourish for its cattle, a fact that is a constant source of envy, conflict and unhappiness within the tribe" (Stoecker 1986: 62). While the relationship of the German colonists with the territory was supposedly characterized by a constant struggle with nature, in an attitude of affirmation of willpower that rooted the settlers in the earth (*bodenständig*), the Herero were viewed as nothing more than passive beings, submissive to nature and doomed to wander in order to satisfy the needs of their livestock.

German authorities did recognize that the Herero were in fact semi-nomadic. But as long as their economy was based on the indiscriminate accumulation of cattle, they would continue to belong to the lowest level of civilization. The German civilizing mission therefore consisted of a process of progressive solidification of frontier zones, through the advance of sedentary settlements (Stoecker 1986). After the extermination of 80 percent of the Herero population and 50 percent of the Nama population of South West Africa in genocides following the same dynamics described by Pélissier for South West Angola, much of the land was distributed to demobilized German soldiers, who were expected to settle the land by becoming Karakul sheep farmers (Schmokel 1985; Weigend 1985).

The interest in Karakul sheep lay in the value of their pelts, which, due to their characteristic curly fur, could be sold in markets in Leipzig, London, and New York at exorbitant prices, mainly intended for the manufacture of luxurious coats (Bravenboer 2007). A native of the steppes of Central Asia, this fat-tailed breed is especially resistant to semi-desert conditions, such as those found in Namibia and South West Angola.[8] German scientists at Halle University had tried, at the turn of the century, to acclimatize Karakul sheep to the sandy soils of eastern Germany, with the intention of freeing Leipzig fur traders from the need to import raw pelts from Asia. In 1909, the same scientists were responsible for bringing Karakul sheep to South West Africa, envisioning a sustainable community of German settlers in the desert (Saraiva 2013). Sheep imported by German scientists from Turkestan to South West Africa would thrive, living on large farms with over 5,000 hectares, fenced off by barbed wire. The rising importance of sheep as a source of income for German settlers meant that they became as animal-centered and animal-dependent as Hereros had been in relation to oxen (Weigend 1985). In the late 1940s, more than three decades after Germany lost the colony, livestock activity continued to occupy more than half of the 40,000 white people living in Southwest Africa (Krogh 1955).

I have provided elsewhere a detailed analysis of the social dimensions of breeding Karakul in German South West Africa and its later connections to Nazi Germany (Saraiva 2013, 2016). Here, I will follow instead the tracks of the Karakul sheep to the north, crossing the Cunene river, which separates Angola from Namibia.

After returning from a recreational visit to South West Africa in 1944, which at the time was under the control of the South African Union, the Portuguese governor of the Huila province in South West Angola, Captain Bustorff Silva, asked Manuel dos Santos Pereira, the veterinarian in charge of the Humpata zootechnical station in the plateau zone, about the possibility of reproducing the German experience with Karakul sheep in Angola. Santos Pereira (1955) promptly gave a positive response, and indicated the Mozamedes desert—the strip between the ocean and the plateau that had just been pacified after the decimation of the Kuvale tribe—as the most promising area for the venture because of its weather conditions, which were similar to the semi-desert steppes of Turkestan where Karakul came from, as well as the availability of land. As in South West Africa, the genocide of the Herero opened up the colonial imagination for a community of white settlers thriving on the desert by breeding Karakul sheep.

Santos Pereira's (1955: 6) answer was indeed enthusiastic: "The SW [South West Africa] mainly at the expense of the Karakul, which is by far its main wealth, managed to occupy more than two-thirds of its arid territorial extension. More than 50 percent of its 40,000 Europeans and the majority of its 300,000 indigenous people live from livestock, and related industries ... It is a symbol, and an example worth imitating." The veterinarian did not hesitate to trade his comfortable life on the temperate Huila plateau for the harsher conditions of the desert, and became the director of the Karakul Experimental Post—the PEC—which was founded in 1948 (see Illustration 5.1). This was the institution responsible for reproducing in Angola the German example that the veterinarian guaranteed was "worth imitating."

A law published in 1948, the same year that the PEC was founded, demarcated a Karakul reservation and defined concessions of 5,000 hectares—exactly the same size as had been used by Germans. These concessions were considered to be a private farm, provided that the holder owned more than 700 sheep, had built a permanent house there, and had at least one foreman who could speak and write Portuguese (AGU 1959). The reservation occupied about 9 million hectares, an area that is roughly equivalent to the size of Portugal. According to Santos Pereira, around 1,600 Portuguese families could be established there, who would own about 2 million sheep. This semi-desert region—an area completely open for colonization, previously occupied by the Kuvale tribe—would now become a source of foreign currency for the economy of the Portuguese Empire. On the occasion of the First Karakul Exhibition, held in Lisbon in 1959 to convince metropolitan investors and lure future settlers, the director of the PEC promised that the reservation would cover most of Portugal's needs in luxury pelts. The country, in the 1950s, imported over 90,000 pelts per year,

ILLUSTRATION 5.1: 'Indigenous village' of the Karakul Experimental Station, ca. 1960. Source: Arquivo Histórico Ultramarino (AHU/IPAD/MU/DGE/RRN/1548/06127).

of which over 11,000 were Karakul pelts.[9] But Santos Pereira insisted that the colonial meaning of Angola's Karakul sheep went far beyond import/export statistics. The grid of concessions that would occupy the entire reservation area expanded from the original core of the PEC (AGU 1959).[10] The PEC was built with the intention of constituting the first materialization of an exemplary white settlement, a model farm to be replicated throughout the desert.

Joyful Luso-Tropical Sheep

The PEC soon gained the status of a mandatory place to visit in South West Angola for every distinguished guest of the Portuguese colonial administration, such as the Brazilian anthropologist Gilberto Freyre. Since the 1930s, Freyre had been probing his theory that the Portuguese had developed a particularly benign form of imperialism—luso-tropicalism—that was based not on racial differentiation, as the empires of northern European countries allegedly were, but on miscegenation of whites and tropical populations, with Brazil as the best historical example. Under growing international isolation after the defeat of fascist powers in World War II, the authoritarian New State regime would incorporate Freyre's luso-tropicalism in its official discourse from the 1950s onward, justifying the retention of Portuguese colonies in Africa. In January 1952, Freyre visited the PEC on his journey through Portugal and the Portuguese colonies, at the invitation of the Portuguese government. In his travelogue-style book that collects his impressions and reflections, *Aventura e Rotina: Uma Viagem à Procura das Constantes Portuguesas de Carácter e Acção* (Adventure and Routine: A Journey in Search of the Portuguese Constants of

Character and Action), Freyre ([1953] 1980: 374) describes for the reader the "unforgettable" sight "of the Post that combined corrals with an ultra-modern laboratory. In the pastures, thousands of sheep roaming have already adapted themselves to the desert. The cross-breeding ended up revealing a kind of ecological sheep. A desert sheep."

At the end of his book, Freyre ([1953] 1980) refers to the moment when he offered to the president of Brazil a gift entrusted to him by the Portuguese president—a chest containing a rare and ancient edition of *The Lusiads*—the sixteenth-century epic poem recounting the voyage of Vasco da Gama from Lisbon to India in 1498, which launched the Portuguese Empire in the Indian Ocean. The chest was made of materials summarizing Portugal imperial history, "consisting of diamonds from Angola, ivory from Mozambique, gold from Guinea, silver from Portugal, pearls from the Portuguese Orient, wood from Cape Verde—all of which radiates the pan-Lusitanian affection for Brazil from Portugal and the Portuguese Overseas territories" (ibid.: 444). The chest was encased in Karakul fur from Angola.[11] It is therefore worth exploring Freyre's unexpected reference to Karakul and the role of this sheep breed in materializing the alleged "Portuguese constants of character and action" that the anthropologist analyzed in his book. In other words, Freyre's reference suggests the importance of investigating the *luso-tropical* nature of the Karakul sheep.

In Freyre's opinion, this "ecological sheep" was the result of cross-breeding of local sheep breeds with the exotic breeds introduced by the Portuguese, thereby forming a hybrid animal that demonstrated the Portuguese constant ability to adapt to the conditions found in the tropics—that is, the constant of action with which the Brazilian was obsessed. Freyre ([1953] 1980) praised the hybrid sheep he found in South West Angola with compliments similar to those he showered on the plants he saw in the new Overseas Garden (Jardim do Ultramar) in Lisbon. He described the latter as a "revolution in the sociology of plant life ... New ecological adjustments have been achieved. Admittedly, they were almost always favored by these transplantation adventures, in the pan-tropical sense of life that at the beginning, and still today, is the core aspect of Portuguese activity in its overseas territories" (ibid.: 19–20).

According to Freyre, reproduction practices of cross-breeding of animals and plants were an expression of the unique Portuguese skills for adaptation in the tropics across the globe; breeding was a fundamental luso-tropicalist practice. In an inspired, and inspiring, text by Cristiana Bastos (1998: 420), Freyre's "joyful luso-tropicalism" is viewed in contrast to Lévi-Strauss's *Tristes Tropiques* (Sad Tropics), wherein Bastos interprets the former as an attempt to overcome "otherness and contradiction, dualism, opposition," which are anthropological characteristics highlighted by the latter.[12] Bastos's proposal is not, of course, to resume Freyre's gesture to see joyful miscegenation and hybridization where others see only otherness. Instead, the author invites us to revisit the "icons and themes" of luso-tropicalism, and recommends critical distance in relation to "the myth of non-racism and the great humanism of the Portuguese" (ibid.: 431). She proposes an ambitious program of work around the very peculiar luso-tropicalist iconography, which consists of "Albuquerque's soldiers marrying Indians" and "assorted natives, holding hands, with smiles on their lips" (ibid.). The Karakul sheep, whose furs encased the luso-tropicalist reliquary offered by the Portuguese President Américo Tomás to the Brazilian President Getúlio Vargas—with Gilberto Freyre as the ritual officiant—pertains to the family of these icons, which are part of the program proposed by Bastos in the late 1990s.

Pedigree Karakul Sheep

Let us take a closer look at the desert sheep breed to try to put in perspective Freyre's views on the nature of Portuguese colonialism. In light of the above, it should be remembered that the Karakul sheep were introduced in Angola after the decimation of the Kuvale and their herds in the deserts of South West Angola. Perhaps more importantly, at least from the standpoint of Freyre's luso-tropicalism obsessed with Portuguese unique characteristics, Portuguese violence mimicked the German initiatives in South West Africa, which certainly did not involve any 'luso-tropical' joyfulness. Moreover, detailing the animal breeding practices developed at the PEC reveals a very different story from the cross-breeding and miscegenation that was so dear to Freyre. It ultimately reveals a colonial history of purification and violence.

Any commercial exploitation of Karakul sheep had to begin by securing a ram whose pedigree was certified by the world's major centers of animal genetics, such as the University of Halle in Germany until the outbreak of World War II (Saraiva 2016). The exploitation of Karakul sheep in German South West Africa had also developed from Halle's certified pedigree rams. Certified pedigree rams ensured the reproduction of sheep with the curly pelts that made Karakul coats a luxury consumer item. Animal geneticists had demonstrated the dominance of the curly pelt trait, which made it possible to carry out the cross-breeding of expensive imported certified Karakul rams with more easily obtained sheep of a local breed that did not have curly hair. The so-called desert sheep referred to by Freyre was the result of cross-breeding pedigree animals with local breeds, but this practice required careful registration and control of each instance of cross-breeding, always ensuring that fertilization was achieved by a pedigree ram.

This was not a simple mixture of the European with the tropical, of the foreign with the local, or of the colonizer with the native. There was an imperative need to ensure and maintain the purity of the colonizer—the certified pedigree Karakul ram—to produce lambs with the pelt that was so coveted by the elite of the fascist regime in Lisbon. The production of these colonial sheep, capable of supporting Portuguese settlers, depended on the active vigilance of the purity of the stud animals imported from Europe. Purity could never disappear in a joyful process of acclimatization.

It is highly revealing that one of Santos Pereira's main tasks as director of the PEC was to guard and distribute purity. Not only did the veterinarian freely loan the certified rams to the owners of the various farms; he also fostered artificial insemination as an efficient way of distributing the genes of his pedigree Karakul rams throughout the Karakul reservation area. Whereas hybrid females, resulting from different instances of cross-breeding, could be inseminated with the semen from pedigree rams, all hybrid males had to be sacrificed before reaching breeding age to avoid contaminating the herd and not compromise the viability of the entire farm.[13] In fact, all lambs intended for the production of pelts were sacrificed at the latest on the second day after birth, because after this point the curly pattern of the pelt disappeared and lost almost all its commercial value.

In addition to mimicking German purification practices, sustaining a Karakul farm also involved mimicking the Kuvales. Notwithstanding all the colonial rhetoric about the civilizing virtues of the sedentary lifestyle over nomadism, which demonstrated the superiority of white settlers over black shepherds, the exploitation of Karakul sheep did demand that shepherds guide the sheep herds across the farms' many thousands of acres. While criticizing the lack of interest of the Kuvale tribes for sheep and their preference for cattle manifested in their custom of reserving sheep herding for children, Santos Pereira (1957) did not hesitate from suggesting that the colonial state had to supply Karakul farms with wage workers responsible for herding the sheep, thus reproducing the systems of forced labor that were common in the Portuguese colonial world. In Santos Pereira's accounts, each indigenous shepherd would look after 100 sheep, which over the long run meant that about 20,000 shepherds would be mobilized for the Karakul reservation (ibid.).

It is important to bear in mind that mimesis does not necessarily entail a faithful copy of the original; it relied here instead on the production of crude imagery of indigenous practices. Sheep grazing in a Karakul barbed wire fenced farm following standardized rotations was not the same as the transhumance practices of Kuvale cattle. Displacements between the different parts of the farm were established by a pasture management system, which governed the movements of the shepherds and their herds.

The importance of mimetic processes in the colonial history of Angola's Karakul sheep is most evident in the houses built in the Post for black shepherds to live in, which was called the PEC's 'indigenous village' (Pereira 1958).[14] Santos Pereira was very proud of a new model hut that he developed. He described these round houses with conical roofs, built with brick and mortar, as being built in 'Karakul style'. Their principal original feature was the replacement of the traditional conical thatched roofs by bricks and cement, applied in ever-tighter concentric rows. In order to build these houses. "there was no need for iron, supports, frameworks, or molds " (ibid.: 7). The veterinarian even developed a standardized process for building these 'Karakul style' dwellings, which, in addition to being built in the various farms, were also built in Mozamedes, where an 'indigenous village' composed entirely of 'Karakul style' dwellings was inaugurated in 1958. The uniform character of the round dwellings hid three different interior topologies: there was "[no] partition for assimilated married blacks; a central partition for two couples without children; three partitions to be used by four single indigenous people" (ibid.: 8).

The description of the 'indigenous village' at the PEC may be fruitfully compared with the complexity of an *onganda* (homestead), "the most fixed mode of residence of the Kuvale tribe" (R. Carvalho 1997: 25). Anthropology, especially that written by Ruy Duarte de Carvalho, has already given a good account of the social functions maintained by an *onganda* used by the Kuvales (ibid.: 29):

> Enclosures surrounded by a circular fence of branches of shrubs that can attain up to 70m in diameter, within which the livestock sleep overnight, complemented by conical and low houses and a smaller enclosure used by the calves. Each *onganda* is used by two or three family groups that may or

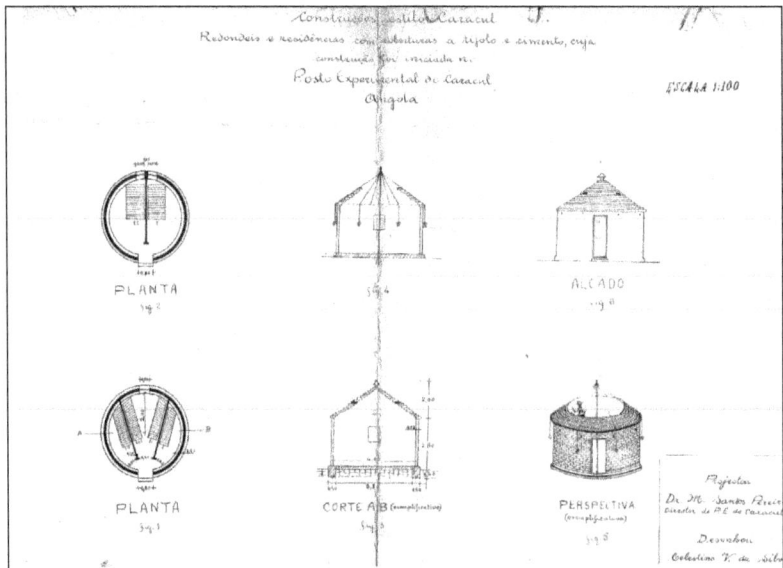

ILLUSTRATION 5.2: Manuel dos Santos Pereira's plans for 'Karakul style' constructions, Karakul Experimental Station, July 1958. Source: Arquivo Histórico Ultramarino (AHU/IPAD/MU/DGE/RRN/1548/16195).

may not be related to one another, and may or may not include the presence of adult children, or nephews, or other dependents of the older men who are the chiefs and establish partnerships between them that involve joint exploitation of the livestock that they hold under their immediate command.

The perimeter of an *onganda* also included cemeteries and places of worship.

It is thereby now easier to understand the above reference to the notion of impoverishment achieved through the mimetic process—as well as its corresponding violence. The apparent local sensibility of the veterinarian in charge of the PEC, expressed in the creation of the 'Karakul style' inspired by the local practices (see also Bastos 2014, this volume), masks in fact a denial of Kuvale sociability, which was now resumed in the domestic sphere as a dichotomy of married/single and reduced the indigenous people to the status of a farm wage worker of the white settler.

A Portuguese House in the Mozamedes Desert

When Gilberto Freyre visited the PEC, this 'indigenous village' had not yet been built. But it is not difficult to imagine the eulogies that Freyre might have showered on the hybrid dwellings designed by Santos Pereira, while ignoring the actual denial of local practices they demonstrated. Freyre ([1953] 1980: 374) was nevertheless able to call attention to the architectural features of the director's house which, according to his description, showed "that it was possible for a Portuguese to live in Karakul in a true oasis ... This was the residence of the director of the Station, surrounded by vines, including a trellis with clusters of grapes that were so lusitan fresh at first glance they appeared to be fake ... the grapevines burst into fat grapes near the porch of the houses, and were within easy reach of the boys and of adults who are the ones who are most homesick for the fruit and aromas of Portugal."

The 'overseas Portuguese house', in the words of the technicians of the Colonial Urbanization Office responsible for the architectural designs for the dwellings of officials of the colonial administration, should be more Portuguese than the 'Portuguese house' (Milheiro 2012). The mimesis of Portuguese life—materialized through the architecture in the traditional style of the 'Portuguese house' of the director's residence, with its balcony and trellis—rather than transplanting Portugal to Africa, constituted an element of construction of the 'imagined community' (Anderson 1983) of the white settler. The veterinarian Santos Pereira took care of maintaining and distributing the purity of the Karakul rams through artificial insemination and by accumulating miles in his Chevrolet van across the vast reservation area. Meanwhile, his wife back at the Post served "magnificent lunches with the grace and dignity of those who presided over a dinner in

ILLUSTRATION 5.3: Director's house, Karakul Experimental Station, ca. 1960.
Source: Arquivo Histórico Ultramarino (AHU/IPAD/MU/DGE/RRN/1548/06127).

Lisbon or Porto" (Freyre [1953] 1980: 375). Much has been written about the excesses of reproducing the customs of the European metropole in the colonies due to the fear of going native (Stoler 2002). Malinowski ([1945] 1966: 14) had already pointed out in the 1940s that the white settler "community is by no means a direct replica of its community back home." The Post thus combined mimesis by default of the 'indigenous neighborhood' and excessive mimesis of Portugal, which was intended, as Santos Pereira (1959: 39) himself claimed, to "reproduce breeders of Karakul sheep." The PEC was therefore the first nucleus of a colonization project conceived not only to occupy a territory whose size was similar to that of metropolitan Portugal, but also to ensure that it would be more Portuguese than Portugal itself.

The breeding of the Karakul sheep was meant to reproduce Portuguese settlers. The life of the white settlers in the colonial reservation of Karakul was no less organized around the function of animal breeding than the life of the Kuvale tribe with their herds of oxen. The breeding techniques of Karakul sheep are therefore not only a metaphor of colonial social life; they also establish a formal correspondence between the lack of cross-breeding among animals and the lack of human miscegenation. Maintaining a farm of Karakul sheep meant that settlers had to follow the zootechnical precepts disseminated by Santos Pereira. They also had to construct a specific colonial space, exemplarily modeled by the PEC: settlers' houses, the 'indigenous villages', and pastures separated by barbed wire, for careful management of the pasture land.

At first sight, the Karakul Experimental Post seemed to respect local customs, with clean, orderly rustic dwellings and indigenous natives who looked after the animals. But it actually followed the teachings of European genetics, rather than elaborate Kuvale genealogies. One only has to scrape a bit at this surface of appearances, and Freyre's joyful mimesis takes on the darker shades of Taussig's colonial mimesis. The Kuvales had their livestock stolen and were exterminated because they were considered to be violent savages and cattle thieves. The 'indigenous villages' were built to resemble the Kuvale *ongandas*, but they were nothing more than cheap barracks for salaried labor. Huge Karakul sheep farms enmeshed the landscape with barbed wire, between whose rows the surviving Kuvale shepherds were entitled to drive their cattle, thus upholding the Portuguese myth of respect for the other. Freyre's vision of luso-tropicalism, contrary to his claim, was not based on hybridization processes, but on a violent triple mimesis: of other European imperial experiences, materialized through the Karakul sheep imported from Germany; of the local social structures, reproduced in a standardized manner in the station's 'indigenous neighborhood'; and, finally, of Portugal, translated in the director's luso-tropical house. The Karakul Experimental Post reminds us that 'luso' and 'tropicalism' are ultimately the products of the operation of these three forms of colonial mimesis.

Acknowledgments

This chapter is the result of the project "Colonial Mimesis in Portuguese-Speaking Asia and Africa," which was developed at the Institute of Social Sciences of the University of Lisbon (ICS-UL) and funded by Portugal's Foundation for Science and Technology (FCT) (PTDC/CS-ANT/101064/2008). A Portuguese-language version of this chapter was originally published in 2014 in the journal *Etnográfica* as "Mimetismo colonial e reprodução animal: Carneiros caracul no Sudoeste Angolano." This English-language version was translated by Martin Dale.

Tiago Saraiva is an Associate Professor in the History Department at Drexel University. He was a Research Fellow at the Institute of Social Sciences of the University of Lisbon (2005–2012) and a Visiting Professor at University of California, Los Angeles (2007/2008 and 2011) and at University of California, Berkeley (2011/2012). He is the author of *Fascist Pigs: Technoscientific Organisms and the History of Fascism* (2016), which was awarded the Pfizer Prize by the History of Science Society in 2017. He is the editor, together with Amy Slaton, of the journal *History and Technology*. E-mail: tsaraiva@drexel.edu

Notes

1. Among the many possible references, one example is the journalist Ana Sofia Fonseca's (2009) book *Angola, Terra Prometida* (Angola, Promised Land) on the sociability of white settlers in Angola made of cinema, beaches, lobsters, beer, car racing, soccer, and radio. The author refers to Sá da Bandeira and Mozamedes on various occasions. Memories produced by the returnees usually paint a darker picture, such as those by Salvador de Figueiredo (2006). The editorial phenomenon associated with colonial memories was discussed by Raquel Ribeiro (2010) in the newspaper *Público*. Concerning the so-called serious novel revisiting of Africa, see Gould (2008). For the history of the Portuguese occupation of Southern Angola, the works of W. G. Clarence-Smith (1979) and René Pélissier (1997) continue to be indispensable. Ruy Duarte de Carvalho (1997, 1999), toying with ethnography and fiction, is undoubtedly the author who in recent years has done the most to ensure that Southwestern Angola gains literary and scientific relevance. Cristiana Bastos (2011), in the wake of the migration from Madeira, wove unexpected relations between the Huila plateau and other parts of the globe.
2. In a similar vein, Reviel Netz (2004), in his transnational history of barbed wire, draws attention to the obvious fact that the life of the cowboys on the Great Plains of the United States had much in common with that of the Native Americans they exterminated, whereby social organization associated with the buffalo was superseded by an equally nomadic life associated with cattle. In other words, the importance of mimesis has not been sufficiently valued in the history of the Far West.
3. This is a path similar to that followed by Ricardo Roque in his work on mimesis, governmentality, and savagery. See Roque (2015, 2020, this volume).
4. The suggestion of associating science with the impoverishment of the world has a long tradition, of which the most distinguished practitioner is undoubtedly Martin Heidegger. In relation to the vast literature devoted to this subject, see, for example, Cathryn Carson (2010).
5. In Angola, a *funante* (bush trader) is an individual who sells goods in remote locations.
6. Quoting Ruy Duarte de Carvalho (1997: 1): "The Kuvale are Herero, therefore, embedded in the aridity and the sand, they are 'residuals', survivors of a total war ... Today's Herero come from Bantu-speaking pastoral populations who will have reached the western coast of Africa, from the east, at the level of the Benguela parallel, and having reached the steppes near the sea, diverted south, deeper and deeper into the borders of the Namib desert and then east to the Kalahari."
7. See Carvalho (1997).
8. Italian colonization in Eastern Libya using Karakul sheep followed the same pattern as the German experience in South West Africa.
9. These figures suggest the urgent need for a study of luxury consumption in Portugal during the New State regime.

10. There are multiple cases in which agricultural experiment stations assumed this role of an advance station of the colonization process. On this subject, see in particular the articles by Christophe Bonneuil (1999, 2000) and Saraiva's (2016) *Fascist Pigs*.
11. I owe this reference to Karakul in Gilberto Freyre's work to the intellectual generosity of Cláudia Castelo.
12. Cristiana Bastos does not suggest that Freyre's ([1953] 1980) work *Aventura e Rotina* is a direct response to that of Lévi-Strauss, not least because it was written before *Tristes Tropiques* was published in 1955.
13. For more details on how the Karakul sheep farms operated, see the descriptions by M. Santos Pereira (1953, 1959) and Mario Garutti (1951).
14. In this volume, Cristiana Bastos also explores the concept of mimesis through the architecture of hut-hospitals shaped like *cubata* round dwellings.

References

AGU (Agência Geral do Ultramar). 1959. *O Karakul*. Lisbon: Agência Geral do Ultramar.

Almeida, João de. 1912. *Sul de Angola: Relatório de Um Governo de Distrito (1908–1910)* [Southern Angola: Report of a district government (1908–1910)]. Lisbon: Tip. Anuário Comercial.

Anderson, Benedict. 1983. *Imagined Communities: Reflections on the Origin and Spread of Nationalism*. London: Verso.

Bastos, Cristiana. 1998. "Tristes trópicos e alegres luso-tropicalismos: Das notas de viagem em Lévi-Strauss e Gilberto Freyre" [Sad tropics and happy luso-tropicalisms: From the travel notes in Lévi-Strauss and Gilberto Freyre]. *Análise Social* 33 (146–147): 415–432.

Bastos, Cristiana. 2011. "Ilhas, planaltos e travessias: Os fluxos de madeirenses entre plantações e colónias" [Islands, plateaus, and crossings: The flowers of Madeirans between plantations and colonies]. In *As Ilhas da Europa, a Europa das Ilhas* [The islands of Europe, the Europe of the islands], 187–196. Funchal: Centro de Estudos de História do Atlântico.

Bastos, Cristiana. 2014. "'No género de construções cafreais': O hospital-palhota como projecto colonial" [The hut-hospital as a colonial project]. *Etnográfica* 18 (1): 185–208.

Bhabha, Homi. 1984. "Of Mimicry and Man: The Ambivalence of Colonial Discourse." *October* 28: 125–133.

Bonneuil, Christophe. 1999. "Penetrating the Natives: Peanut Breeding, Peasants and the Colonial State in Senegal (1900–1950)." *Science, Technology and Society* 4 (2): 273–302.

Bonneuil, Christophe. 2000. "Development as Experiment: Science and State Building in Late Colonial and Postcolonial Africa, 1930–1970." *Osiris* 15: 258–281.

Bravenboer, Brenda. 2007. *Karakul: Gift from the Arid Land, 1907–2007*. Windhoek: Karakul Board of Namibia and Karakul Breeders' Society of Namibia.

Carson, Cathryn. 2010. "Science as Instrumental Reason: Heidegger, Habermas, Heisenberg." *Continental Philosophy Review* 42: 483–509.

Carvalho, Eduardo Cruz de. 1974. "'Traditional' and 'Modern' Patterns of Cattle Raising in Southwestern Angola: A Critical Evaluation of Change from Pastoralism to Ranching." *Journal of Developing Areas* 8 (2): 199–226.

Carvalho, Ruy Duarte de. 1997. *Aviso à Navegação: Olhar Sucinto e Preliminar sobre os Pastores Kuvale da Província do Namibe com Um Relance sobre as Outras Sociedades Agropastoris do Sudoeste de Angola* [Notice to navigation: Succinct and preliminary look at the Kuvale pastors of the Namibe Province with a glance at the other agropastoral societies in Southwest Angola]. Luanda: Instituto Nacional do Livro e do Disco.

Carvalho, Ruy Duarte de. 1999. *Vou Lá Visitar Pastores: Exploração Epistolar de Um Percurso Angolano (1992–1997)* [I go there to visit pastors: Epistolary exploration of an Angolan route in Kuvale territory (1992–1997)]. Lisbon: Cotovia.

Castelo, Cláudia. 2007. *Passagens para África: O Povoamento de Angola e Moçambique com Naturais da Metrópole (1920–1974)* [Tickets to Africa: The settlement of Angola and Mozambique with naturals from the metropolis (1920–1974)]. Porto: Afrontamento.

Clarence-Smith, W. G. 1979. *Slaves, Peasants and Capitalists in Southern Angola 1840–1926*. Cambridge: Cambridge University Press.

Evans-Pritchard, E. E. (1940) 1965. *The Nuer: A Description of the Modes of Livelihood and Political Institutions of a Nilotic People*. Oxford: Oxford University Press.

Feio, Mariano. 1998. *As Causas do Fracasso da Colonização Agrícola de Angola* [The causes of the failure of agricultural colonization in Angola]. Lisbon: Ministério da Ciência e Tecnologia /Instituto de Investigação Científica Tropical.

Figueiredo, Salvador de. 2006. *Angola, O Último Café* [Angola, the last coffee]. Torres Vedras: ABC–Impressão Côr de J. Grilo.

Fonseca, Ana Sofia. 2009. *Angola, Terra Prometida: A Vida que os Portugueses Deixaram* [Angola, promised land: The life of the Portuguese left]. Lisbon: Esfera dos Livros.

Franklin, Sarah. 2007. *Dolly Mixtures: The Remaking of Genealogy*. Durham, NC: Duke University Press.

Freyre, Gilberto. (1953) 1980. *Aventura e Rotina: Sugestões de Uma Viagem à Procura das Constantes Portuguesas de Carácter e Acção* [Adventure and routine: A journey in search of the Portuguese constants of character and action]. Lisbon: Livros do Brasil.

Garutti, Mario. 1951. *Relazione sul PEK: Osservazioni del Dott. Mario Garutti* [Report on PDK: Observations of Dr. Mario Garutti]. Arquivo do Istituto Agricola per l'Oltroemare, Fasc. 1027.

Gerwarth, Robert, and Stephan Malinowski. 2009. "Hannah Arendt's Ghosts: Reflections on the Disputable Path from Windhoek to Auschwitz." *Central European History* 42 (2): 279–300.

Gould, Isabel Ferreira. 2008. "Decanting the Past: Africa, Colonialism, and the New Portuguese Novel." *Luso-Brazilian Review* 45 (1): 182–197.

Griffiths, Tom, and Libby Robin, eds. 1997. *Ecology and Empire: Environmental History of Settler Societies*. Seattle: University of Washington Press.

Haraway, Donna J. 2008. *When Species Meet*. Minneapolis: University of Minnesota Press.

Krogh, D. C. 1955. "Economic Aspects of the Karakul Industry in South West Africa." *South African Journal of Economics* 23 (2): 99–113.

Malinowski, Bronislaw. (1945) 1966. "Dynamics of Cultural Change." In *Social Change: The Colonial Situation*, ed. Immanuel Wallerstein, 11–24. New York: John Wiley and Sons.

Medeiros, Carlos Alberto. 1976. *A Colonização das Terras Altas da Huíla (Angola): Estudo de Geografia Humana* [Colonization of the Highlands of Huíla Angola): A study of human geography]. Lisbon: Centro de Estudos Geográficos.

Melo, Daniel. 2001. *Salazarismo e Cultura Popular (1933–1958)* [Salazarism and popular culture (1933–1958)]. Lisbon: Imprensa de Ciências Sociais.

Milheiro, Ana Vaz. 2012. *Nos Trópicos sem Le Corbusier: Arquitectura Luso-Africana no Estado Novo* [In the Tropics without Le Corbusier: Luso-African Architecture in the New State]. Lisbon: Relógio d'Água.

Netz, Reviel. 2004. *Barbed Wire: An Ecology of Modernity*. Middletown, CT: Wesleyan University Press.

Pélissier, René. 1997. *História das Campanhas de Angola: Resistência e Revoltas, 1845–1941* [History of campaigns in Angola: Resistance and revolts, 1845–1941]. Lisbon: Estampa.

Pereira, M. Santos. 1953. "Plano de Fomento do Karakul de Angola" [Promotion plan for the Karakul of Angola]. Lisbon: Unpublished manuscript.

Pereira, M. Santos. 1955. *O Que Pode Valer o Karakul na Economia e Ocupação de Angola* [What Karakul can be worth in the economy and occupation of Angola]. Lisbon: Centro de Estudos Económicos.

Pereira, M. Santos. 1957. "Plano de Acção para o Desenvolvimento do Caracul de Angola" [Action plan for the development of the Karakul of Angola]. Archive of the Portuguese Institute for Development Support (IPAD).

Pereira, M. Santos. 1958. "Construções de estilo Karakul: Como construir economicamente casas circulares com tetos de tijolo" [Karakul-style constructions: Economic solutions for building circular houses with brick ceilings]. Archive of the Portuguese Institute for Development Support (IPAD 16195).

Pereira, M. Santos. 1959. "Situação do Karakulo Angolano" [Situation of the Angolan Karakul]. *Boletim Geral do Ultramar* 406: 27–56.

Ribeiro, Raquel. 2010. "Os retornados estão a abrir o baú" [The returnees are opening the trunk]. *Público*, 12 August. https://www.publico.pt/2010/08/12/culturaipsilon/noticia/os-retornados-estao-a-abrir-o-bau-263209.

Roque, Ricardo. 2015. "Mimetic Governmentality and the Administration of Colonial Justice in East Timor, ca. 1860–1910." *Comparative Studies in Society and History* 57 (1): 67–97.|

Roque, Ricardo. 2020. "The Name of the Wild Man: Colonial *Arbiru* in East Timor." In *Swearing and Cursing: Contexts and Practices in a Critical Linguistic Perspective*, ed. Nico Nassenstein and Anne Storch, 209–235. Berlin: De Gruyter.

Saraiva, Tiago. 2013. "The Production and Circulation of Standardized Karakul Sheep and Frontier Settlement in the Empires of Hitler, Mussolini, and Salazar." In *New Natures: Joining Environmental History with Science and Technology Studies*, ed. Dolly Jørgensen, Finn Arne Jørgensen and Sara B. Pritchard, 135–150. Pittsburgh, PA: University of Pittsburgh Press.

Saraiva, Tiago. 2016. *Fascist Pigs: Technoscientific Organisms and the History of Fascism*. Cambridge, MA: MIT Press.

Schmokel, Wolfe W. 1985. "The Myth of the White Farmer: Commercial Agriculture in Namibia, 1900–1983." *International Journal of African Historical Studies* 18 (1): 93–108.

Stoecker, Helmuth, ed. 1986. *German Imperialism in Africa: From the Beginnings until the Second World War*. Trans. Bernd Zöllner. London: Hurst.

Stoler, Ann Laura. 2002. *Carnal Knowledge and Imperial Power: Race and the Intimate in Colonial Rule*. Berkeley: University of California Press.

Taussig, Michael. 1987. *Shamanism, Colonialism, and the Wild Man: A Study in Terror and Healing*. Chicago: University of Chicago Press.

Taussig, Michael. 1993. *Mimesis and Alterity: A Particular History of the Senses*. New York: Routledge.

Vieira, António da Silva. 1967. *Trigo de Morais Segundo Alguns Depoimentos* [Trigo de Morais according to some testimonies]. Lisbon: Agência Geral do Ultramar.

Weigend, Guido G. 1985. "German Settlement Patterns in Namibia." *Geographical Review* 75 (2): 156–169.

Zimmerer, Jürgen. 2005. "Annihilation in Africa: The 'Race War' in German Southwest Africa (1904–1908) and Its Significance for a Global History of Genocide." *German Historical Institute Bulletin* 37: 51–57.

Zimmerer, Jürgen. 2011. *Von Windhuk nach Auschwitz?: Beiträge zum Verhältnis von Kolonialismus und Holocaust* [From Windhoek to Auschwitz? Contributions to the relationship between colonialism and the Holocaust]. Münster: LIT Verlag.

Chapter 6

THE COLONIAL STATE AND CARNIVAL
The Complexity and Ambiguity of Carnival in
Guinea-Bissau, West Africa

Christoph Kohl

In history and the social sciences, carnival phenomena have attracted much
research interest. Their multi-layered meanings and associated ritual inver-
sions have revealed divergent views about social and political conditions. On
a general level, these aspects converge to reproduce carnival as a complex
arena of political, social, and symbolic negotiation and resistance. Carnival has
also proved attractive for scholarly reflection due to its performative, mimetic
character. In this sense, analyzing carnival within the context of mimesis and
the colonial state can pave the way for an understanding of the ambiguities of,
and challenges to, colonial rule as much as it can illuminate the indigenous

Notes for this chapter begin on page 163.

dynamic of appropriation and subversion of colonial authority. In this chapter, carnival, crises, mimesis, and colonial representations constitute the 'ingredients' of an inquiry into how the colonial state engaged with the threats of mimetic carnival performances. The analysis focuses on two periods of Portuguese colonialism in Guinea-Bissau, West Africa—the late nineteenth century, when effective colonial seizure was yet to be accomplished, and the heyday of anti-colonial struggle in the 1960s and early 1970s—in order to explore the multiple and ambivalent meanings of Guinean carnival, both within and beyond issues of criticism and opposition to colonial state authority. The chapter suggests that the performance of carnival could become politicized in the colonial encounter in Guinea-Bissau, particularly in times of crisis. Luso-African creole communities, I will argue, were important agents in this history of colonial crisis and carnival mimesis.

In the former Portuguese Guinea—today the independent state of Guinea-Bissau—creole groups have played key roles, both as mediators of colonial trading interests and state administration and as activists in anti-colonial developments. In the literature, they are known for their 'rebellious' stance toward the colonizers, and they figure prominently in historical accounts of the liberation movements that finally achieved independence in 1973–1974 after more than a decade of armed struggle (Dhada 1993; Duarte Silva 1997; Galli and Jones 1987).[1] Systematic historical research on the emergence and development of carnival in colonial Guinea-Bissau is still lacking, yet it can be hypothesized that Guinea's carnival has its roots in the numerous European coastline trading posts established since the sixteenth century, where creole communities settled and prospered (see Brooks 2003; Havik 2004; Kohl 2009; Mark 2002). These communities came into being when people of heterogeneous geographical and cultural origins (European, African, Cape Verdean) met in those trading posts, thereby giving rise to new cultural expressions, including a Luso-creole language, Kriol, nowadays the *lingua franca* in Guinea-Bissau.

It is all but certain, though, that carnival was already an established tradition among European and creole groups in these former trading outposts at the turn of the nineteenth century. Until the 1960s, carnival was largely restricted to these communities in the former trade settlements. When Luso-African creoles began to pose a threat to colonially defined boundaries, colonizers responded with a colonial ideology that sought to maintain inequality and the subordination of creoles. As I have argued elsewhere (Kohl 2016), the African and creole groups were able to develop limited agency and to partly resist such colonial representations and practices. Here, I will explore how this interplay between African and creole claims to cultural and political autonomy, on the one hand, and Portuguese colonizing orientations to power and control, on the other, played a decisive role in carnival performances. Anxious about the fact that the Africans and creoles did not conform to the images and roles that were intended for them, colonial rulers attempted to suppress carnivalesque activities as a subversive form of mimesis. As a result, the former were to become subject to a set of tactical measures to regulate mimesis, examples of a colonial governmentality, albeit a fragmentary one (Pels and Salemink 1994; 1999: 19–20; see also Ladwig and Roque, this volume).

In the beginning of this chapter, I set the analytical framework for the study of colonial rule, mimesis, and carnival in the context of colonial Guinea-Bissau.[2] As part of this elaboration, I consider the ambivalent significance and manifold meanings of carnival performances, past and present, and the ways in which they can be handled as political issues by state authorities. The second part of the chapter is dedicated to the analysis of the concurrence of colonial crises and carnival in Guinea-Bissau, using two major examples. The first case illustrates how creoles—serving the European colonizers as auxiliaries—lampooned colonial politics through carnival and its performances of inversion and critique in the late nineteenth century. Basically, they were accentuating the weak position of the early yet ground-gaining colonial state by accusing the Portuguese colonizers of betraying the colony's interests to the French. The second example is based on an analysis of archival material and eyewitness recollections from the late-colonial period, the 1960s and early 1970s. By then, carnival—still largely restricted to the former trading posts and centers of creole culture—had turned into a platform of open and mimetic protest against the ongoing colonial presence and repression, and of rising nationalism dominated by creoles. In both cases, creoles acted as if they were the actual masters of the country, highlighting the potential impact they would have on nation building, which was to be realized following independence.

Colonialism and Resistance, Mimesis and Carnival

At first glance, the allegedly rational colonial state and its forms of governmentality[3] appear to be the complete antithesis of carnival, which can generally be regarded as marked by a reversal of common orders. While the state tends to be associated with order, classification, and control, carnival signifies disorder, parody, and subversion. Thus, from this point of view, carnival in colonial situations can be looked on as a ritual of resistance, as a reaction to foreign domination per se. However, caution is recommended here. In his study on Cape Verdean *tabanca* associations, Wilson Trajano Filho (2006: 11–17) concludes that framing colonialism and carnival in a simple binary opposition of domination and resistance does not convey the complex relationship between colonizers and subjects that emerges in these performances. From this perspective, shades of gray between black and white were largely absent. Since the 1990s, historians have increasingly questioned such strict dichotomies, pointing out that colonial states and their ideologies were heterogeneous and marked by ambivalence, inefficiency, and fragility (Cooper 2005; Scott 1995: 197; Stoler and Cooper 1997; Thomas 1994). European colonial actors could have differing and sometimes competing agendas and follow diverse rationalities at different times. In their turn, indigenous groups could use and manipulate colonial systems for their own purposes in ways that did not involve opposition and resistance to the colonial presence. Moreover, it could happen that colonial rulers simply lacked the manpower and bureaucratic capacities to enforce prohibitions and regulations. Yet even under more structured conditions, it is often impossible to "assume anything like a coherent ensemble of strategies" (Pels and Salemink 1999: 20) in relation to colonial governmentality.[4]

This was often the case in the Portuguese colony of Guinea-Bissau, one of the smallest West African countries. Situated between Senegal to the north and the Republic of Guinea to the southeast, Guinea-Bissau's coastal areas are marked by riverine lowlands, into which Portuguese navigators first entered in the mid-fifteenth century. Subsequently, Europeans identified the coast as suitable for establishing a handful of small commercial settlements for trade, laying the foundations for colonization. Until the late nineteenth century, Portugal's presence in what now constitutes Guinea-Bissau was underfinanced, understaffed, and thus very weak. The colonial authorities were repeatedly confronted with popular resistance to Portuguese misgovernment, neglect, or interventions, often uncovering metropolitan Portugal's weakness to enforce its will. One of the first manifestations against colonial rule was the dismissal of the colonial administrator and his immediate replacement by an elected board of creole traders in the trading post of Cacheu in 1684–1685, when local traders opposed a proposed state-sponsored trading company (Brooks 2003: 149). Portugal's weak and negligent colonial presence in the few trading posts along the coast repeatedly prompted mutinies of soldiers (most of them local creoles and Cape Verdeans) and rebellions of the creole population throughout the late eighteenth and the nineteenth centuries (Bowman 1997; Hawthorne 2003: 180–181; Pélissier 1989).

The effective occupation of the entire territory was not achieved until the 1930s, against fierce but sporadic armed resistance. Attempts to set up a proper colonial state administration had been gradually made since 1879, after Guinea-Bissau gained its administrative autonomy from Cape Verde, which had supervised it until then. However, the colonial state remained administratively inefficient and continued to push forward its few infrastructures by force. Forced labor was common. Corruption was generally high and prevented various projects from being completed. New crises for the colonial power arose in the early twentieth century. From 1911 until its dissolution in 1915, the Liga Guineense (Guinean League)—regarded by some scholars as a proto-nationalist movement dominated by creoles—actively advocated the social, political, and economic interests of local, urban, middle-class Cape Verdeans and other creole traders (Mendy 1994: 329–339; Pélissier 1989: 295–302; Trajano Filho 1998: 228–313). Nevertheless, the colonial state managed to consolidate its structure from the 1920s to the 1950s, integrating a small number of Africans (many of them Cape Verdean and Bissau-Guinean creoles) into its administration.

In spite of these efforts, the presence of the Portuguese remained weak (Forrest 1992: 16–21). In general, Portugal invested very few resources to develop its neglected colony (Galli and Jones 1987: 28). To date, thick volumes of law gazettes continue to testify to the colonizers' claim to regulate aspects of social, economic, and political life, even though, as in Cape Verde, the colonial state was never able to completely enforce these provisions and therefore had to tacitly compromise. Nonetheless, its commitment to exerting power and controlling local life persisted after World War II. The colony's ultimate colonial crisis started in 1963 when the independence movement Partido Africano da Independência da Guiné e Cabo Verde (PAIGC, African Party for the Independence of Guinea and Cape Verde), which was co-founded and led by Amílcar Cabral (himself a creole of Cape Verdean ancestry), launched its first attacks as part of the struggle for independence, signaling the beginning of a liberation war that lasted for more than a decade (Dhada 1993; Forrest 1992; Galli and Jones 1987). Beforehand, a new wave of nationalism had washed over the country, severely challenging colonial domination (Duarte Silva 1997). Hence, as in colonial territories elsewhere, Portugal's Guinea-Bissau remained in constant crisis, with the colonial power more or less successively repelling local attempts to control, appropriate, change, deter, or undermine colonial political force.

One means to channel these efforts and thwart colonial domination was that of carnival performances. Carnival's potential to act as a medium of resistance and criticism of authority has been famously pointed out by Mikhail Bakhtin (1984). Carnivalesque rituals aim to engage in a dialogue with everyday life, thus disclosing the discrepancy between real and carnivalesque life. By displaying abnormal behavior, aberrant costumes, and mummery, individuals can metamorphose into other characters and slip into new roles. This allows for new, unusual opportunities for communication since the anonymity granted by costumes and masks can serve to disguise one's own origins, social status, and personality—thereby also facilitating the display of social critique (Mezger 1980: 220–223). It is therefore not surprising that, in a wide variety of historical situations, carnival oscillated between acceptance and constraint, or that carnivalesque events were forbidden or subject to restrictions and regulations (Braun 2002: 10; Mezger 1980: 205–211; 2000: 129–131).

In many settings, the original significance of carnival as a social critique has been largely concealed as a result of a process of class or state domestication. In Europe, for instance, the ruling class appropriated medieval carnival, transforming formerly wild rituals into courtly masquerades, parades, and feasts; as a consequence, the original medieval forms disappeared (Bakhtin 1984: 28). A comparable situation of carnival domestication may have occurred in Guinea-Bissau after independence. Carnival parades held in contemporary Guinea-Bissau have little in common with overt rebellion and subversion, although many masks caricature current social, political, and economic events and problems. Instead, authorities grant the fools and their associations the right to parade through cities and towns, with police accompanying them for security reasons. At the same time, the country's Ministry of Culture organizes carnival as a countrywide contest, thus imposing a controlling structure on a ritual that is commonly associated with disorder and anti-structure. In other words, not only the populace but also the state can appropriate carnival, remodeling the actually subversive performance into a 'domesticated' one, as occurred not only in late-colonial Guinea-Bissau, but also—and especially—in post-colonial times.

The available documented references to carnival in colonial Guinea-Bissau date from the late nineteenth century. Here, carnival—locally known by the Portuguese terms *carnaval* or *entrudo*—was possibly first performed in a handful of littoral settlements that were connected to Portugal by seaway. Elderly Guineans remembered that carnival was already a well-liked festivity among Europeans and the creole population (both Cape Verdeans and Bissau-Guinean creoles) as early as the 1920s and 1930s, especially among the youth (Kohl 2016). In any event, rebellious expressions of carnival had become popular in Guinea-Bissau by the late nineteenth century (Crowley 1989: 143–144, 146–147). In Portugal itself, carnival has been a very popular festivity for centuries, at times acquiring violent expressions, even in some early-twentieth-century zones of Lisbon (Coelho 1993: 299–300; Lahon 1999: 170–171; Leite de Vasconcellos 1982: 145–170). Thus, many Portuguese colonial officials may have remembered this kind of unruly carnival, regarding it as a threat to (colonial state) order.[5] Comparable regional examples also existed. Guinea-Bissau's neighboring countries, such as Senegal, Gambia, and Sierra Leone, celebrated lantern (*fanaal*) festivals that displayed some carnivalesque features, revealing transatlantic connections to the Caribbean (Bettelheim 1985; De Jong 2009; Nunley 1982, 1985; Oram 1998, 2002). It is possible that the colonized Bissau-Guineans, particularly creoles in the former trade settlements, challenged colonial representations through carnival performances.

Yet rather than straightforward manifestations of resistance, carnival performances in Guinea-Bissau should instead be read as ambivalent and multi-layered cultural expressions. My field observations during the Bissau carnival season in 2007 and 2013, for instance, suggest that some individuals take part in carnival because of the possibilities that participation creates for sociability and conviviality, that is, for *communitas* (Turner 1969). Other individuals, especially children and youth, may participate simply for amusement and fun. On the grounds of these considerations drawn from the contemporary period, one could argue that carnival performances in colonial West Africa did not necessarily have to be associated with resistance. Nevertheless, carnival's potential to challenge and criticize state authority remains very much alive in the Guineans' repertoire. People can use carnival as a vehicle to openly or tacitly criticize the government for bad governance, as happens frequently in Bissau through artistic, fanciful papier-mâché headpieces, the best being awarded a prize by a jury.

An early instance of the political potential of carnival for criticizing the state in Guinea-Bissau can be found in late-nineteenth-century Portuguese documentation. In 1888, in the colonial settlement of Bolama, carnival performance served as a platform for creole groups and the local military to criticize the colonial governor's policies and even imperial politics more broadly. It is to an analysis of this historical episode that I now turn.

A Carnival Disorder in Bolama, 1888

The following carnivalesque episode was described in a confidential telegram sent by the colonial governor of Portuguese Guinea, Francisco Teixeira da Silva, to the Portuguese Overseas Ministry.[6] In it, the governor complained that a big masquerade had taken place in Bolama—then the capital of Portuguese Guinea—on Friday, 17 February. Bolama is situated off the Bissau-Guinean coast on an island of the same name. The masquerade was composed of local soldiers under the leadership of an Angolan commander, Colonel Eusébio Catella do Valle, head of the Bolama-based Riflemen Battalion No. 1 and, for a brief period in April 1887, the colony's interim governor and secretary-general.[7] Presumably, most of those taking part in the masquerade were Cape Verdeans, as they were strongly represented in the armed forces in Portuguese Guinea. The governor charged the locals in general—and Catella do Valle in particular—of wanting "to govern this province." Catella do Valle was accused of populism, treason, and of possibly being the author of the masquerade that had turned into "an element of disorder" since the moment Teixeira da Silva had started to govern the province of Portuguese Guinea. Catella do Valle had reportedly "lost his head" and even recommended to replace the governor. His "wrongdoing" was not perceived as a mere carnivalesque "crossing the line" but as a serious threat to colonial domination, since it involved individuals of African and creole origins in the service of Portugal. Instead of defending colonial authorities as auxiliary agents, the local soldiers had appropriated an originally European performance in ways considered undesirable by superior officials. Although carnival linked its colonial performers to the Portuguese metropole, the way in which it was performed in Bolama was completely unwanted by Teixeira da Silva, who viewed it as questioning colonial representation and betraying the colonial project.

Significantly for the interpretation of this carnivalesque disorder, the same document also alludes to the Franco-Portuguese commission that had been installed to accurately delimit the Portuguese colonies' borders with French Senegal in the aftermath of the Berlin Conference of 1884–1885. Both countries had signed a treaty in May 1886 that stipulated an exchange of territories. The new boundaries were to the disadvantage of the Portuguese; however, the delimitation was not implemented until after February 1888 (Esteves 1988; Pélissier 1989: 172–174), that is, around the time of the portrayed carnival episode. According to the contents of the telegram, the crowd parodied French officials and caused general disorder. The delimitation commission included two French officials—Captain Henri Brosellard Faidherbe, the head of the French mission, and Lieutenant Clerc (indicated as "Clerk" in the document) (Esteves 1988: 183–186)—both of whom were mentioned in the telegram. On 28 January, the French mission had reportedly arrived in Bolama, and on 4 February left for the Rio Nunes area in the southern part of present-day Guinea-Bissau (ibid.: 186–187). On Shrove Tuesday, 14 February, also known as Pancake Day, the report continued, a masquerade (organized by local soldiers, possibly of Cape Verdean origin) emerged from the casern and passed in front of the Government House without permission. The crowd carried along a banner bearing Portugal's national colors and the word "Commission." This was accompanied by a safe that bore the inscription "Money, a Lot of Money" and by a big box labeled "Cape Roxo," a reference to the cape that marks the Senegalese–Bissau-Guinean border. A buoy labeled "Mind the Buoy" was followed by five masked figures representing members of the commission. Finally, the masquerade dissolved itself.

It is notable that the telegram accused both the indigenous population and the local soldiers of treason. Eventually, Bolama's municipal administrator was interviewed by Teixeira da Silva, who asked why permission had been granted for the masquerade. The administrator replied that he had been convinced that it would be something "innocent." The governor, however, did not accept this justification and dismissed the administrator who had breached his responsibilities as, *de jure*, only the secretary-general, apparently of the provincial administration, was allowed to grant permissions. In a subsequent letter to the ministry, the governor explained that Catella do Valle had justified his involvement in the parody, that he wanted to "defend himself" and "distract from his responsibilities." Catella do Valle declared that he lived together in the barracks with his officers, possibly also Bissau-Guinean, Cape Verdean, and/or Angolan creoles, who knew how to produce masquerade pieces.[8] As a consequence of these investigations, Catella do Valle was discharged by a decree dated 28 February 1888 from his position as commander of the riflemen regiment and was retired in 1890.

Admittedly, a single telegram does not permit a 'thick' description of what happened in Bolama during the carnival in 1888: many statements remain sketchy and contexts unclear. Therefore, it is hardly possible to fulfill Sherry Ortner's (1995) demand for thick and detailed ethnographic analyses. Nonetheless, some preliminary conclusions can be drawn. First, this vignette illustrates well the ambiguity of colonial domination, showing the administration to be deeply divided by personal animosities, prejudices, mistrust, and diverging interests. The bureaucratic complexity and the pronounced yet often pretended rigidity of sticking to legal-bureaucratic principles were expressed by the governor's insistence on how to correctly issue licenses. In a small colonial capital like Bolama, whose population never exceeded more than a few thousand individuals and where distances were generally short, the picture that emerges reveals at once the colonial regulatory zeal and the prevalent confusion in applying the legislation. This account confirms the weak nature of Portuguese colonialism in Guinea-Bissau at the time, along with the ambiguity of colonial armies. It prompted military officials to accuse the metropolitan Portuguese government of corruption and mismanagement, resulting in concerns that the natives would strive to gain power. As suggested by Stoler and Cooper (1997: 24): "One of the most basic forms of colonial control—by the military— depended on soldiers who were simultaneously coerced and coercing, who enforced the will of the elite yet made demands themselves."

Second, the episode points to the creativity of the carnival mimicry of colonial events. In one stroke, it criticized both the French members of the border delimitation commission and the Portuguese administrators who had supposedly accepted to 'play the game' and were seen as guilty of betraying the interests of the colony. Criticizing the French might have been acceptable from an 'official' Portuguese point of view, but for creoles to accuse the Portuguese administration itself of corruption was definitely too much. Hence, the episode also reveals how the actors, predominantly creoles, strove for recognition and power after they witnessed the colonizers squandering territory that many may have considered as their own property and homeland. Indeed, the creole carnival manifestations can be read as a nationalistic reaction of a small local group that was unhappy with the terms set by the Luso-French border commission, reacting with outrage against both the Portuguese metropolitan authorities and their branch in Bolama that had not, in their eyes, properly defended the cohesion of the colony. Revealing a (proto-)nationalist stance, they were angry that the important trading post of Ziguinchor, which was mainly inhabited by fellow creoles, and its hinterland, the fertile Casamance region, were annexed to French Senegal. These occurrences thus anticipated to some extent the foundation of the Liga Guineense about two decades later. This case brings to light both the subversive and transgressive character of mimetic processes of appropriation of colonial power and identities (Ferguson 2002: 557; Taussig 1993: 129, 252). Furthermore, the mimetic masquerades enacted by the local African and creole officials fundamentally disturbed—and even put into question the existence of—colonial orders of representation and the actions of the colonial state.

The next example takes us to Bissau some decades later to explore another state attempt at interfering with carnival festivities. In Guinea-Bissau, the colonial state had continued to extend its influence gradually, seeking to control the social and cultural life in the coastal settlements. In 1961, as the winds of anti-colonialism and African liberation movements were growing stronger, the Portuguese government made efforts to further supervise and manage carnival festivities.

Controlling Carnival in Bissau, 1961

Especially after the effective colonial seizure of the territory was completed in the 1930s, the Portuguese autocratic regime, known as the Estado Novo (New State), attempted to restrict the people's freedom. Whereas street carnival remained a unique creole cultural representation limited to a few semi-urban settlements in the colony, increasingly segregationist and racist policies (although implemented in only a rudimentary fashion as compared to Angola or Mozambique) were reflected in my informants' comments. After the promulgation of the Native Statute in the 1920s, which set 'civilized' citizens apart from 'uncivilized' natives, carnival revelers began to be popularly identified with the civilized population (comprising Europeans and Cape Verdeans). However, in reality many creoles who did not hold citizenship also participated in the festivities, thus indicating the limitations of colonial legal restrictions in practice.

Another colonial crisis was about to erupt in Guinea-Bissau. After World War II, most African colonies, which had been quite arbitrarily demarcated and seized by European colonial powers only a few decades before, turned into arenas of rising nationalism and liberation struggles. The national question was raised by numerically small groups of local elites. In Guinea-Bissau, creoles, including Cape Verdeans, figured prominently among those aspiring to independent statehood and nationhood. A new batch of clandestine nationalist movements emerged after 1945. These groups were increasingly and vehemently advocating self-rule and independence for the autocratically ruled colony. Most of these movements were short-lived and formed through fission or fusion with other movements.[9] Some, like the precursors of the later victorious independence movement PAIGC, were directly related to the Liga Guineense (Dhada 1993: 212, 216). In the 1950s, these movements were usually led by creole urban residents. Protests against the colonial state reached their peak in 1959, when a violently quelled dockworkers' strike became known as the Pidjiguiti Massacre. The nationalist movements continued their agitation, and in January 1963, the independence war began. As early as the mid-1950s, however, the colonial authorities must have become increasingly nervous about these developments that challenged the authority of the state. It follows that the colonial state authorities probably feared carnival as a means to cover politically subversive activities to promote a nationalist agenda.

According to oral accounts I collected in the field, carnival seems to have been banished in the 1950s from the capital's oldest part, Bissau Velho (Old Bissau), which is characterized by high housing, population density, and narrow streets. Carnival was moved away from Bissau Velho to the newer parts of the capital's city center where streets are wider and easier to supervise. It is likely that this move by the colonial state did not yield the desired results. The fear that carnival could be used to channel subversive nationalist and anticolonial ideas and performances eventually became deeply rooted among the colonial representatives, especially in the context of the volatile political atmosphere of the 1950s–1960s. In its urge for regulation, the administration possibly found itself in a bit of a dilemma, because carnival was very popular not only among Africans (especially creoles), but also among the European community in the colony—albeit celebrated in a completely different way, mostly involving private functions. For this reason, it seemed to be very difficult, if not impossible, to completely prohibit the celebration of carnival. Accordingly, a middle way was taken when legal measures were adopted in 1961. In mid-January, about four weeks before carnival was scheduled to take place on 13 and 14 February, the colonial governor, Commander António Augusto Peixoto Correia, issued a decree that aimed to curtail—but not entirely forbid—the *entrudo*, the Portuguese term by which carnival was locally known.[10] This was apparently a unique occurrence as no carnival-related laws from other Portuguese colonies such as Angola and Cape Verde decreed around the same time are known to date.[11]

This decree stipulated that "carnivalesque events" had to obey a number of restrictions. Alongside uncontroversial clauses, such as the prohibition on blocking traffic or using dangerous or inflammable objects in public spaces, the regulation also issued a ban on "masks and other disguises that occult or garble the bearers in a form that does not permit her/him to be identified rapidly." Moreover, the "usage of personal costumes of administrative authorities, the army, the navy, police officers, customs officials, Portuguese Youth, and the fire brigade by individuals who do not belong to these institutions" was henceforth forbidden.[12] Thus, the administration attempted to regulate mimesis to prevent the appropriation of colonial representations of domination and authority by the colonized in general, and by creoles, who figured prominently in the independence movement, in particular. The decree was aimed at the maintenance of the colonized's recognizability as 'Others'. By trying to regulate appearances, it was intended to make society 'legible'. Finally, the performance of any dance or entertainment event, whether in public or private spaces, needed a special license from then on.

We do not know how or to what extent this decree was implemented on the occasion of the carnival in 1961. Perhaps, and similarly to the case of Cape Verde discussed by Trajano Filho (2006), both carnival revelers and representatives of the colonial authorities entered into a silent compromise that facilitated the realization of carnival in public as long as a line drawn by the colonial officials—that is, mimicking government officials and questioning the status quo of colonization—was not crossed. Nevertheless, I think that this represents one further possible way in which "alternative governmentalities" (Pels 1997: 177; see also the introduction to this volume) can evolve from such a specific situation, where colonial state regulation and carnival performances face each other.

One of my interlocutors remembered that during a carnival in Bissau in the 1960s, one of his friends was arrested because he had worn a military police uniform as a costume. In any case prohibited by the decree, a civilian wearing a military uniform in a carnival context must have been unthinkable in the eyes of the colonial authorities after the outbreak of the struggle for independence. Another contemporary witness affirmed that the confinement of the carnival had also occurred because some papier-mâché masks caricatured members of the Portuguese government and their local colonial representatives. This informant suggested that the Portuguese colonial authorities had already lost control over the carnival by 1970. Obviously, even the celebration of street carnival in the newer parts of Bissau's city center appears to have eventually proven to be a hotbed of subversion. On this account, it seems, street carnival was eventually entirely banished from Bissau's city center, from where it was moved to the Chão de Pepel neighborhood about 500 to 1,000 meters to the north (Rambout Barcelos et al. 2006: 183). The quarter of Santa Luzia also became known as a carnival hotspot, even if only because some bars there were highly popular during the *entrudo* season.

It is quite possible that, following Homi Bhabha (2005: 266), the Portuguese colonial officials may have discounted the imitation of colonial and Portuguese government officials as a sophisticated form of subversion and considered it merely as 'aping' or parody, as mockery rather than mimicry. As I have argued above, perspectives such as Bhabha's underestimate and underemphasize the interpretive and multi-layered character of carnival performance. Nevertheless, it is plausible that, in the eyes of the colonizers, carnival, if performed by their subjects in a 'calumnious' manner, was conceived as a 'wrong' and 'bad' manifestation of civilization—an entirely undesirable, European-born but falsely appropriated tradition that contested white European supremacy. This 'wrong imitation' or 'bad copy' (Gable 2002) may indeed have been understood as mockery by the authorities, in contrast to a desired mimicry of European civilization. In this sense, Bissau-Guinean carnival is a good example of James Ferguson's (2002: 553) claim that "colonial imitation always threatened to become excessive and uncontrolled and thereby to unsettle the boundaries and relations of authority between settler and native that the colonial order depended on." Thus, apart from being a potential threat to colonial rule in the politically heated atmosphere between various nationalist groupings and the Portuguese state, the natives who 'aped' carnival were also embarrassing because they threatened the—politically and ideologically claimed—strict hierarchical order between colonizers and the indigenous population (see Bhabha 2005: 266). In other words, some subjects' attempts to fight for recognition and to claim political participation by (mis)using the ambiguity of carnival were not only menacing but also embarrassing (Ferguson 2002: 553). After all, and despite official statements, colonizers aimed at producing "perfected natives, not imitation Europeans" (Dutch colonial official, quoted in Stoler and Cooper 1997: 7) as a result of their self-proclaimed civilizing mission. Hence, proclamations to educate and civilize natives and to eventually dissolve boundaries soon reached their limits. Such commitments were revealed to be rhetorical and thus mere lip service, further highlighting the ambiguity of colonialism in general and of carnival in particular.

Traces of this ambivalence can also be found in evidence concerning the socially differentiated forms of celebrating carnival in Guinea-Bissau, differences that followed colonial, ethnic, and class lines and divides. Portrayals of carnival celebrations in Bissau that I collected during field research reveal the divided experience among carnival revelers in the late-colonial period when nationalist 'insurrection' struck Guinea-Bissau. The memories of my (African) interviewees suggest that private parties and festivities of a non-suspicious nature were excluded from the 1961 prohibition on carnival celebrations in the streets. Such carnival balls were often organized by formal associations close to the colonial state and were chiefly frequented by European and Lebanese merchants. These orderly carnival proms stood in sharp contrast to popular street carnival. Proms were organized, for example, by sports clubs like the União Desportiva Internacional de Bissau (International Sports Union of Bissau) and Benfica (named after the famous Lisbon football club), and by the colony's traders' association, Associação Comercial, Industrial e Agrícola da Guiné (Commercial, Industrial, and Agricultural Association of Guinea).

These 'divided experiences' also manifested themselves in the fact that the majority of the Europeans living in Bissau remained in the city center during carnival, although some European residents used to go to the street carnival hotspots in order to take photographs, as an informant recounted. As far as the proms were concerned, it was primarily the elite, including a few Africans, many of them of creole background, who attended these balls, and tickets were comparatively expensive, this serving as an exclusion mechanism. Accordingly, these carnival balls appear to have had little in common with subversion of the prevalent social order or mordant criticism of colonialism. Instead, they seem to configure another historical instance of what Bakhtin (1984) calls the 'domestication' of wild, low-class carnival by the ruling classes, through which the latter appropriated and transformed previously popular and disorderly activities into upper-class events.

From Carnival to Carnivals and Their Multiple Meanings

Edward Schieffelin (1985: 722) has highlighted the complex conflation—or multi-layeredness—of various meanings in cultural representations. From this perspective, African popular involvement in street carnival could entail other meanings beyond resistance, subversion, and mimicry against colonial rule. For many participants, sociability and rambunctious partying were at the very fore. Moreover, it is noteworthy to point out that in late-colonial times members of the urban Bissauan middle class often organized private carnival gatherings. Colonial carnival was not an African or creole event alone. A descendant of a long-established upper-middle-class creole family who was born in the early 1950s told me about his carnival experiences in the Chão de Pepel neighborhood, situated close to the city center, in the late 1950s and 1960s. This quarter used to be inhabited by many European and creole middle-class families. As in his father's time, informal networks among circles of friends and co-workers, usually craftsmen, still existed at the time. Co-workers used to party together after pooling their money to pay for food, drinks, and costumes. The private carnival gatherings began at night, with people having drinks in bars, taverns, or the backyards of their residences. This suggests that not all aspects of popular carnival were politicized during the colonial period. Rather, many individuals, especially if they had come to an arrangement with the colonial state, simply enjoyed carnival as an opportunity to take a break from their work routine and to socialize with their peers, relatives, and friends.

   Not only in this regard can we speak of heterogeneity and multi-layeredness of carnival. Since colonial times, Bissau-Guinean carnival has translated representations from across the Atlantic and from the continent's interior, absorbing these features into its own repertoire. In this way, individuals of various cultural and ethnic backgrounds can identify with carnival because they recognize features with which they are already familiar. Masks, for instance, are used in various ceremonies throughout the region. *Kumpó* and *kankurang* masking induces social control. In a comparable vein, the motif of an upside-down world, frequently ascribed to carnival, is associated with masking, where social rules are temporarily and selectively suspended (De Jong 1999: 57; 2000: 154). Moreover, mimesis is a crucial component of lantern and *fanaal* parades, which have been celebrated in West Africa for at least 150 years (Bettelheim 1985: 50). Nunley (1985: 48) notes that, similarly to maskers in the interior of Sierra Leone and Nigeria (where many of the ancestors of Freetown's inhabitants originated), the identity of the lantern operator is kept secret, thus demonstrating parallels between these rituals and various other cultural representations that can imply a conflation of meanings. The aspect of mimicry is even more present in the *fanaal* that is performed annually in the Senegalese city of Saint Louis. De Jong (2009: 50) argues that, when performed by the Senegalese, the *fanaal* "still conveys a sense of belonging to a realm of French civilization, but not quite." Clearly, the motif of resistance does not appear to be prominent in this kind of performance.

Vice versa, carnival revelers from Guinea-Bissau's hinterland could identify themselves with certain elements appearing in the celebration of carnival that—coincidentally or not—resembled manifestations that those engaged in urban carnival celebrations knew from their own cultural background, that is, their ancestral villages. This integrative heterogeneity of carnival, which at the same time points to the event's ambiguity, can be demonstrated by the following examples. Many of my informants remembered large masks popularly known as *entrudos* that caused a big stir at the time. These *entrudos* were usually worn by elderly men. At times, the *entrudo* was referred to as a *homem morcego* (lit., 'batman', possibly alluding to the well-known comic book hero) if he was dressed in ugly and messy black clothes. These masked figures were feared by some, especially by children: they used to scare minors by growling and symbolically beating them with *chicotes* (whips). At the time, this sort of whip came to be rarely used by the *entrudos* because the instrument was popularly associated with the colonial police, who employed it to punish individuals and disperse groups of people. Sometimes the masked figures wavered back and forth, uttering cries that sounded like "boom-boom-boom." According to this informant, these maskers occasionally clashed with Portuguese soldiers in the late 1960s and early 1970s. If we take this information seriously, the colonial administrators interpreted the carnivalesque 'batman'—rightly or wrongly—as a mockery of their seemingly unpopular security forces, with the "boom-boom-boom" utterances possibly alluding to grenade impacts. However, different interpretations are possible, corresponding to the multi-layeredness of carnival. The element of punishment is also well known from the aforementioned *kankurang* masquerade, in which the player dressed in a grass robe and displayed cutlasses as elongations of his arms (De Jong 2000: 155). In both rituals, the personality of the masker remains secret while violence symbolically comes to the fore. Just like the *kankurang* (and *kumpó*) masked figures that hunt children in order to punish them, the *entrudo* (symbolically) whipped children and scared adults with impunity because the mask had conferred an identity beyond the mask wearer's personality.

There are at least two potential interpretations of the 'batman': it can be seen as a parody of colonial policemen, or as an 'urbanized' *kankurang*. Hence, carnival enthusiasts disguised as batman make clear the ambiguous character of carnivals whose features can be interpreted in one way or another. Yet bat-man and cowboy costumes, as well as the use of industrially fabricated masks since the 1960s, also illustrate the degree to which colonial Guinea-Bissau and a part of the local population—including notably the creoles in (semi-) urban settings—were linked not only to the metropole but also to a more cosmopolitan, Portuguese identity, further illustrating the ambiguities and internal divisions experienced by the colonized. Africans and creoles may simply have been taking advantage of a way to claim membership in wider European culture or even in colonial society. They asserted rights because these urban Bissau-Guineans wanted to be "full and equal citizens of a modern and urban society" and to be looked on as "civilized men," not merely "decorative barbarians" (Ferguson 2002: 555). This recognition as equals, in Bhabha's (2005: 266; italics in the original) words, as subjects *"of a difference that is almost the same, but not quite,"* however, was denied to the majority of Africans, thereby severely restricting their room for political maneuver to demand alterations of the status quo.[13]

The restriction or partial prohibition of carnival in 1888 and again in the late 1950s, 1960s, and early 1970s—at a time when social and political discontent challenged the colonial state's rule—also illuminates the relationship between different groups in colonial contexts. The above-mentioned divided experience of carnival shows the growing drifting apart and physical separation of groups populating Bissau, underlining the colonial state's divide-and-rule policy, although ethno-racial distance in colonial Guinea-Bissau was never as all-embracing and strict as in other African settler colonies. Despite attempts to maintain social boundaries—and in contrast to the officially voiced ideology—a certain space existed within which to negotiate the relationships between Europeans, Africans, and Cape Verdeans, among others. Against this backdrop, colonial authorities certainly had the freedom to interpret carnivalesque performances either as overtly hostile or as undesired mocking or foolish misbehavior, interpretations that resulted in the meting out of different punishments. This left space for arbitrariness, depending on who the perpetrators were and on the personal relationship they had with the law enforcers. The increasing segregation along (anything but static) social and ethnic lines in formerly mixed neighborhoods like Chão de Pepel, for example, is illustrated by the fact that members of different social classes and ethnic groups (Europeans and Lebanese, Cape Verdeans and creoles) celebrated carnival in different ways. Many Bissau-Guineans did not know how the European Portuguese residents used to celebrate carnival.

This segregation of carnival may have been facilitated by real and reputed nationalist activities and infiltrations that accelerated and deepened the colonizers' inclination to treat Africans with a generalized suspicion during the liberation war. Since the colonial state seemingly feared the appropriation of street carnival by masked nationalist followers, the festival must have represented a political risk. In this way, the role of carnival extended far beyond simple public masquerading and boisterous partying in the streets. Instead, it constituted a social performance that merged both private and political spheres.

Conclusion

Both in the early and the late days of effective colonial control of the territory of present-day Guinea-Bissau, carnival not only reflected crises of colonial power and domination, but also, and more importantly, triggered colonial responses to carnivalesque performances in general, and to its specific mimetic aspects in particular. These responses were essentially a reaction to the dangers and challenges that carnival posed to the colonizers' representations. Although the colonized were not homogeneous but rather an ambiguous category of people, and despite the fact that many observers regarded carnival as an apolitical festivity, carnivalesque mimicry was nevertheless perceived as having the potential to eradicate or weaken the boundaries between the colonizers and the colonized. Carnival in the late-nineteenth and then again in the mid-twentieth century can be regarded as a reversal of the social order—but only to a limited extent. The reversed social order and the perceived threat to colonial rule were, in the first case above, illustrated by the local soldiers who criticized the corrupt behavior of colonial officials under the disguise of carnival celebrations.

In the 1880s, carnival was appropriated by African army officials, who used its mimetic power to challenge colonial politics and accuse European officials of corruption. In this way, creoles tacitly presented themselves as the 'genuine' masters who actually governed the colony. Although carnival was originally an imported European tradition, it came to incorporate various local meanings and therefore appeared as a multi-layered cultural manifestation. This metamorphosis reinforced the threat to colonial representation, as carnival appealed not only to the small European and creole populations, but (potentially) also to a wider African audience. The colonizers were aware of carnival's subversive potential and reacted in an outright nervous manner. Their fear was all the greater because colonial rule at the time was not yet well established and was largely limited to a handful of trade settlements. Moreover, fragile colonial rule and order (and thus representations) had been challenged repeatedly by Africans, among them notably local creoles. This reversal was also epitomized by the figures of carnival fools dressed as soldiers and, in particular, by the figures of *entrudos*, which can be interpreted according to a variety of meanings.

Apparently, it was the *entrudo* as a parody of colonial police officers that led the oppressive, fascist colonial state to suppress carnival, starting in the late 1950s. In earlier periods, this was often not the case.[14] By the 1960s, both international and local colonial constellations had changed, and the colonizers' nightmare came to pass as the creole-led independence movement began to fight colonial rule. The measures taken by the Portuguese to constrain mimesis and the challenge to colonial representation were no longer an effective method to counter ambitions for independence. While in the 1880s the colonial administration reacted with disciplinary measures, in the 1960s the ranks appeared to have been closed. Now, the colonizers attempted to regulate what they could not prevent, trying to end ambivalence and ambiguity in an attempt to negate the oppositional potency entailed in mimetic practice.

Ortner (1995: 173, 183–187) laments the lack of an ethnographic perspective in most influential studies of resistance. More precisely, she criticizes the neglect of the 'internal politics' of the colonized. In the cases I have described, a number of distinct perceptions clashed not only during times of carnival, but during the entire colonial period as well. Whereas the colonial state authorities may have generally regarded carnival, when performed by the dominated African population, as a potential threat to colonial rule, many African, creole, and European carnival enthusiasts alike—taking the conflation of meanings into account—considered carnival as a heterogeneous spectacle in which they were able to detect traces of their respective cultural repertoires. While a few may have used the complex ambivalences of carnival to stage performances that bore political meaning or that came to be understood as anti-colonial by the administration, most saw it as an occasion to have fun and party together.

Furthermore, the cases presented here suggest that carnival performances did not simply and solely 'ape' the colonialists. They thus alert us to the fact that one should not overstress carnival in colonial situations as a mere feature of subversion and resistance to European authority per se—as underlined, among others, by Michael Taussig (1993) and by Paul Stoller (1984) in his study on the Hauka movement in Niger. It could be even be suggested that colonial Guinea-Bissau may not have actually possessed a subversive character that was observed and therefore fought by the colonizers. Instead, subversion may have been a feature that was anticipated or imputed to local carnival performances by European colonial officials. In many cases, some colonized individuals or groups of people may even have enacted subversive mimetic performances out of group dynamic effects, without employing it as a conscious practice of resistance. When we perceive imitation not simply as an effort of mechanical copying but as a creative and underdetermined act, many interpretations of carnival and its mimetic potentials are conceivable. To suggest otherwise would do little justice to the complexity, multi-layeredness, and interpretive ambiguity of these performances.

Acknowledgments

The findings presented in this chapter result from literature research and a year's fieldwork in Guinea-Bissau, completed in May 2007, as part of my PhD project "Creole Identity, Interethnic Relations, and Postcolonial Nation-Building in Guinea-Bissau," supported by the Max Planck Institute for Social Anthropology and the Graduate School "Society and Culture in Motion," both located in Halle (Saale), Germany. The author wishes to express his thanks to Cristiana Bastos, Patrice Ladwig, Ricardo Roque, and Oliver Tappe for intensive discussions, comments on, and suggestions regarding earlier versions of this piece, which were presented as papers at conferences. Special thanks go to Silvia Gerlinger for proofreading and comments. This chapter is dedicated to my friend and colleague, the late Christian Kordt Højbjerg.

Christoph Kohl studied at the Johannes Gutenberg University Mainz and the Ecole des Hautes Etudes en Sciences Sociales (EHESS), Marseille. He conducted his PhD project on Guinea-Bissau for the Max Planck Institute for Social Anthropology, Halle/Saale. He was a Research Fellow at the Institute of Sociology for a project on returned refugees in Angola at the Ludwig Maximilian University of Munich and for the research group "The Cultural Dynamics of Political Globalisation" at the Peace Research Institute Frankfurt (PRIF). Ultimately, he was a Research Fellow at the Georg Eckert Institute for International Textbook Research (GEI), Braunschweig. He now works as an independent researcher. E-mail: christoph_a_kohl@hotmail.com

Notes

1. Until the late nineteenth century, Portuguese colonization remained limited to a few trading posts (e.g., Bissau, Cacheu, Farim, Geba, and, later, Bolama) along the coastal line where commodities and slaves were traded. Pervasive colonization began only from about the 1920s and encountered resistance. Portugal's refusal to gradually grant its colonial territories independence or at least autonomy after 1945 radicalized nationalist movements, leading to the outbreak of the Guinea-Bissau War of Independence in 1963.
2. Please see the introduction by Ladwig and Roque for the dichotomous categories I am using here. I hope that in the course of this chapter it will become clear that 'colonizers' and 'colonized' are ideal types I am employing to highlight a contrast that in fact often becomes blurred.
3. According to Max Weber (1978: 1:56, 65), core characteristics of the modern state include the existence of administrative and legal order, citizens,

a territorial basis, and a monopoly on the legitimate use of physical force. Charles Tilly (1990: 74–75, 98–99) stresses the state's authoritative allocation of values via taxation, whereas Christian Lund (2006: 690–691) points to the symbolism and performance of modern statehood. Michel Foucault (1995) emphasizes the repressive and productive character of the state. See Ladwig and Roque's points on colonial governmentality in the introduction and especially the chapter by Roque, which discusses the notion in more detail.

4. On the difference between strategy as a form of power enacted by institutions, for example, and the subversive nature of tactics employed with reference to Michel de Certeau's (1984) work, see Tappe's chapter in this volume.

5. Personal communications, Ricardo Roque and Cristiana Bastos, December 2012.

6. Telegram No. 55, dated 20 February 1888, reproduced in a registry book, Arquivo Histórico Ultramarino (hereafter AHU), Fundo da Guiné, Livro 102. I am deeply indebted to Wilson Trajano Filho, who called my attention to this document and provided me with his transcript. See also AHU, Sala 12, 2.1 Secção-D1, No. 923.2, Pasta 10.

7. According to his military record card (AHU, Sala 12, 2.1 Secção-D1, No. 923.2, Pasta 10.A, Processo 97), Catella do Valle was born in Luanda, the capital city of Angola, in 1844, presumably into a creole family, as no ethnic identity is indicated and his parents bore Portuguese names. Since he is insulted as a *sobba* (the Angolan-Portuguese term meaning 'chief') in the telegram, he appears to have been of at least part-African origin. After he had entered the army in 1857, he made a career in the military and was transferred to Portuguese Guinea in 1885. He died in 1917. Interestingly, carnival appears to have been well established in Luanda for centuries and was embraced by creole inhabitants (Birmingham 1988).

8. AHU, Sala 12, 2.1 Secção-D1, No. 923.2, Pasta 10.A, Processo 95. I thank Carlos Almeida at AHU for his valued assistance.

9. For an overview of these movements, see, for example, Chilcote (1972: xxxvi, 603–607), Dhada (1993), Duarte Silva (1997: 28–34), and Pereira (2003: 80–88, 113–126).

10. Portaria No. 1301 of 18 January 1961, in Boletim Oficial da Guiné Portuguesa, supplement (18 January 1961) to No. 2 (14 January 1961); my translation.

11. Birmingham (1988), the only historical text on Angolan carnival known to me, is primarily dedicated to post-independence carnival and only briefly touches on colonial developments. Similarly, no information on Cape Verdean carnival celebrations and colonial interventions could be found.

12. Portaria No. 1301 of 18 January 1961, in Boletim Oficial da Guiné Portuguesa, supplement (18 January 1961) to No. 2 (14 January 1961).

13. Ferguson and Bhabha challenge earlier theorists of imitation like the Martinique-born Frantz Fanon (1980: 136, 145), whose works dealt with political, cultural, and mental decolonization. Fanon accused Africans of wanting to be like their white colonial masters. Arguing from a normative point of view, Fanon saw the colonized as dependent (ibid.: 146–148)—unlike Bhabha and

Ferguson, who stressed their agency. Fanon's view largely suppressed the ambiguity of colonialism and the manifold, albeit hidden, fields of action that were open to many Bissau-Guineans at the time.

14. In the late 1880s, the colonial authorities appeared to be quite helpless when faced with this kind of critique. Only after 1910 did the colonial state manage to effectively control the population and its activities. By the late 1960s and early 1970s, the colonial state had already lost its credibility. Incapable of reform and openness, colonial authorities closed a 'social relief valve', attempting to deny the population certain socio-psychological needs. This, along with the inability to deal with critique, finally fueled resistance and opposition, contributing to an escalation of the late-colonial crisis, which led to violent decolonization by 1974.

References

Bakhtin, Mikhail. 1984. *Rabelais and His World*. Trans. Hélène Iswolsky. Bloomington: Indiana University Press.

Bettelheim, Judith. 1985. "The Lantern Festival in Senegambia." *African Arts* 18 (2): 50–102.

Bhabha, Homi. 2005. "Of Mimicry and Man: The Ambivalence of Colonial Discourse." In *Postcolonialisms: An Anthology of Cultural Theory and Criticism*, ed. Gaurav Desai and Supriya Nair, 265–273. New Brunswick, NJ: Rutgers University Press.

Birmingham, David. 1988. "Carnival at Luanda." *Journal of African History* 29 (1): 93–103.

Bowman, Joye L. 1997. *Ominous Transition: Commerce and Colonial Expansion in the Senegambia and Guinea, 1857–1919*. Aldershot: Avebury.

Braun, Karl. 2002. "Karneval? Karnevaleske! Zur volkskundlich-ethnologischen Erforschung karnevalesker Ereignisse" [Carnival? Carnivalesque! Folkloristic ethnological research on carnival events]. *Zeitschrift für Volkskunde* 98: 1–15.

Brooks, George E. 2003. *Eurafricans in Western Africa: Commerce, Social Status, Gender, and Religious Observance from the Sixteenth to the Eighteenth Century*. Athens: Ohio University Press.

Certeau, Michel de. 1984. *The Practice of Everyday Life*. Trans. Steven F. Rendall. Berkeley: University of California Press.

Chilcote, Ronald H. 1972. *Emerging Nationalism in Portuguese Africa: Documents*. Stanford, CA: Hoover Institute Press.

Coelho, Adolfo. 1993. *Obra Etnográfica*. Vol. 1: *Festas, Costumes e outros Materiais para uma Etnologia de Portugal* [Ethnographic work. Vol. 1: Festivities, customs and other materials for an ethnology of Portugal]. Lisbon: Dom Quixote.

Cooper, Frederick. 2005. *Colonialism in Question: Theory, Knowledge, History*. Berkeley: University of California Press.

Crowley, Daniel J. 1989. "Carnival as Secular Ritual: A Pan-Portuguese Perspective." In *Folklore and Historical Process*, ed. Dunja Rihtman-Auguštin, 143–148. Zagreb: Institute of Folklore Research.

De Jong, Ferdinand. 1999. "Trajectories of a Mask Performance: The Case of the Senegalese *Kumpo.*" *Cahiers d'Études Africaines* 39 (1): 49–71.

De Jong, Ferdinand. 2000. "Secrecy and the State: The Kankurang Masquerade in Senegal." *Mande Studies* 2: 153–173.

De Jong, Ferdinand. 2009. "Shining Lights: Self-Fashioning in the Lantern Festival of Saint Louis, Senegal." *African Arts* 42 (4): 38–53.

Dhada, Mustafah. 1993. *Warriors at Work: How Guinea Was Really Set Free.* Niwot: University Press of Colorado.

Duarte Silva, António E. 1997. *A Independência da Guiné-Bissau e a Descolonização Portuguesa: Estudo de História, Direito e Política* [The independence of Guinea-Bissau and Portuguese decolonization: The study of history, law, and politics]. Porto: Edições Afrontamento.

Esteves, Maria Luísa. 1988. *Cacheu, Cidade Antiga: A Questão do Casamansa e a Delimitação das Fronteiras da Guiné* [Cacheu, ancient city: The Casamance question and the delimitation of Guinea's borders]. Lisbon: Centro de Estudos de História e Cartografia Antiga.

Fanon, Frantz. 1980. *Schwarze Haut, weiße Masken* [Black skin, white masks]. Frankfurt am Main: Syndikat.

Ferguson, James. 2002. "Of Mimicry and Membership: Africans and the 'New World Society.'" *Cultural Anthropology* 17 (4): 551–569.

Forrest, Joshua B. 1992. *Guinea-Bissau: Power, Conflict, and Renewal in a West African Nation.* Boulder, CO: Westview Press.

Foucault, Michel. 1995. *Discipline and Punish: The Birth of the Prison.* Trans. Alan Sheridan. New York: Vintage Books.

Gable, Eric. 2002. "Bad Copies: The Colonial Aesthetic and the Manjaco-Portuguese Encounter." In *Images and Empires: Visuality in Colonial and Postcolonial Africa*, ed. Paul S. Landau and Deborah D. Kaspin, 294–319. Berkeley: University of California Press.

Galli, Rosemary E., and Jocelyn Jones. 1987. *Guinea-Bissau: Politics, Economics, and Society.* London: Francis Pinter.

Havik, Philip J. 2004. *Silences and Soundbites: The Gendered Dynamics of Trade and Brokerage in the Pre-colonial Guinea Bissau Region.* Münster: Lit Verlag.

Hawthorne, Walter. 2003. *Planting Rice and Harvesting Slaves: Transformations along the Guinea-Bissau Coast, 1400–1900.* Portsmouth, NH: Heinemann.

Kohl, Christoph. 2009. "Creole Identity, Interethnic Relations, and Postcolonial Nation-Building in Guinea-Bissau." PhD diss., Martin Luther University of Halle-Wittenberg.

Kohl, Christoph. 2016. "Limitations and Ambiguities of Colonialism in Guinea-Bissau: Examining the Creole and 'Civilized' Space in Colonial Society." *History in Africa* 43: 169–203.

Lahon, Didier. 1999. *O Negro no Coração do Império: Uma memória a resgatar, séculos XV–XIX* [The Black in the heart of the empire: A memory to be redeemed, 15th–19th centuries]. Lisbon: Secretariado Coordenador dos Programas de Educação Multicultural-Ministério de Educação.

Leite de Vasconcellos, José. 1982. *Etnografia Portuguesa: Tentame de Sistematização* [Portuguese ethnography: An attempt at systematization]. Vol. 8. Lisbon: Imprensa Nacional-Casa da Moeda.

Lund, Christian. 2006. "Twilight Institutions: Public Authority and Local Politics in Africa." *Development and Change* 37 (4): 685–705.

Mark, Peter. 2002. *"Portuguese" Style and Luso-African Identity: Precolonial Sene-gambia, Sixteenth–Nineteenth Centuries.* Bloomington: Indiana University Press.

Mendy, Peter Karibe. 1994. *Colonialismo Português em África: A Tradição de Resistência na Guiné-Bissau (1879–1959)* [Portuguese colonialism in Africa: The tradition of residence in Guinea-Bissau (1879–1959)]. Bissau: Instituto Nacional de Estudos e Pesquisa.

Mezger, Werner. 1980. "Fasnacht, Fasching und Karneval als soziales Rollenexper-iment" [Fasnacht, Fasching, and Karneval as a social role experiment]. In *Nar-renfreiheit: Beiträge zur Fastnachtsforschung* [Jester's license: Contributions to carnival research], ed. Hermann Bausinger and Manfred Fuhrmann, 203–226. Tübingen: Tübinger Vereinigung für Volkskunde.

Mezger, Werner. 2000. "Masken an Fastnacht, Fasching und Karneval: Zur Geschichte und Funktion von Vermummung und Verkleidung während der när-rischen Tage" [Masks during Fastnacht, Fasching and Karneval: On the history and function of disguise and mummery during the foolish days]. In *Masken und Maskierungen* [Masks and masking], ed. Alfred Schäfer and Michael Wim-mer, 109–134. Opladen: Leske & Budrich.

Nunley, John W. 1982. "Images and Printed Words in Freetown Masquerades." *African Arts* 15 (4): 42–46, 92.

Nunley, John W. 1985. "The Lantern Festival in Sierra Leone." *African Arts* 18 (2): 45–103.

Oram, Jenny. 1998. "Float Traditions in Sierra Leone and the Gambia." *African Arts* 31 (3): 50–96.

Oram, Jenny. 2002. "Urban Float Traditions in West Africa: A Museum Perspec-tive." In *Museums and Urban Culture in West Africa*, ed. Alexis B. A. Adandé and Emmanuel Arinze, 77–95. Oxford: James Currey.

Ortner, Sherry B. 1995. "Resistance and the Problem of Ethnographic Refusal." *Comparative Studies in Society and History* 37 (1): 173–193.

Pélissier, Réne. 1989. *Naissance de la Guiné: Portugais et Africains en Sénégambie (1841–1936)* [The birth of Guinea: Portuguese and Africans in Senegambia (1841–1936)]. Orgeval: Editions Pélissier.

Pels, Peter. 1997. "The Anthropology of Colonialism: Culture, History, and the Emergence of Western Governmentality." *Annual Review of Anthropology* 26: 163–183.

Pels, Peter, and Oscar Salemink, eds. 1994. "Introduction: Five Theses on Ethnog-raphy as Colonial Practice." *History of Anthropology* 8 (1–4): 1–34.

Pels, Peter, and Oscar Salemink. 1999. "Introduction: Locating the Colonial Sub-jects of Anthropology." In *Colonial Subjects: Essays on the Practical History of Anthropology*, ed. Peter Pels and Oscar Salemink, 1–52. Ann Arbor: University of Michigan Press.

Pereira, Aristides. 2003. *O meu Testemunho: Uma Luta, um Partido, dois Países. Versão documentada* [My testimony: One fight, one party, two countries. Documented version]. Lisbon: Editorial Notícias.

Rambout Barcelos, Manuel, Nicolau Fara Gomes, Félix Sigá, Harriet C. McGuire, and Simon Ottenberg. 2006. "Masked Children in an Urban Scene: The Bissau Carnival." In *Playful Performers: African Children's Masquerades*, ed. Simon Ottenberg and David A. Binkley, 181–206. New Brunswick, NJ: Transaction Publishers.

Schieffelin, Edward L. 1985. "Performance and the Cultural Construction of Reality." *American Ethnologist* 12 (4): 707–724.

Scott, David. 1995. "Colonial Governmentality." *Social Text* 43: 191–220.

Stoler, Ann L., and Frederick Cooper. 1997. "Between Metropole and Colony: Rethinking a Research Agenda." In *Tensions of Empire: Colonial Cultures in a Bourgeois World*, ed. Frederick Cooper and Ann L. Stoler, 1–56. Berkeley: University of California Press.

Stoller, Paul. 1984. "Horrific Comedy: Cultural Resistance and the Hauka Movement in Niger." *Ethos* 12 (2): 165–188.

Taussig, Michael. 1993. *Mimesis and Alterity: A Particular History of the Senses*. London: Routledge.

Thomas, Nicholas. 1994. *Colonialism's Culture: Anthropology, Travel, and Government*. Princeton, NJ: Princeton University Press.

Tilly, Charles. 1990. *Coercion, Capital, and European States: AD 990–1990*. Cambridge, MA: Blackwell.

Trajano Filho, Wilson. 1998. "Polymorphic Creoledom: The 'Creole' Society of Guinea-Bissau." PhD diss., University of Pennsylvania.

Trajano Filho, Wilson. 2006. "Por uma Etnografia da Resistência: O Caso das *Tabancas* de Cabo Verde [For an ethnography of resistance: The case of the *tabancas* of Cape Verde]." *Série Antropologia* 408: 1–36.

Turner, Victor. 1969. *The Ritual Process: Structure and Anti-Structure*. Brunswick, NJ: Transaction Publishers.

Weber, Max. 1978. *Economy and Society*. 2 vols. Trans. and ed. Guenther Roth and Claus Wittich. Berkeley: University of California Press.

Chapter 7

MIMETIC PRIMITIVISM
Notes on the Conceptual History of Mimesis

Patrice Ladwig

When thinking of major theoreticians of mimesis and imitation in philosophy and the social sciences, thinkers like Plato, Erich Auerbach, Walter Benjamin, and many others come to mind. However, when we conceptualize the work of mimesis as an inter- or transcultural process, which is marked by encountering cultural 'Others', what is the position and influence of these Others in Western writings and thinking on mimesis? When we take for granted that during Western expansion and the colonial encounter information about the imitative practices of societies outside the West fed into the theorizing of mimesis, can we flesh out what could be called an alternative, or at least de-centered, genealogy of mimesis as a concept? Despite the diversity of these encounters and their distorted representations in the context of colonialism, missionary work, travel accounts, and early anthropological research, it is important to take into account that the information and imaginaries attached to the allegedly 'primitive'[1] also fed into Western theories of mimesis. Confrontations with different systems of thinking in which mimetic processes could be observed spurred wider discussions on what mimesis might mean in human culture beyond the 'West'.[2] Matthew Potolsky (2006) proposes that, through this encounter, remarkable differences from the Western Enlightenment and its ideas of mimesis and representation became apparent. The mimetic behavior attributed to indigenous people was considered foreign to the scientific worldview of the Enlightenment, as in these systems of thinking "magical copies have real properties and genuine powers on their own. They belong to a network of reciprocal sympathies and material embodiments, not a hierarchical ladder of rational forms and material embodiments" (ibid.: 139)

This chapter sets out to explore the primitive sources of mimetic theory. Referring to Enlightenment discourses, early anthropological accounts of indigenous societies, and critiques of modernity in the critical theory of the early Frankfurt School, the text will take a consciously generalizing approach, loosely inspired by Edward Said's (1979) and Michel Foucault's (2002) genealogical method. My endeavor is also related to Reinhardt Koselleck's (1979) version of conceptual history. I want to explore the larger semantic shifts in the understandings of mimesis over time, and analyze how descriptions of mimesis in indigenous, non-Western societies contributed to its theoretization. By taking as a red thread the two interrelated questions of mimesis and representation, I hope to show that the reflection on and appropriation of descriptions of primitive mimesis were essential for the constitution of its modern theoretical discourse.

I position this transcultural history of the concept of mimesis between two poles, which create a field in which theoretical discussions of mimesis unfold. On the one hand, I refer to accounts of the primitive, in which practices of imitative magic and the belief in fetishes or effigies are understood as superstition. Early anthropology, comparative religion, and scholars such as Edward Tylor and James Frazer postulated that these cultures represented mankind in its early stages, similar to European prehistoric cultures.[3] Magical thinking and its imitative rites were considered to be the lowest evolutionary stage of mankind. On the other hand, I will discuss theories that use images of the noble savage and romanticizing notions of primitivism. Some of these accounts argue that the primitive Other is still capable of mimetic and animistic thinking, but that it is allegedly lost in civilized and rationalized societies. Consequently, indigenous populations and their mimetic cultures were also used as a contrast to modern life, perceived to be marked by alienation, social fragmentation, and the disappearance of mimesis. I therefore argue that the reception, interpretation, and subsequent theorizing of descriptions deriving from mimetic behavior observed among primitives are strongly embedded in modernity's ambivalent self-reflections. On the one hand, we deal with discourses of superiority and progress and, on the other hand, with melancholic self-critiques circling around ideas of loss and alienation. One could say that the philosophical, anthropological, and social science discourses here underwent a process similar to those in the arts: in various epochs primitive art was used to substantiate, expand, or undermine certain modern aesthetic positions, often without referencing or giving voice to the producers of these artworks (see Flam and Deutsch 2003; Meyers 2006). In the arts and philosophical movements, primitivism "always involves a going back, a return to, a recovery of some early state of being that is perceived to be simpler or more vital or more innocent" (Connelly 1998: 338). Primitivism "always has at its core a sense of loss" (ibid.). However, I would add that primitivism always has two interrelated sides: it might be understood as overcoming an earlier stage of mankind like in evolutionary and Enlightenment thinking, or as a melancholic loss accompanied by alienation in modernity (see also Torgovnick 1990).

In order to explore the reception of primitive mimesis, the first part of this chapter will discuss some basic definitions of mimesis, especially its Platonic and Enlightenment genealogies. Here, I will show that the evolvement of the hierarchical relationship of original and copy and the negative connotations of imitation and representation are based on important epistemic shifts linked, for example, to the Reformation and the Enlightenment. I understand these developments as laying the groundwork for crucially influencing the perceptions of allegedly savage and primitive societies. The understanding of primitive fetishes in the eighteenth century among thinkers like, for example, Immanuel Kant and G. F. W. Hegel, are singled out as examples here. I deem these developments in the Enlightenment and Idealism as crucial for understanding the formation of an hegemonic intellectual apparatus feeding colonial discourses of cultural superiority. The subsequent part will discuss early anthropological theories of magic and their reference to imitative behavior, such as James Frazer's notion of 'sympathetic magic' and Lucien Lévy-Bruhl's notion of 'mystical participation'. They will be explored with reference to several ethnographic examples featuring in their work in order to show that an evolutionary and pejorative account of primitive mimesis slowly gave way to a more serious engagement with non-Western forms of mimetic behavior. The final part will explore to what extent certain forms of primitivism became crucial for critiques of the Enlightenment and modernity. Max Horkheimer and Theodor W. Adorno's ([1947] 2002) notion of mimesis in the *Dialectic of Enlightenment* and Walter Benjamin's work on the mimetic faculty will here serve as examples. Proposing that over-rationalization and alienation have led to a loss of mimetic capacities in modern society, they used snippets of ethnographies of primitive mimesis to show that what modernity had lost was still prevalent among indigenous societies. In conclusion, I argue that despite greater theoretical reflexivity, modernity and many of its contemporary discourses on authenticity and alienation have not yet escaped the spell of mimetic primitivism.

The Evolvement of Negative Mimesis

Mimesis has a long genealogy in theorizing art and society; several excellent studies that give an overview of the diverse histories of the concept have been published (Gebauer and Wulf 1995; Potolsky 2006). For centuries, the concept was dominant in discussions relating to art, theatre, painting, and literature.[4] The *Oxford English Dictionary* defines mimesis as "imitative representation of the real world in art and literature," and as "the deliberate imitation of the behavior of one group of people by another as a factor in social change." Behind these seemingly straightforward definitions lingers a history that covers an intellectual terrain reaching from classical Greek philosophy, in Plato's and Aristotle's works, to issues of copyright and originality in the contemporary digital age. But with every inclusive concept that has such a long and diverse history, its applications and uses have undergone crucial changes.

If Alfred North Whitehead's (1979: 39) exaggerated dictum that "the safest general characterization of the European philosophical tradition is that it consists of a series of footnotes to Plato" contains at least some truth, then a critical reflection on the concept of mimesis and its various transformations has to take Plato's essentially ambivalent understanding into account. Plato's view of mimesis is manifold and not as reductionist as I might depict it here. It operates on several levels, and at times with contradictory implications.[5] Generally speaking, in Plato's (1992) *Republic* we are told that positive mimesis has educational and socializing functions.[6] However, uncontrolled and chaotic mimesis (unnecessary craft-making, imitating nature sounds, etc.) is viewed critically (ibid.: Book II, 395c–397e; see also Gebauer and Wulf 1995: 25–30). Homer's images of gods and demi-gods are seen as blasphemous, and presented as an imitation of bad examples that have to be controlled by the guardians of the *polis* (Plato 1992: Book II, 377e–392c). Here, the link between mimesis and ideas about representation becomes relevant: like in Plato's allegory of the cave, art is seen as an imitation of an imitation in the sense that art copies the world of phenomena, which in itself is already an imitation of the 'real'.[7] Art and its imitative representations of 'original reality' are therefore subject to a double removal, and the illusion produced by art is seen as potentially deceptive and therefore inferior (ibid.: Book X, 596e–602c). Hence, mimesis and its produced representations are understood as an act that potentially corrupts and deceives the real, and therefore has to be controlled.[8]

I think that some of Plato's 'negative' features of mimesis have had a crucial influence on Enlightenment discourses, and have also laid the groundwork for the evaluation of cultural Others during the colonial expansion and Western hegemony. The mimetic practices observed among non-Western colonial subjects were often described in pejorative terms that clearly reflect the negative stance we find in works that discuss fetishism and magical thinking.

Beyond these earlier encounters, one can also argue that the negative features of mimesis are still present in modern disguise. Potolsky (2006) has detected traces of this understanding of mimesis in a variety of modern theories, and rightly points out that mimesis is, in some of these approaches, still a slave to its (at times distorted) Platonic genealogy. The implicit assumption is that mimetic behavior produces inferior copies of something else more original, and that it results in misrepresentations. In Marx's view, for example, Potolsky argues that "the accounts of social mimesis ... remain within the Platonic tradition of treating mimesis as a source of deception and a false representation of reality" (ibid.: 138).

How were these Platonic features of mimesis transmitted, and in which social and philosophical context did this transmission take place? While the Aristotelian-inspired view of mimesis remained crucial until the Middle Ages,[9] traces of Plato's account of mimesis and its negative connotations resurfaced later in a variety of approaches. Especially with the coming of the Renaissance, we witness a turn to Plato and a re-evaluation of mimetic behavior. The translation of mimesis into the Latin *imitatio* puts the focus on the mechanical and 'fake' character of mimesis (Wulf 1997: 1020), and Renaissance writers discover imitation as a central concept but not as original and creative behavior. Imitation becomes a topic of parodies of outdated, mechanical behavior, such as in Cervantes's *Don Quixote*. This and other works explore "the failure of imitation" (Potolsky 2006: 60) in an age where old social orders—like knighthood in Cervante's case—became destabilized and gave way to new ideas and values. Michel Foucault (1994: 49) interprets Don Quixote's mad behavior in epistemic terms. In the context of the great epistemological shift of the late sixteenth century, when the interplay of resemblance and sign was redefined, "language breaks off its old kinship with things and enters into that lonely sovereignty." Don Quixote still acts according to the old order of things and epistemes,[10] and therefore appears as a madman.

Stephen Halliwell (2002: 13) argues that the translation to imitation (and, one might add, its embeddedness in the ruptures of social orders and new epistemes) changed the concept to such a degree that, for several centuries, its negative connotations became dominant: "No greater obstacle now stands in the way of a sophisticated understanding of all the varieties of mimeticism, both ancient and modern, than the negative associations that tend to colour the still regrettably standard translation of mimesis as 'imitation,' or its equivalent in any modern language." In an overgeneralizing manner, one could state that, especially with the coming of Enlightenment, many of the negative features of imitation again come to the fore. The Enlightenment and modernity put emphasis on an independent, rational subject,[11] which has itself freed from superstition and the bonds of tradition. According to Immanuel Kant ([1784] 2013: 8), who famously defined Enlightenment as "the escape of men from their self-imposed immaturity, especially set in matters of religion,"[12] one of the main reasons for the regrettable condition of mankind is the habit of imitating the traditions of previous generations.[13] As I will discuss later, this also became a defining feature of Kant's view of African culture, which according to him is marked by the superstitious belief in fetishes.

During the Enlightenment, however, it is not only the transformation of the understanding of mimesis that signals a change; the shift primarily becomes visible in new ideas about representation and perception. A self-conscious subject that surveys the outer world arises, and sets new standards for how the world as an objectified entity is perceived. Concomitantly, representation evolves as a separation of essence and external form, of truth and its various appearances. In Kant's philosophy,[14] the things in themselves (*Dinge an sich*) are now unknowable:

> In reinterpreting the cognitive object, Kant extends the modern causal loop between things and ideas at the cost of introducing a distinction between what appears and what is. In calling attention to the difference between objects of experience and knowledge on the one hand, and things in themselves on the other, Kant formulates a new and very powerful version of the old Platonic dualism between objects of experience and knowledge, between the world in which we live and the world we invoke to explain that world. This results in new conceptions of the subject, the object, and the relation between them. (Rockmore 2011: 45)

As Webb Keane (2006: 198) elaborates, in this perspective objects are basically of interest because they "materialize and express otherwise immaterial or abstract entities, organizing subjects' perpetual experiences and clarifying their cognitions. The very materiality of objects, their availability to the senses, is of interest primarily as the condition for the knowability of otherwise abstract or otherwise invisible structure." This binary dimension of representation implies the division of truth and appearance.[15] Therefore, imitation is inextricably bound up with the question of representation, and again viewed as potentially corrupting, as it is in Plato. The anthropologist Johannes Fabian (1990: 753–754) adds important points to this problematic epistemological gap: "Taken as a philosophical issue, the idea of representation implies the prior assumption of a difference between reality and its 'doubles.' Things are paired with images, concepts, or symbols, acts with rules and norms, events with structures. Traditionally, the problem with representations has been their 'accuracy,' the degree of fit between reality and its reproductions in the mind."

I think that the Kantian stance described above can be seen as one of the endpoints of century-long problematizations that also had very concrete, historical implications. Whereas my reading of the changes that mimesis and representation underwent from the perspective of Enlightenment epistemology has been rather limited and selective due its focus on philosophical questions, these changes were not present in discourses among philosophy experts alone. The question to what extent, if at all, images could actually represent gods, holy objects, and so forth is of an earlier date. Historically speaking, the numerous theological discussions that circle around the problem of imitation and representation were part of major shifts in the understanding of religion in Europe.[16] Ralph Giesey's (1960) excellent discussion on changes in the understanding of effigies as representing the king in the royal funeral ceremonies in France and Ernst Kantorowicz's ([1957] 1997) famous exploration of the notion of the 'king's two bodies' in medieval political theology are works that have discussed these shifts in concrete historical contexts. Another important point of crystallization of these questions can be located in the transformations that came with the Reformation. In some interpretations of Protestantism, the outer world, and especially its religious iconicity as in Catholicism, becomes devalued, and belief is increasingly defined as an inner condition located in the subject.[17] Some Protestant movements—led by Calvin or Zwingli, for example—developed strong forms of iconoclasm. In the years following the initial Reformation (especially between 1520 and 1570), iconoclastic riots took place all over Europe.[18]

Although these processes were never overarching or complete, and did not follow a simple teleology, one could state in general terms that, at the end of these complex developments, we arrive at a rather new epistemology. After centuries of religious and philosophical quarrels, new ways of conceptualizing the relationship between the external world and the subject evolved with the Enlightenment and the Reformation. The subject has to free itself from the bonds of tradition and belief, and the gap between subject and object widens. Objects can still 'symbolize' meanings and 'stand for something'.[19] However, the notion of an active presence of a living entity in, for example, an effigy gradually disappears. Concomitantly, mimesis undergoes a similar shift—from a term that at the beginning denoted an act of creatively forging links between subject and object, to a more reductionist, even pejorative understanding of imitation.

Primitive Mimesis: Fetishes and Evolution in Kant and Hegel

Although these theoretical developments were by no means universal, they laid out the intellectual groundwork for the cultural encounter with indigenous societies, as many of the discussed intellectual and religious developments were paralleled by an increasing European domination in various parts of the world. An increasing amount of reports by travelers and colonial officials described (and more often imagined) societies that were said to cling to mimetic practices and to believe in the living qualities of certain objects that came to be subsumed under the category of the fetish. Although overseas colonialism started earlier, the eighteenth, nineteenth, and early twentieth centuries became an era in which depictions of indigenous, allegedly primitive societies were worked into a variety of European ideas surrounding mimesis and representation.

The theorizing of mimesis on the basis of accounts of cultural Others is exposed to power relations, which are already visible in the production of ethnographic information itself and its reception among European thinkers and artists. The overwhelming part of the data was drawn from travel descriptions and missionary reports, and not from ethnographic fieldwork. Fritz Kramer (1981: 111) has coined the term "imaginary ethnography" in relation to nineteenth-century accounts. He sees in them "moments of a naive metaphysics, that in some respects continue the fantasies of heaven and hell of European Christianity." However, after the rise of the natural sciences and the Enlightenment, he also locates in these ethnographic narratives a longing for a counterpart to the "radical rational culture of Europe" (ibid.). One of the best examples of establishing a distinction between Enlightenment civilization and its primitive antipodes is the discourse that was constructed around 'fetishes'. Taken to be emblematic of the pre-logical thinking of, for example, 'Africans', fetishism was, in popular evolutionary schemes, located at the lowest level of development, with polytheism and monotheism being later stages of development. Fetishes were taken to be false copies of something they could not be. Objects such as stones, Voodoo dolls, amulets, and so forth were, in indigenous conceptions, seen as active and living copies of persons. They were produced through acts of imitation, in which mimesis created a lasting link between original and copy. Often replicating not external forms but their spiritual essence, Enlightenment thinking understood them as false representations that were grounded in the illogical thinking of the natives. William Pietz (1985) has traced the genealogy of the idea of the fetish to the sixteenth and seventeenth centuries, in the context of Portuguese and Dutch expeditions to West Africa. He defines the fetish as "the problematic of the social value of material objects as revealed in situations formed by the encounter of radically heterogeneous social systems" (ibid.: 7) but also works out a history-of-ideas approach to fetishism, and speaks of the fetish in terms of the "general Enlightenment theory" (ibid.: 1) that evolved at the end of the eighteenth century. Interestingly, the belief in fetishes not only was attributed to primitives, but also delivered fodder for the Protestant critiques of idolatry in Catholicism that I already briefly alluded to in the context of iconoclasm. Primitive superstition was found not only in the colonies, but also at home (ibid.: 14):

> The discourse of the fetish has always been a critical discourse about the false objective values of a culture from which the speaker is personally distanced. Such was the negative force of revaluation when Portuguese Catholics named African religious and social objects "feiticos," and such was the force when commodity-minded Dutch, French, and English Protestants identified African religious objects and Catholic sacramental objects equally as fetishes, thereby preparing the way for the general fetish theory of the enlightenment.

The reports of travelers, merchants, slave traders, and missionaries also found their way into the philosophical writings of the Enlightenment, and accounts of fetishism became one of the preferred markers of distinction between civilization and primitiveness. Immanuel Kant gives us an excellent example. First, he discusses the alleged lack of development among 'the negroes of Africa' due to their racial inferiority. One implicit assumption here is, I think, that the reproduction of traditions through imitation produces a kind of stasis. Second, he postulates that the difference regarding mental capacities produces a kind of cognitive distortion in which 'things' are taken for living entities (fetishes) worthy of veneration. In *Observations on the Feeling of the Beautiful and Sublime*, Kant ([1764] 1960: 110–111) elaborates:

> The Negroes of Africa have by nature no feeling that rises above the trifling. Mr. Hume challenges anyone to cite a single example in which a Negro has shown talents, and asserts that among the hundreds of thousands of blacks who are transported elsewhere from their countries, although many of them have even been set free, still not a single one was ever found who presented anything great in art or science or any other praiseworthy quality ... So fundamental is the difference between these two races of man, and it appears to be as great in regard to mental capacities as in colour. The religion of fetishes so widespread among them is perhaps a sort of idolatry that sinks as deeply into the trifling as appears to be possible to human nature. A bird's feather, a cow's horn, a conch shell, or any other common object, as soon as it becomes consecrated by a few words, is an object of veneration and of invocation in swearing oaths. The blacks are very vain but in the Negro's way, and so talkative that they must be driven apart from each other with thrashings.

In a similar way, Hegel analyzed non-Christian religion and fetishes. His extensive treatment of fetishes and idols has a central role in the making of Eurocentric world history (cf. Tibebu 2011). Hegel (1975) proposed in his *Lectures on the Philosophy of World History*, given between 1821 and 1831, that Africans are not capable of imagining anything greater than man, and therefore concluded that fetish worship was the only cult they were able to develop.[20] Like Kant, his theorizing takes a pejorative turn, and in his overarching evolutionary march of mankind to the Absolute, indigenous populations and the religion of Asia are deemed to cling to superstition based on polytheism. In a lecture given in 1824, Hegel places the magic of Eskimos (who according to him have no religion) below that of the Africans (cf. Tibebu 2011), and then proceeds to discuss Hinduism and Chinese religion. Here he proposes that alienation and misrecognition derive from their idol worship (*Götzendienst*). In his *Encyclopedia of the Philosophical Sciences*, one of the foundational works of German Idealism, Hegel ([1817] 2010) ridicules the worship of cows, monkeys, and Brahmins in Indian and Chinese religions, equating it with the idol worship of the Old Testament (see also Fromm [1959] 1999: 209). Hegel's major attack, however, aims at pantheism, because his vision of Christianity was based on the belief in one God, and in a kind of religion that under the aegis of the state would produce moral citizens. The belief in effigies and living representations blocks this development. In one of his numerous discussions on Hinduism as pantheism, Hegel (1920: 90) extrapolates that in Hinduism the absolute can take the form of sensuous objects (i.e., fetishes), which he calls a product of "fantastic symbolism." This leads the Hindus to "live and move among *simulacra*" (ibid.: 51). Then, again, the non-moderns live in a world of fake representations. For him, "this only proves actually the incapability of the people entertaining these false conceptions to free themselves from the belief in the independency, the absoluteness of the finite, being unable to comprehend what really is" (Hegel, cited in Rathore and Mohapatra 2017: 130). He contrasts this with the true symbolism of his understanding of monotheism, in which sign and signifier are distinguished. Here again, we can link this point to the previous discussion on representation. While mimetic thinking and fetishes collapse the division of subject and object, of sign and signifier, their distinction is actually understood by Hegel and Kant as a prerequisite for understanding the real, and also for developing a civilization. Both Kant's and Hegel's abstract philosophies, and their recourse to fetishes and superstitious representations of primitive religions, can be understood as a kind of intellectual supplement of European hegemony, and in the end also as fostering the superiority of colonizing powers.

However, we also have to note the differences between Hegel and Kant here. Hegel showed great interest in India, and produced an astonishing amount of writing on it. In *Hegel's India: A Reinterpretation, with Texts*, Rathore and Mohapatra (2017) outline Hegel's ambition to systematize knowledge on different cultures into one system, and show that his account was not always dismissive (ibid.: 24). Moreover, Hegel's writings on India were foundational for German Romanticism, which turned Hegelianism on its head and developed a primitivist-Orientalist critique of industrial society.

Early Anthropology and Mimetic Theory: James Frazer and Lucien Lévy-Bruhl

Anthropology's relationships with colonial projects have taken on a variety of forms, oscillating between deep compliance and resistance (Asad 1973; Said 1989). However, what is of interest to me here is not the ethical dimension of these processes, but the fact that in several well-known ethnographies and theory schools arising in early anthropology, mimesis and imitation feature prominently. Some of the most influential studies in early anthropology that have taken mimesis as a core concept have been carried out in the context of colonial encounters. They have had enduring effects in reversed form in the post-colonial theorizing of mimesis, namely, as resistance.

Closely linked to the idea of the fetish that I outlined in the previous part, magic became another favorite topic of analysis, and also marks the beginning of the anthropological theorizing of religion under the influence of evolutionism and colonialism.[21] James Frazer surveyed a mass of ethnographic reports and mythologies from all around the world, and a great number of descriptions related to beliefs and rituals in which a created image (effigies, puppets, etc.) is thought to catch the essence of an object it represents, so that what is done to the image is thought to be done to the object. Through mimetic enactment, the object 'represents' what is perceived as absent from the perspective of the Enlightenment thinker; it gives the object a sort of life and reality, invoked through mimesis. In his major work *The Golden Bough*, Frazer (1894) subsumes mimetic enactment under the notion of 'sympathetic magic'. He proposes that, in these magical practices, imitation and similarity play a key role (ibid.: 52). He elaborates:

> If we analyze the principles of thought on which magic is based, they will probably be found to resolve themselves into two: first, that like produces like, or that an effect resembles its cause; and, second, that things which have once been in contact with each other continue to act on each other at a distance after the physical contact has been severed. The former principle may be called the Law of Similarity, the latter the Law of Contact or Contagion. From the first of these principles, namely the Law of Similarity, the magician infers that he can produce any effect he desires merely by imitating it: from the second he infers that whatever he does to a material object will affect equally the person with whom the object was once in contact, whether it formed part of his body or not. (ibid.: 48)

One of the first efforts to systematize a large body of ethnographic and historical accounts, Frazer's work also included an exegesis of Greek mythology. However, his perspective on magic was still close to accounts of fetishism. From the standpoint of the Enlightenment, Frazer (1894: 39) concluded that "magic is a spurious system of natural law as well as a fallacious guide of conduct; it is a false science as well as an abortive art." He saw magic as the most basic level in the evolution of mankind. Religion was already a sign of a higher complexity of thinking, superseded by the scientific view of the world. As a "dispassionate observer" who had studied magic, he nevertheless concluded that one "can hardly regard it otherwise than as a standing menace to civilisation" (ibid.: 56). Originally published in 1890, *The Golden Bough* became a large success and was widely read beyond purely academic circles. Intellectuals like T. S. Elliot and Sigmund Freud were inspired by the work. The latter used some of Frazer's ideas and descriptions, and in 1913 incorporated them into his *Totem and Taboo*, with the telling subtitle *Resemblances between the*

Psychic Lives of Savages and Neurotics, comparing the level of consciousness among primitives with that of children.

Whereas parts of the British school of social anthropology still adhered to an evolutionary paradigm, the French philosopher Lucien Lévy-Bruhl (1859–1939) had a somewhat different agenda. Trained as a philosopher, but also active in French sociology and anthropology, he is mainly known for his works on the 'primitive mentality' and concepts such as 'mystical participation'. His major publications—for example, *Les fonctions mentales dans les sociétés inférieures* (Mental Functions in Lower Societies), published in 1910, and *La mentalité primitive* (Primitive Mentality), published in 1922—seem to suggest a strong evolutionary bias, which later anthropologists described as "a horrific example for the miscomprehension of a scientific discourse" (Muenzel 2001: 250–251).[22] As an armchair anthropologist, he assembled (similar to Frazer) a huge mass of ethnographic reports and tried to explore the mental functions at the base of a wide range of phenomena, such as totemism, magic and magically loaded objects, shamanism, belief in ghosts and effigies, and the return of the dead. He understood his work not as an effort to classify primitives into an evolutionary scheme like Frazer, but as an attempt to compare modern ways of thinking about the world with primitive ones. The latter also included references to Chinese, ancient Greek, and Hindu traditions. Postulating a great gap between primitive and scientific thinking, he especially referred to phenomena of non-distinction and suggested that primitive man lives in a non-dual, animistic universe in which matter and mind are not divided—a standpoint that has been heavily criticized due to its generality and exoticizing effects.[23]

This "prelogical mentality," as Lévy-Bruhl (1923: 55) labeled it, constitutes the "collective representations of the primitive" that "differ profoundly from our ideas or concepts; nor are they the equivalent of them" (ibid.: 7) Unlike in societies where scientific thinking has become the dominant way of seeing the world, these collective representations are based on animistic principles and do not distinguish between dream and reality, subject and object, mind and matter. Although missionaries, travelers, and anthropologists had crafted reports on these beliefs from all around the world, Lévy-Bruhl's (1985: 76–77) starting point is that the facts described mostly remain alien to *our* form of thinking: "In the collective representations of primitive mentality, objects, beings, phenomena can be, though in a way incomprehensible to us, both themselves and something other than themselves. In a fashion which is no less incomprehensible, they give forth and they receive mystic powers, virtues, qualities, influences, which make themselves felt outside, without ceasing to remain where they are."

As in Frazer's account, things can become doubled via imitation, and mimetic behavior and representation play an important role in Lévy-Bruhl's theorizing.[24] I will here discuss two sets of examples analyzed by Lévy-Bruhl. The first relates to his extensive treatment of ritual and religious dance performances that imitate ancestors and the departed. The second group of examples discusses the use of objects such as amulets that imitate the qualities of other objects or persons. Both discussions also relate to the concept of representation and ideas about fetishes.

In his book *Primitives and the Supernatural,* in the chapters titled "Ceremonies and Dances" and "The Worship of Ancestors and of the Dead," Lévy-Bruhl (1935: 113–114, 134–135, respectively) focuses on a notion of mimesis that today would be labeled performative.[25] As an example, he takes an annual festival performed by the Kiwai (of Papua New Guinea), in which the masked males dress up as animals. Lévy-Bruhl cites the ethnography by Gunnar Landtman, who states that, among the Kiwai, "nearly all the outdoor dances can be called mimetic, inasmuch as they imitate actions from real life" and display "great ingenuity, for the dancers do not just copy the various movements in a mechanical way" (ibid.: 122). In opposition to Frazer and other accounts of mimesis, imitation is not seen as mechanical here but as a kind of aesthetic expression. Lévy-Bruhl then explores another example of a dance ritual in more detail, taken from Theodor Koch-Grunberg's study of the Baniwa in Northwest Brazil:

> The idea of magic influence is at the basis of all these mimetic representations. They are destined to bring to the village and its inhabitants, their plantations, and to all the surrounding nature, blessing and fertility ... From the circumstance that the dancer in his movements and gestures imitates, as faithfully as it is in his power to do, the being whom he endeavours to represent, he identifies himself with him. The magic power dwelling in the mask is transferred to the dancer, makes him a masterful 'demon,' capable of subduing 'demons' or making them favourable to him. (ibid.: 127)

The performance of the rite demands an effort to copy the movements of other beings, and the mask worn during the rite gives the dancer a new identity via mimetic transfer. Moving on to his analysis of this and similar rites, Lévy-Bruhl states that "by imitating what their mythical ancestors have done in certain circumstances, and reproducing their gestures and their acts, these natives are in communion with them and actually participating in their substance" (ibid.: 115). He elaborates further:

> Is it possible to penetrate yet further into the significance of these ceremonies and these magico-propitiatory dances? ... For there seems to be no doubt that in nearly all such dances the wearers of these masks represent "ghosts," that is, save in exceptional cases, the dead or the ancestral spirits. Now the word "represent" must be understood here in its literal etymological sense—that in which the primitives would take it if they used it: to re-present, to cause to reappear that which has disappeared. As long as the actors and dancers wear these masks, and from the mere fact that they cover their faces, they are not only the representatives of the dead and the ancestors whom these

masks portray: for the time being, they actually become these dead and these ancestors. To primitives, as we know, bi-presence is not an inconceivable, or even unnatural idea. (ibid.: 123–124)

Here, imitating the moves of ancestors is not just a mere representation or performance but a kind of immersion into a role that does not allow for any distance between past and present, self and other, the living and the dead. Mimesis here mediates between these (at least to our perception) separate domains. In the quote above, Lévy-Bruhl alludes to the fact that the word 'representation' has, etymologically speaking, an interesting double meaning, which Carlo Ginzburg and Raymond Williams refer to as well: on the one hand, it describes, in an older translation, "the efficacious presence of something"; on the other hand, it stands for "something that is actually not present" (Ginzburg 1991: 1219–1220; see also Williams 1983: 267). Lévy-Bruhl deems the first meaning as more suited to his case. Then, *pace* the concept of representation that evolved during the Enlightenment and the Reformation,[26] Lévy-Bruhl sees imitative acts as ritual performances that have an efficacious character and are not mechanical acts that produce inferior copies of originals.

Coming back to the discussion of the fetish as a living object, we can note that a similar conclusion is drawn by Lévy-Bruhl in relation to magically charged objects and the principle of what he (somewhat misleadingly) labels 'mystical participation'. Imitation here is not necessarily a copy of another object's exterior form, but the act of copying aims at the force inherent in that object. Giving the example of the production of amulets among the Eskimos of Greenland,[27] in which certain qualities of animals are copied into an object, Lévy-Bruhl (1935: 339–340) notes:

The amulet does more than merely represent the animal or human being which it imitates or by which it is made. The amulet is alive, because it has been made during the recitation of a charm or spell, when the dominating qualities of the animal or the part of the body have been invoked; the power of these qualities is at any rate potentially present in the animal. It evidently makes no great difference whether it is the thing (animal) itself or an imitation which is used as an amulet; it has the same power.

Lévy-Bruhl gives numerous other examples that are comparable to the relationship between an 'original' human being and its effigy-copy. He understands them as expressions of the *mentalité primitive* in which "the reality of the similitude is of the same kind as that of the original—that is, essentially mystic" (Lévy-Bruhl 1985: 52). Christopher Bracken (2002: 333) refines the explanation given by Lévy-Bruhl, stating: "The likeness does not stand in for what it imitates, it participates in what it imitates. The thing contains its likeness, and the likeness, the thing for both contain a force communicated along the pathway of mimesis." Significant here is that Lévy-Bruhl did not consider imitative representations as mere 'symbols' that 'stand for something'—an approach that was dominant in anthropology for several decades.[28]

Despite the evolutionary tendencies of his theory, and the overstretched, generalizing distinction between the modern mind and primitiveness,[29] Lévy-Bruhl can be credited for pointing out that Western ideas about rationality, and certain divides that were emerging in the context of the Enlightenment and Reformation, are far from general. Lévy-Bruhl understands his own modern and scientific culture and its understandings of imitation and representation as being culturally specific, and not, like Kant and other Enlightenment thinkers, as epistemological universals. This theme was picked up his pupil Maurice Leenhardt, and actually has regained importance in recent discussion in anthropology.[30] Although Lévy-Bruhl does not theorize mimesis explicitly, his concept of participation shows that he understood these practices of imitation and representation as a challenge to, and extension of, Western mimetic theory. In opposition to Enlightenment discourses on fetishism and to Frazer's pejorative account of imitative magic as a false science as well as an abortive art, Lévy-Bruhl implicitly recognized that the negative connotations of mimesis and representation were only of limited value when trying to understand systems of thinking positioned outside the context of modernity.

I have here given only a snapshot of early anthropological works that dealt with mimetic practices. Anthropological research in the post-colonial period rediscovered mimesis from the perspective of resistance. The most famous and influential works were probably the film *Les maîtres fous* (The Mad Masters) from 1955 by Jean Rouch and the writings of Michael Taussig.[31] In other anthropological writings, the theoretical developments became increasingly diversified and complex, and like in other subjects, the long and open genealogy of mimesis produced a certain fuzziness. However, as Michael Lempert (2014: 380) notes, imitation and mimesis have been included in a variety of other discussions in anthropology, and attest to the centrality of the concept:

> For good and for ill, anthropology has not tried to tame this disorder because imitation has rarely been a central or well-established topic for much of the field. In ethnographies, imitation appears in familiar guises: parodies, piracies, counterfeits, historical reenactments, pantomime, quotation, vocal mimicries. In stressing the local, strategic deformations introduced as actors draw on but invariably depart from globalizing discourses such as human rights, many anthropologists embrace analytic tropes that have mimetic dimensions, such as translation, appropriation, vernacularization, sampling, and dubbing.

Outside of anthropology, Michael Taussig's work gained prominence. Inspired by the works of Walter Benjamin, Taussig's *Shamanism, Colonialism and the Wild Man* (1987) and *Mimesis and Alterity* (1993) gave mimesis a central position. The latter book is of a more theoretical nature and continues to develop Benjamin's work on the mimetic faculty.[32] Here, Taussig took on mimesis as a concept that essentially became a tool of the critique of colonialism, violence, exploitation, and perhaps modernity at large. The precursors of his theorizing—Benjamin and various members of the Frankfurt School—will be discussed in the following part.

Primitive Mimesis as a Critique of Modernity: The Frankfurt School

It is rather easy to detect in Lévy-Bruhl's notions of the primitive mentality and mystical participation, with their non-dualistic features, a form of extreme primitivism. Do such theories, in the end, tell us more about our own desires than explain the logics of other cultures? It is rather obvious that the contrast between the rationality of modernity and that of true representation and mimetic thinking can easily become a sort of lament about what has been lost through the Enlightenment and modernity. Indeed, various movements in art and philosophy have exposed what Ben Etherington (2018) has called "primitivism's reverse teleology," which he describes as a "kind of utopianism." The use of ethnographic accounts of allegedly primitive societies here has a strong parallel in the realm of art, where primitivism was a multifaceted and dispersed but nevertheless strong movement. Although Pablo Picasso's famous painting *Demoiselles d'Avignon*, for example, was inspired by primitive art, in the end Picasso did not refer to or credit any primitive sources directly (Connelly 1998: 342), and many theoreticians of mimesis do likewise. They might refer to some travel accounts or in the best case to early ethnographies, but they are mainly pursuing projects that look for 'contrast material' that helps them to expose a lack or loss in modernity. As Robert Goldwater (1938: 173) explained in one of the first synthetic books on primitivism in modern art: "Primitive art only served as a kind of stimulating focus, a catalytic which, though not itself used or borrowed from, still helped the artists to formulate their own aims because they could attribute to it the qualities they themselves sought to attain."

As I will outline in this part, the Enlightenment and its move to an objectified world surveyed by an interior subject have been critiqued by several theorists from the perspective of mimetic theory, and with reference to the encounter with non-Western societies. Some propagators of the Frankfurt School have suggested that we witness a decrease of mimetic practices in modern, industrial society, and that that one consequence of this process is increasing alienation.[33] It is this kind of reverse perspective that Max Horkheimer and Theodor W. Adorno ([1947] 2002) suggest in *Dialectic of Enlightenment*. Written during World War II and originally published shortly afterward, the work can be seen as an effort of critical theory trying to come to terms with high modernity's inherent barbaric and exploitative dimensions, exemplified by Nazi Germany and the Holocaust, one the one hand, and by mass production and the cultural industry, on the other. Horkheimer and Adorno undertake a polemical reading of the Enlightenment and argue that we witness a decline of mimesis in modernity. In a world in which the self becomes more and more an inner property of the individual, and in which the outer world and nature are reduced to the analytical reason of modernity, mimesis, animistic, and magical beliefs become repressed. In their account, "the disenchantment of the world means the extirpation of animism" (ibid.: 2) and "for civilization, purely natural existence, both animal and vegetative, was the absolute danger. Mimetic, mythical, and metaphysical forms of behavior were successively regarded as stages of world history which had been left behind" (ibid.: 24). They argue that the Enlightenment and the spread of scientific worldviews 'flatten' the world, thereby disenchanting it:

> The whole ambiguous profusion of mythical demons was intellectualized to become the pure form of ontological entities. Even the patriarchal gods of Olympus were finally assimilated by the philosophical *logos* as the Platonic Forms. But the Enlightenment discerned the old powers in the Platonic and Aristotelian heritage of metaphysics and suppressed the universal categories' claims to truth as superstition. In the authority of universal concepts the Enlightenment detected a fear of the demons through whose effigies human beings had tried to influence nature in magic rituals. From now on matter was finally to be controlled without the illusion of immanent powers or hidden properties. For enlightenment, anything which does not conform to the standard of calculability and utility must be viewed with suspicion. (ibid.: 3)

However, in their view, modernity does not progress toward greater freedom, but toward a pure, immanence-based rationality, paving the way for domination and totalitarian rule. Magic is linked to deeper truth, but it is not a universal and dominant truth.[34] Mimesis becomes controlled and bureaucratic, cutting off the subject from objects under the pretext of rationality.[35] In order to contrast this disenchanted world of 'fake Enlightenment' with that of magic and animism among primitives, Horkheimer and Adorno do not discuss ethnographic details, but make several references to the anthropological research. Robert H. Lowie, Marcel Mauss, Emile Durkheim, and Edvard Westermarck are cited with reference to totemism, *mana*, sacrifice, and so forth. As I outlined before with reference to theoreticians of mimesis, the question of representation also takes a central position in these arguments. With reference to language, Horkheimer and Adorno ([1947] 2002: 7) state:

> The manifold affinities between existing things are supplanted by the single relationship between the subject who confers meaning and the meaningless object, between rational significance and its accidental bearer. At the magical

stage dream and image were not regarded as mere signs of things but were linked to them by resemblance or name. The relationship was one not of intention but of kinship. Magic like science is concerned with ends, but it pursues them through mimesis, not through an increasing distance from the object.

When mimesis is understood as a process of appropriation and as an exchange, as it is here, it has the capacity to bridge the gap between world and consciousness, between subject and object. The loss of mimesis therefore implies a larger distance between these dualities. Consequently, a hierarchy of rationalities, in which cultures that still believe in mimesis supposedly occupy a lower position in the civilizational scale, is introduced:

> The superseding of the old diffuse notions of the magical heritage by conceptual unity expresses a condition of life defined by the freeborn citizen and articulated by command ... Along with mimetic magic it tabooed the knowledge which really apprehends the object. Its hatred is directed at the image of the vanquished primeval world and its imaginary happiness. The dark, chthonic gods of the original inhabitants are banished to the hell into which the earth is transformed. (ibid.: 10)

Although mimesis and imitation are conceptualized as positive features, Horkheimer and Adorno's image of pre-modern societies still follows a trope similar to that of other evolutionists. Their concept of natural or animistic mimesis is embedded in a "schematic version of the history of modern consciousness" in which "human understanding progresses in three stages, from magical to mythic/epic to modern/scientific self-understanding" (Miller 2011: 24). By depicting modernity, similar to Max Weber ([1930] 1992: 123), as an "iron cage" (*stahlhartes Gehäuse*) in which formal-procedural rationality (*Zweckrationalität*) and efficacy progress, it seems that Horkheimer and Adorno were in need of a counter-image. They found this in allegedly pre-modern, non-capitalist societies that had not yet undergone Enlightenment and rationalization. One the one hand, this view might be seen as having rather romantic undertones that postulate a non-alienated form of existence, in which mimesis can give access to authentic experience. Ernesto Verdeja (2009: 494) thinks that Adorno's idea of mimesis "relies on a problematic, unmediated conception of authenticity." On the other hand, recent discussions in philosophy and anthropology have raised similar topics with reference to ontology. Bruno Latour's idea of purification and Eduardo Viveiros de Castro's emphasis on ontologies are in some respects not that far away from Adorno's reasoning.[36]

The understanding of mimesis in the *Dialectic of Enlightenment* partially also resonates with the thoughts of another member of the Frankfurt School, Walter Benjamin. Benjamin has a less coherent account of mimesis and actually changes his definition according to the context of its application. This tendency reflects his methods of working and thinking, which are marked by fragments, collage, and the simultaneity of past and present.[37] In his essay "On the Mimetic Faculty" (a revised version of "Doctrine of the Similar"), Benjamin ([1933] 1999: 722) defines language in terms of mimesis, but already sees language as evolving from another stage of development, that of non-sensuous similarity: "In this way, language may be seen as the highest level of mimetic behavior and the most complete archive of nonsensuous similarity: a medium into which the earlier powers of mimetic production and comprehension have passed without residue, to the point where they have liquidated those of magic." Benjamin ([1920–1921] 1996: 274) postulates that, in pre-historic times and among "druids, brahmins and shamans," words and names did not refer to things (as in Saussurian linguistics), but magically participated through sound in things, a capacity that is inevitably lost. But for Benjamin, this is a process that has been at work for ages, not only since the encroachment of modernity. Generally speaking, through any expression in a language, an original state of total immersion into nature becomes fragmented. It is not the unity of word and thing, of subject and object that is at the center of his interest in language, but the subject's process of becoming in the course of acquiring a language. What we are left with today is the gift of seeing resemblances, only a "rudiment of the once powerful compulsion to become similar and to behave mimetically" (Benjamin [1933] 1999: 720).

In Benjamin's other works we find examples where the mimetic and magic capacities of the primitives are equated with those of children. In "Berlin Childhood around 1900," the child mixes dream, fantasy, and reality, and the differentiation of self and external world is not yet accomplished (Benjamin [1938] 1990).[38] He also refers to primitive forms of play, ritual, and dance (ibid.). Children and primitives still have a sense for magical correspondence. Like Adorno, Benjamin sees a decline of mimesis: "The perceptual world [*Merkwelt*] of modern human beings seems to contain far fewer of those magical correspondences than did that of the ancients or even that of primitive peoples. The question is simply: Are we dealing with a dying out of the mimetic faculty, or rather perhaps with a transformation that has taken place within it?" (Benjamin [1933] 1999: 695).

How can we contextualize Benjamin's use of the primitive in his philosophy of language and his account of mimesis? In 1915, Benjamin had already attended the lectures of Walter Lehmann on ancient Peruvian art in Munich. Lehmann presented clay heads that resembled decapitated heads. He interpreted them as trophies from headhunting; it was not an exact likeness that was crucial, but the strength of the victim that one could absorb while holding the head imitation (see Brodersen 1996: 81). So it was not only representation, but the belief in efficacy that Lehmann emphasized. Benjamin's interest in anthropological accounts and his primitivism surfaced again in the summer of 1918, when he immersed himself in history and anthropological accounts that later formed the groundwork for his essay on the mimetic faculty (see

Gess 2007: 305). Nicola Gess has argued that Benjamin's ideas on language are little, if at all, influenced by Lévy-Bruhl's notion of primitive or mystic participation (ibid.: 308). In contrast, Christopher Bracken (2002) explicitly links Benjamin's philosophy of language to Lévy-Bruhl without, however, delivering direct proof. Benjamin (1935) was well aware of the works of Lévy-Bruhl, and his review of the sociology of language discusses the concept of mystic participation at length. Be that as it may, Benjamin's idea that the process of *naming* things once contained the magical capacity of language finds a strong parallel in Lévy-Bruhl's extensive treatment of this question. Paolo Gabrielli (2004: 323) mentions that one of Benjamin's central ideas, namely, "non-sensuous similarity," had already been used by Lévy-Bruhl in 1927.

Although primitivism was widespread in intellectual circles in Benjamin's times,[39] I think that his version is rather complex. In 1917, Benjamin wrote "On the Program of the Coming Philosophy," in which he attacks Kant's theory of knowledge. Referring to Kant's subject-object distinction, he picks up a thread that was already discussed in a previous part of this chapter and lists 'examples' that contradict Kant's thesis:

> We know of primitive peoples of the so-called pre-animism stage who identify themselves with sacred animals and plants and name themselves after them; we know of insane people who likewise identify themselves in part with objects of their perception, which are thus no longer objecta, "placed before" them; we know of sick people who do not relate the sensations of their bodies to themselves, but rather to other creatures, and of clairvoyants who at least claim to be able to feel the sensations of others as their own. (Benjamin [1917] 1989: 4)

His analogies between primitive people, madmen, and visionaries might be somewhat misleading from today's perspective, but they are an intrinsic part of many accounts of primitivism in the arts. There, the allegedly "excessive imagination and lack of reason" of primitives are set in contrast to the repressive rationality of modernity (Connelly 1998: 340). Benjamin wants to develop a form of 'magical critique' from these cases. Countering Kant, Benjamin sees in ritual, madness, drug-induced states of mind, and Surrealist art possibilities for a return of mimetic capacities.[40] He "conjures up the specter of the primitive neither to condemn it, nor to advise those whose job is to civilize it, but to imitate it. He develops the term magical critique for his thinking" (Bracken 2002: 344). In opposition to Horkheimer and Adorno, he not only laments the disappearance of mimesis in modernity, but also sees opportunities for its return. His work therefore "celebrates and mourns ... the liquidation of tradition" (McCole 1993: 8) at the same time.

This stance is also deducible from Benjamin's ([1936] 2002) account of mimesis that is implicitly contained in one of his more famous essays, "The

Work of Art in the Age of Its Technological Reproducibility." He proposes that modern technologies such as film and photography change the way we perceive the world. While a painting as an original has, according to Benjamin, an 'aura' (substituting the magic of his language philosophy), modern techniques of reproduction (the capacity to produce infinite copies) and mass consumption are not able to incorporate this aura. However, Benjamin here exposes not just a simple melancholia for older times and other cultures; he also sees opportunities opening up through this new concept. The cinema itself, with its fast-moving images and overstimulation, can at first create a shock that frees the masses from their routines. Then, Benjamin suggests, through these technologies, the masses develop a greater desire to get closer to the image and to annihilate the uniqueness of the object by mimetically appropriating it (ibid.: 105). I agree with Michael Taussig (1993: 20), who proposes that it is not only melancholia and loss that surround Benjamin's notion of mimesis: "Instead, modernity provides the cause, context, means, and needs for the resurgence—not the continuity— of the mimetic faculty." This differentiates Benjamin's idea of mimesis from Adorno's account, which simply sees its decline in modernity.

Conclusion

I began this selective and generalizing conceptual history with an overview of the genealogies and transformations of the concepts of mimesis and representation. By postulating a close link between mimesis and representation, I argued that in Kant's philosophy of Enlightenment and Hegel's Idealism, the negative connotations of mimesis (first pronounced in Plato's philosophy) became dominant. These Enlightenment discourses also laid the groundwork for the transcultural exchanges that influenced the subsequent theorizing of mimesis. However, as I showed, these exchanges were of a rather asymmetric nature, and depictions of primitive mimetic practices and fetish worship were interpreted as proof of the illogical thinking of the natives, of their lack of rationality. Enlightenment theories of fetishism and Frazer's notion of primitive imitative magic also provided substance for the evolutionary theories of the nineteenth century, and, moreover, a legitimation for colonial hegemony and civilizational superiority. For Eric Hobsbawm (1994: 46), 'barbarism' is seen as "the reversal of what we may call the project of the eighteenth-century Enlightenment, namely the establishment of a *universal* system of such rules and standards of moral behaviour, embodied in the institutions of states dedicated to the rational progress of humanity."

With Lévy-Bruhl's theories, I outlined an approach that still exoticizes the mimetic and representational thinking of indigenous societies, and draws a dividing line between modernity and primitiveness, but nevertheless seriously tries to understand the difference between systems of thinking. Moreover, we here find a strong (armchair) engagement with ethnographies. With Horkhheimer and Adorno, and finally Walter Benjamin, primitive mimesis is transformed into a counter-image of the Enlightenment and modernity. The objectification of nature, the increased bureaucratization of society, and the repression and disappearance of mimesis in modernity were made visible by pointing to societies in which mimesis is supposedly still alive. Whereas Horkheimer and Adorno mainly accused modernity and Enlightenment thinking of oppressing mimesis, I argued that Benjamin has a somewhat less pessimistic perspective. In both approaches, however, "'mimesis' sounds a muted and half-forgotten, but still *optimistic* tone in that it signals a force both primitive and irrational, prior to and resistant to the encroachment of full-on modernity" (Miller 2011: 23). Especially in Benjamin (and later in Taussig) we find a hope to escape the rationality and the iron cage of modernity through the reactivation of mimesis. As in primitivist movements in the arts, a return to something more simple and immediate through mimetic practices was considered an antidote to the hyper-rationality of modernity.

The encounters between Western theories of mimetic behavior and more or less fictional ethnographies of primitives can in this sense be understood as an appropriation of a cultural Other, as a process of mimesis itself. Depending on a multiplicity of factors, such as reception, power constellations, and so forth, I argued that these appropriations create discourses that move between two poles: one the one side, a strengthening of European superiority and colonial hegemony; on the other, a critique of modernity and rationality. It is rather obvious that, in the case of critiques of modernity and the Enlightenment, we deal with a form of primitivism expressed as a lack of real mimesis and representation. Primitivism, alongside Orientalism, was a popular trope of the nineteenth and twentieth centuries, and has been well documented in art history and literature.[41]

The question, however, why certain accounts of primitive mimesis held such an attraction for Adorno, Benjamin, and the theoreticians of mimesis discussed in this chapter probably has many answers. There was obviously the need for a counter-image. But to be more specific, one could argue that this image had to embody a certain kind of authenticity, which could either be classified as something anachronistic (an *Urform*), or as a loss or lack. Charles Lindholm (2008) suggests that the marked desire for authenticity in our time is rooted in the modern loss of faith and meaning—a proposition that resonates very well with critical stances on the Enlightenment and modernity. Anthropologist Dimitrios Theodossopoulos (2013: 338) states that there is often a "presupposition that authenticity lies at an inaccessible level below the surface of social life, deep within oneself or among societies 'uncontaminated' by modernity." Moreover, he argues that "authenticity encodes the expectation of truthful representation" (ibid.: 339). With a return to an older notion of mimetic representation in Lévy-Bruhl, Adorno, and Benjamin, a return to something more 'real' and original was imagined. However, according to Gustave Ribeiro (2017), this longing for authenticity is still prevalent in the current age, but again exposed to shifts. Living in an age where the original is increasingly disappearing, he imagines two outcomes of this process (ibid.: 34):

> The first could be called hyperfetishism, meaning the hyper efficacy of fetishism in a world completely colonized by copies without originals ... In such a realm no one would really care about alienation. The current almost complete disappearance of the term is an indication of this. The other outcome is what I would call hyperanimism, or a return of the metaphysics of animism among the moderns. One expression of hyperanimism is the prestige currently enjoyed by some theories that attribute agency to things. Perhaps it is a reaction to a world where copies have no originals ... a reaction to the possibility of a shallow world, finally and completely disenchanted.

In this view, modernity—post-, late-, or whatever—seems to be caught up in an endless loop, moving between a world of copies without originals and resistance efforts to re-enchant these soulless copies with animistic capacities.

Acknowledgments

This chapter's argument is partially based on research previously published in "Mimetic Theories, Representation, and 'Savages': Critiques of the Enlightenment and Modernity through the Lens of Primitive Mimesis" in *The Transformative Power of the Copy*, edited by Corinna Forberg and Philipp Stockhammer (Heidelberg: University Publishing, 2017). I thank Philipp and Corinna for their invitation to the workshop in Heidelberg, and Christoph Brumann for the final reading of the original text. Thanks as well to Berghahn's excellent editors, who helped with the German-English referencing of Walter Benjamin's work. In comparison to the previous text, this version has a stronger focus on the notion of primitivism and is structured as a conceptual history.

Patrice Ladwig studied social anthropology and sociology and obtained his PhD from the University of Cambridge. He has worked at the University of Bristol, the Max Planck Institute for Social Anthropology, and the University of Zurich. His work focuses on the anthropology of Buddhism (Laos and Thailand), death and funeral cultures, colonialism, the link of religion to communist movements, and general social theory. He currently works at the Max Planck Institute for the Study of Religious and Ethnic Diversity and carries out research on economic modernization, religion, and ethics in the context of the Max Planck Cambridge Centre for the Study of Ethics, Human Economy and Social Change. E-mail: ladwig@mmg.mpg.de

Notes

1. Throughout this chapter, I will use the term 'primitive' without quotation marks. From anthropology's beginnings as an academic subject, as well as in public discourse, this term designated small-scale, mostly non-literate tribal societies that are today variously labeled as 'indigenous peoples', 'ethnic minorities', and so forth. As will become clear in the course of this chapter, many of the accounts of these societies, especially in the time frame under discussion here, were products of the Western ethnographic imagination, which at times had little to do with the societies in question.

2. Although the simple opposition of the 'West' and the 'Other' is a crude simplification, I think it makes sense in the generalizing context I will discuss here. See also the preceding note.

3. For the process of 'Othering' based on ideas of time and progress, see Fabian (1983).

4. For literature, see Erich Auerbach's ([1953] 2003) classic account.

5. See also Gebauer and Wulf (1995: 25–30) on the plurality of meanings of mimesis in Plato. They state that "in addition to imitation, representation, and expression, there is also emulation, transformation, the creation of similarity, the production of appearances, and illusion" (ibid.: 25).

6. See Plato's (1992) *Republic*, especially Books II and III on the basic and vague definition of imitation. The ban of certain forms of poetry from the *polis* is treated in Book III. In Book X, this ban is extended to all poetry.

7. For the allegory of the cave, see Plato (1992: Book VII).

8. On the corrupting features of mimesis, see Plato (1992: Book X, 602c–608b).

9. We find Aristotle's work on poesies a more positive account of mimesis. Aristotle understood mimesis as a natural behavior and considered representations as essential for processes of learning and socialization in general, for example, as in the cathartic functions of theater. Mimesis is conceptualized as a natural human inclination or instinct.

10. Foucault (1994: 168) defines episteme as *a priori* knowledge. A matrix on which knowledge and discourses becomes possible is always only one episteme that defines the conditions of the possibility of all knowledge.

11. Modernity here acts as a term defining a period that, depending on one's perspective, starts with the French Revolution and the Enlightenment. In these pages, it also comes to take on meanings that delineate modernity from primitiveness and act as a specific narrative to legitimize Western domination. Similar to the idea of civilization, the term has now become pluralized in order to weaken its Eurocentric associations. See Eisenstadt (2003) on the idea of 'multiple modernities'.

12. In this understanding, a large part of humanity was still marked by their "minority of age" (*Minderjährigkeit*) and "legal or civil immaturity" (Kant [1784] 2013: 19).

13. Kant's ([1784] 2013) account of innovation and genius in Western history here serves as a good example: imitation is seen as the antidote to innovation, as true

innovation progresses through the genius who, in an authentic manner, advances through his own reason without imitating others. See also Potolsky (2006: 67).

14. Philosophers and experts of Kantian and Platonic thought would probably dismiss my superficial reading here. Whether Kant returned to certain aspects of Plato's ideas (e.g., *noumenon*) has been discussed with much controversy. For a position that conforms to my understanding, see Rockmore (2011). For an opposing perspective that reads Kant in terms of his *Erkenntnistheorie* as essentially anti-Platonian, see Walter Patt (1997: 38–39).

15. Foucault (1994: 43) has traced this development and its shifts in the sixteenth and seventeenth century in terms of the relationship between signifier and signified: "This new arrangement brought about the appearance of a new problem, unknown until then: in the sixteenth century, one asked oneself how it was possible to know that a sign did in fact designate what it signified; from the seventeenth century, one began to ask how a sign could be linked to what it signified. A question to which the Classical period was to reply by the analysis of representation; and to which modern thought was to reply by the analysis of meaning and signification."

16. Carlo Ginzburg (1991) gives a very interesting overview of the changing connotations of representation to which I will return later.

17. See, for example, the discussions on belief and their applicability in anthropology in Needham (1972) and, more recently, in Lindquist and Coleman (2008).

18. See Besançon's (2009) study on the intellectual history of iconoclasm.

19. See Ladwig (2012) for different understandings of symbols and representations in modernity.

20. On Hegel's images of Africa in these lectures, see Susan Buck-Morss (2009).

21. See also Fabian (1983: 11–12) on notions of time and evolution in early anthropology.

22. Elsewhere, Lévy-Bruhl (1985: 76) proclaimed: "Let us abandon the attempt to refer their mental activity to an inferior variety of our own." See also Evans-Pritchard ([1934] 1970) for a more balanced view of Lévy-Bruhl's works.

23. For an overview of critiques of Lévy-Bruhl and reinterpretations, see Mousalimas (1990: 40–41).

24. In his posthumously published notebooks, Lévy-Bruhl (1975:) also makes more explicit references to Greek philosophic notions such as mimesis.

25. Gebauer and Wulf (1995: 316) have linked performativity to mimesis and focus on body-related motions, rhythms, gestures, and sounds.

26. Ginzburg (1991: 1226–1227) has argued that the evolvement of the second meaning (absence) can, in general, be attributed to the Jewish-Christian vision of icons even before the Reformation.

27. Lévy-Bruhl here cites the ethnography of William Thalbitzer, who spent two years in an isolated Inuit settlement around 1900. Like in the previous case, Lévy-Bruhl in my opinion actually draws on ethnographies that expose a much higher level of refinement than those of Frazer some decades earlier. This might be based in the fact that he—as an armchair anthropologist—seems to have had a different agenda than Frazer and puts more emphasis on detail. Frazer

was, however, a better storyteller. The second explanation might be that, in the course of two decades, the amount of reliable ethnographic material had increased tremendously.

28. I have outlined in an earlier publication that the anthropologists of different generations have usually supported one of the following methods for understanding these imitative representations (Ladwig 2012: 429–430). Either there is a purpose connected to these transformations (functionalism), which show how the brain works (cognitivism) and have to be interpreted (interpretivism), or these transformations are of a metaphorical nature (symbolism). Recent approaches see representation as a way of domesticating 'otherness' into our frameworks of analysis, and advance a reading that is actually very close to that of Lévy-Bruhl. See Henare et al. (2007) for a call to rethink the position of objects and representation.

29. Lévy-Bruhl, however, saw the primitive mentality also at work in our own culture. The British social anthropologist Evans-Pritchard (1965: 91) wrote: "For him, Christianity and Judaism were also superstitions, indicative of prelogical and mystical mentality ['primitive mentality'], and on his definitions necessarily so. But, I think in order not to cause offence, he made no allusion to them."

30. Leenhardt (1979) continued some of these themes in his anthropological accounts of Melanesia, in which the socio-cosmic principles animating the body are described as an essential part of the concept of the person. These principles make it possible to transform the body and actually become another being, as is, for example, often encountered in shamanism.

31. For more details, see our discussion of these works in the introduction to this volume.

32. For Benjamin ([1933] 1999: 720), humans are distinguished by their mimetic faculties and the "gift for seeing similarity is nothing but a rudiment of the once powerful compulsion to become similar and to behave mimetically." Taussig (1993: xiii) extends this definition and defines it as "the nature that culture uses to create second nature, the faculty to copy, imitate, make models, explore difference, yield into and become Other. The wonder of mimesis lies in the copy drawing on the character and power of the original, to the point whereby the representation may even assume that character and that power."

33. For the wider context of the Frankfurt School of critical theory, see the seminal work of Rolf Wiggershaus (2010) and Jay Bernstein (1994).

34. Horkheimer and Adorno ([[1947] 2002: 6) state that "magic is bloody untruth, but in it domination is not yet disclaimed by transforming itself into a pure truth underlying the world which it enslaves."

35. See Potolsky (2006: 144) on the notion of mimesis in this work. For further explorations of Horkheimer and Adorno's notion of mimesis, see Michael Cahn (1984).

36. Latour's work takes a central role in these discussions about the value of ontology for understanding not only science and technology, but also 'pre-modern' societies. Latour (1993: 10–11) suggests that modernity enforces a distinction of various ontological spheres, that purification "creates two entirely distinct ontological zones: that of human beings on the one hand; that of nonhumans on the other." The anthropologist Eduardo Viveiros de Castro (2012: 152) adds,

in a tone that is close to that of Adorno's analysis of the disappearance of mimesis: "Modernity started with it: with the massive conversion of ontological into epistemological questions—that is, questions of representation ... After objects or things were pacified, retreating to an exterior, silent and uniform world of 'Nature', subjects began to proliferate and to chatter endlessly."

37. On Benjamin's notion of mimesis and its contextualization in his working methods and development of ideas, see Taussig (1993: 19–32).
38. See Gess (2007) on Benjamin's primitivism and the context of its time.
39. On Benjamin's use of certain images of the primitive, see Gess's (2013) excellent analysis.
40. See Joyce Cheng (2009) on Benjamin's relation to Surrealism.
41. It is interesting to note that between 1900 and World War I, the term 'primitivism' was used "without reference to tribal societies" (Grijp 2012: 134). It could contain a plethora of figures who stood outside or at the periphery of society, such as "peasants, fishermen ... children and fools" (ibid.). So the primitive was not always to be found overseas or in the colonies, but just around the corner.

References

Asad, Talal, ed. 1973. *Anthropology and the Colonial Encounter*. London: Ithaca Press.
Auerbach, Erich. (1953) 2003. *Mimesis: The Representation of Reality in Western Literature*. Trans. Willard R. Trask. Princeton, NJ: Princeton University Press.
Benjamin, Walter. (1917) 1989. "On the Program of the Coming Philosophy." Trans. Mark Ritter. In *Benjamin: Philosophy, Aesthetics, History*, ed. Gary Smith, 1–12. Chicago: University of Chicago Press.
Benjamin, Walter. (1920–1921) 1996. "Language and Logics." In *Walter Benjamin: Selected Writings, Volume 1, 1913–1926*, ed. Howard Eiland and Michael W. Jennings, 272–274. Cambridge, MA: Belknap of Harvard University Press.
Benjamin, Walter. (1933) 1999. "On the Mimetic Faculty." In *Walter Benjamin: Selected Writings, Volume 2, 1927–1934*, ed. Michael W. Jennings, Howard Eiland, and Gary Smith; trans. Rodney Livingstone et al., 720–722. Cambridge, MA: Belknap of Harvard University Press.
Benjamin, Walter. 1935. "Probleme der Sprachsoziologie: Ein Sammelreferat" [Problems of the sociology of language: A literature review]. *Zeitschrift für Sozialforschung* 4: (2): 248–268.
Benjamin, Walter. (1936) 2002. "The Work of Art in the Age of Its Technological Reproducibility." In *Walter Benjamin: Selected Writings, Volume 3, 1935–1938*, ed. Howard Eiland and Michael W. Jennings; trans. Edmund Jephcott et al., 101–133. Cambridge, MA: Belknap of Harvard University Press.
Benjamin, Walter. (1938) 1990. "Berlin Childhood around 1900." In *Walter Benjamin: Selected Writings, Volume 3, 1935–1938*, ed. Howard Eiland and Michael W. Jennings, 344–415. Cambridge, MA: Belknap of Harvard University Press.

Bernstein, Jay, ed. 1994. *The Frankfurt School: Critical Assessments*. New York: Routledge.

Besançon, Alain. 2009. *The Forbidden Image: An Intellectual History of Iconoclasm*. Trans. Jane M. Todd. Chicago: University of Chicago Press.

Bracken, Christopher. 2002. "The Language of Things: Walter Benjamin's Primitive Thought." *Semiotica* 138 (1/4): 321–349.

Brodersen, Momme. 1996. *Walter Benjamin: A Biography*. Trans. Malcolm R. Green and Ingrida Ligers; ed. Martina Derviş. London: Verso.

Buck-Morss, Susan. 2009. *Hegel, Haiti, and Universal History*. Pittsburgh, PA: University of Pittsburgh Press.

Cahn, Michael. 1984. "Subversive Mimesis: Theodor W. Adorno and the Modern Impasse of Critique." In *Mimesis in Contemporary Theory: An Interdisciplinary Approach*, ed. Mihai Spariosu, 27–64. Philadelphia, PA: John Benjamins.

Cheng, Joyce. 2009. "Mask, Mimicry, Metamorphosis: Roger Caillois, Walter Benjamin and Surrealism in the 1930s." *Modernism/modernity* 16 (1): 61–86.

Connelly, Frances. 1998. "Primitivism." In *Encyclopedia of Aesthetics*, ed. Michael Kelly, 338–342. New York: Oxford University Press.

Eisenstadt, S. N. 2003. *Comparative Civilizations and Multiple Modernities*. 2 vols. Leiden: Brill.

Etherington, Ben. 2018. "The New Primitives." *Los Angeles Review of Books*, 24 May. https://lareviewofbooks.org/article/the-new-primitives/.

Evans-Pritchard, E. E. (1934) 1970. "Lévy-Bruhl's Theory of Primitive Mentality." *Journal of the Anthropological Society of Oxford* 1: 39–60.

Evans-Pritchard, E. E. 1965. *Theories of Primitive Religion*. Oxford: Clarendon Press.

Fabian, Johannes. 1983. *Time and the Other: How Anthropology Makes Its Object*. New York: Columbia University Press.

Fabian, Johannes. 1990. "Presence and Representation: The Other and Anthropological Writing." *Critical Inquiry* 16 (4): 753–772.

Flam, Jack D., and Miriam Deutsch, eds. 2003. *Primitivism and Twentieth-Century Art: A Documentary History*. Berkeley: University of California Press.

Foucault, Michel. 1994. *The Order of Things: An Archaeology of the Human Sciences*. New York: Vintage.

Foucault, Michel. 2002. *The Archaeology of Knowledge*. Trans. A. M. Sheridan Smith. London: Routledge.

Frazer, James G. 1894. *The Golden Bough: A Study in Comparative Religion*. New York: Macmillan.

Fromm, Erich. (1959) 1999. "Das Unbewusste und die psychoanalytische Praxis" [The unconscious in psychoanalytic practice]. In *Erich Fromm Gesamtausgabe* [Collected works of Erich Fromm], vol. 12, ed. Rainer Funk, 201–236. Munich: Deutsche Verlags-Anstalt.

Gabrielli, Paolo. 2004. *Sinn und Bild bei Wittgenstein und Benjamin* [Meaning and image in Wittgenstein and Benjamin], Frankfurt: Peter Lang Verlag.

Gebauer, Gunter, and Christoph Wulf. 1995. *Mimesis: Culture-Art-Society*. Trans. Don Reneau. Berkeley: University of California Press.

Gess, Nicola. 2007. "Magisches Denken im Kinderspiel: Literatur und Entwicklungs-psychologie im frühen 20. Jahrhundert" [Magical thinking and children's games: Literature and development psychology in the early twentieth century]. In *Literatur als Spiel: Evolutionsbiologische, ästhetische und pädagogische Aspekte* [Literature as game: Perspectives from evolutionary psychology, aesthetics, and pedagogy], ed. Thomas Anz and Heinrich Kaulen, 295–314. Berlin: de Gruyter.

Gess, Nicola. 2013. *Primitives Denken: Wilde, Kinder und Wahnsinnige in der literarischen Moderne (Müller, Musil, Benn, Benjamin)* [Primitive thinking: Savages, children, and madmen in literary modernity (Müller, Musil, Benn, Benjamin)]. Paderborn: Fink Wilhelm.

Giesey, Ralph E. 1960. *The Royal Funeral Ceremony in Renaissance France.* Geneva: Librairie E. Droz.

Ginzburg, Carlo. 1991. "Représentation: Le mot, l'idée, la chose" [Representation: The word, the idea, the thing]. *Annales* 46 (6): 1219–1234.

Goldwater, Robert. 1938. *Primitivism in Modern Painting.* New York: Harper & Brothers.

Grijp, Paul van der. 2012. "A Cultural Search for Authenticity: Questioning Primitivism and Exotic Art." In *Debating Authenticity: Concepts of Modernity in Anthropological Perspective*, ed. Thomas Fillitz and A. Jamie Saris, 128–141. New York: Berghahn Books.

Halliwell, Stephen. 2002. *The Aesthetics of Mimesis: Ancient Texts and Modern Problems.* Princeton, NJ: Princeton University Press.

Hegel, Georg Wilhelm Friedrich. (1817) 2010. *Encyclopedia of the Philosophical Sciences in Basic Outline.* Part 1: *Science of Logic.* Trans. and ed. Klaus Brinkmann and Daniel O. Dahlstrom. Cambridge: Cambridge University Press.

Hegel, Georg Wilhelm Friedrich. 1920. *The Philosophy of Fine Art.* Vol. 2. Trans. F. P. B. Oamaston. London: Bell & Son.

Hegel, Georg Wilhelm Friedrich. 1975. *Lectures on the Philosophy of World History: Introduction.* Trans. H. B. Nisbet. Cambridge: Cambridge University Press.

Henare, Amiria, Martin Holbraad, and Sari Wastell, eds. 2007. *Thinking Through Things: Theorising Artefacts Ethnographically.* London: Routledge.

Hobsbawm, Eric. 1994. "Barbarism: A User's Guide." *New Left Review* 206: 44–54.

Horkheimer, Max, and Theodor W. Adorno. (1947) 2002. *Dialectic of Enlightenment: Philosophical Fragments.* Ed. Gunzelin S. Noerr; trans. Edmund Jephcott. Stanford, CA: Stanford University Press.

Kant, Immanuel. (1764) 1960. *Observations on the Feeling of the Beautiful and Sublime.* Trans. John T. Goldthwait. Berkeley: University of California Press.

Kant, Immanuel. (1784) 2013. *Answer the Question: What Is Enlightenment?* Trans. Daniel F. Ferrer. https://archive.org/details/AnswerTheQuestionWhatIs Enlightenment.

Kantorowicz, Ernst H. (1957) 1997. *The King's Two Bodies: A Study in Mediaeval Political Theology.* Princeton, NJ: Princeton University Press.

Keane, Webb. 2006. "Signs Are Not the Garb of Meaning: On the Social Analysis of Material Things." In *Materiality*, ed. Daniel Miller, 182–205. Durham, NC: Duke University Press.

Koselleck, Reinhart, ed. 1979. *Historische Semantik und Begriffsgeschichte* [Historical semantics and conceptual history]. Stuttgart: Klett-Cotta.

Kramer, Fritz. 1981. *Verkehrte Welten: Zur imaginären Ethnographie des 19. Jahrhunderts* [Upside down worlds: On the imaginary ethnography of the nineteenth century]. Frankfurt am Main: Syndikat.

Ladwig, Patrice. 2012. "Ontology, Materiality and Spectral Traces: Methodological Thoughts on Studying Lao Buddhist Festivals for Ghosts and Ancestral Spirits." *Anthropological Theory* 12 (4): 427–447.

Latour, Bruno. 1993. *We Have Never Been Modern*. Trans. Catherine Porter. Cambridge, MA: Harvard University Press.

Leenhardt, Maurice. 1979. *Do Kamo: Person and Myth in the Melanesian World*. Chicago: University of Chicago Press.

Lempert, Michael. 2014. "Imitation." *Annual Review of Anthropology* 43: 379–395.

Lévy-Bruhl, Lucien. 1923. *Primitive Mentality*. Trans. Lilian A. Clare. London: Allen & Unwin.

Lévy-Bruhl, Lucien. 1935. *Primitives and the Supernatural*. Trans. Lilian A. Clare. London: Allen & Unwin.

Lévy-Bruhl, Lucien. 1975. *The Notebooks on Primitive Mentality*. Trans. Peter Rivière. Oxford: Basil Blackwell.

Lévy-Bruhl, Lucien. 1985. *How Natives Think*. 3rd ed. Trans. Lilian A. Clare. Princeton, NJ: Princeton University Press.

Lindholm, Charles. 2008. *Culture and Authenticity*. Malden, MA: Blackwell.

Lindquist, Galina, and Simon Coleman. 2008. "Introduction: Against Belief?" *Social Analysis* 52 (1): 1–18.

McCole, John. 1993. *Walter Benjamin and the Antinomies of Tradition*. Ithaca, NY: Cornell University Press.

Meyers, Fred. 2006. "'Primitivism', Anthropology, and the Category of 'Primitive Art.'" In *Handbook of Material Culture*, ed. Chris Tilley, Webb Keane, Susanne Küchler, Mike Rowlands, and Patricia Spyer, 267–284. London: Sage.

Miller, Gregg D. 2011. *Mimesis and Reason: Habermas's Political Philosophy*. Albany: State University of New York Press.

Mousalimas, S. A. 1990. "The Concept of Participation in Lévy-Bruhl's 'Primitive Mentality.'" *Journal of the Anthropological Society of Oxford* 21 (1): 33–46.

Muenzel, Mark. 2001. "Lucien Lévy-Bruhl." In *Hauptwerke der Ethnologie* [Major works of ethnology], ed. Christian F. Feest and Karl-Heinz Kohl, 250–255. Stuttgart: Alfred Kröner.

Needham, Rodney. 1972. *Belief, Language, and Experience*. Oxford: Basil Blackwell.

Patt, Walter. 1997. "The Synthetic Character of the Moral Law According to Kant." In *Kant: Analysen, Probleme, Kritik*, Vol. 3, ed. Hariolf Oberer, 21–39. Würzburg: Königshausen & Newmann.

Pietz, William. 1985. "The Problem of the Fetish, I." *RES: Anthropology and Aesthetics* 9 (1): 5–17.

Plato. 1992. *Republic*. 2nd ed. Trans. G. M. A. Grube; rev. C. D. C. Reeve. Indianapolis: Hackett.

Potolsky, Matthew. 2006. *Mimesis*. London: Routledge.

Rathore, Aakash Singh, and Rimina Mohapatra. 2017. *Hegel's India: A Reinterpretation, with Texts*. New Delhi: Oxford University Press.

Ribeiro, Gustavo Lins. 2017. "What's in a Copy?" In *The Transformative Power of the Copy: A Transcultural and Interdisciplinary Approach*, ed. Corinna Forberg and Philipp W. Stockhammer, 21–36. Heidelberg: Heidelberg University Publishing.

Rockmore, Tom. 2011. *Kant and Phenomenology*. Chicago: University of Chicago Press.

Said, Edward W. 1979. *Orientalism*. New York: Random House.

Said, Edward W. 1989. "Representing the Colonized: Anthropology's Interlocutors." *Critical Inquiry* 15 (2): 205–225.

Taussig, Michael. 1987. *Shamanism, Colonialism, and the Wild Man: A Study in Terror and Healing*. Chicago: University of Chicago Press.

Taussig, Michael. 1993. *Mimesis and Alterity: A Particular History of the Senses*. New York: Routledge.

Theodossopoulos, Dimitrios. 2013. "Laying Claim to Authenticity: Anthropological Dilemmas." *Anthropological Quarterly* 86 (2): 337–360.

Tibebu, Teshale. 2011. *Hegel and the Third World: The Making of Eurocentrism in World History*. New York: Syracuse University Press.

Torgovnick, Marianna. 1990. *Gone Primitive: Savage Intellects, Modern Lives*. Chicago: University of Chicago Press.

Verdeja, Ernesto. 2009. "Adorno's Mimesis and Its Limitations for Critical Social Thought." *European Journal of Political Theory* 8 (4): 493–511.

Viveiros de Castro, Eduardo. 2012. "Cosmological Perspectivism in Amazonia and Elsewhere." *HAU: Journal of Ethnographic Theory, Masterclass Series* (1): 45–168.

Weber, Max. (1930) 1992. *The Protestant Ethic and the Spirit of Capitalism*. Trans. Talcott Parsons. London: Routledge.

Whitehead, Alfred North. 1979. *Process and Reality*. New York: Free Press.

Wiggershaus, Rolf. 2010. *Die Frankfurter Schule* [The Frankfurt School]. Reinbek: Rowohlt Verlag.

Williams, Raymond. 1983. *Keywords: A Vocabulary of Culture and Society*. Rev. ed. London: Fontana.

Wulf, Christoph. 1997. "Mimesis." In *Vom Menschen: Handbuch historische Anthropologie* [On humans: Handbook of historical anthropology], ed. Christoph Wulf, 1015–1028. Basel: Beltz Verlag.

POSTSCRIPT
The Risks and Failures of Imitation

Patrice Ladwig and Ricardo Roque

In Lévi-Strauss's (1961) passage from *Tristes Tropiques* cited in the opening paragraphs of our introduction to this volume, the Nambikwara chief mimetically appropriated the writing gesture from the ethnographer. The chief understood that writing was a power tool, that it could become a crucial element for enhancing his authority. However, when we again follow Lévi-Strauss's text, we are told that the chief failed to convince his followers of the validity of his mimetic appropriation: "Shortly after my visit the leader lost the confidence of most of his people. Those who moved away from him, after he had tried to play the civilized man, must have had a confused understanding of the fact that writing, on this its first appearance in their midst, had allied itself with falsehood; and so they had taken refuge, deeper in the bush, to win themselves a respite" (ibid.: 293).

The chief's claim to power through imitation was probably undermined by local social structures and forms of behavior that squashed any efforts to centralize power—a reading one may infer from Clastres's (1987: 189–218) account of Amazonian societies. For Clastres, these societies are equipped with political structures and cultural repertoires that actively prevent the accumulation of power. "Chieftainship," Clastres writes, "is not the locus of power" (ibid.: 206). The chief rules through his prestige; he is a kind of symbolic diplomat without the capacity to exert command. This form of statelessness is further perpetuated by small-scale warfare and segmentary structures. From this perspective, the refusal to live under the leadership of a power-hungry imitator

References for this section begin on page 204.

of the 'white man', as described by Lévi-Strauss among the Nambikwara, can be also interpreted as the rejection of writing as an embryonic feature of the state and its forms of governance. The indigenous mimetic practice here was carried out in a situation that could not unfold into a consequential political state of imitation, as it were. Indeed, it seemed condemned to fail because the chief's intention to enhance his authority through copying the stranger's powers was negated by the existing stateless social structures.

Stateless Imitations

The event above is also suggestive of the fact that, in Amazonia as in many other societies, European objects, signs, and tools of statehood—writing included—were not necessarily understood and received mimetically by the indigenous groups on the same cultural terms as Europeans. Nicholas Thomas has long demonstrated that, contrarily to self-celebratory narratives of colonial supremacy, indigenous societies appropriated external things and tools with considerable cultural autonomy. Thomas (1991: 87) concludes that they were not compelled by the "irresistible magnetism of white commodities," for example. Similarly, there was no universal or inherent indigenous desire to imitate the imported power tools of Europeans, including writing as a form of state rule. Cultural interpretations varied and could result in mimetic indifference and refusal, rather than desire, toward the foreign as a source of statehood.

The argument that writing as a technology of power is rejected (more or less consciously) by certain ethnic groups in order to prevent the integration into, or the building of, states is advanced by scholarship concerned with state formation beyond Western colonial expansionism. James Scott (2009) has controversially proposed that attitudes of rejection of the state are characteristic of how some animistic and highly mobile Southeast Asian highland societies relate to the Buddhist states in the lowlands (see also Tappe, this volume). Countless myths circulate in the highlands of mainland Southeast Asia (Michaud 2017) and the Himalayas (Oppitz 2006), recounting that these societies once had a script but lost it due to stupidity or an act of betrayal. According to some interpretations of these myths, writing was abandoned because, for the highlanders (similarly to the Nambikwara rejection of writing described above), accepting it would have represented a first step toward statehood and its early forms of governmentality. It would have implied subordination to external forms of state command in the context of what has been labeled 'internal colonialism' (Hechter 1975).

Although the suggestive equation of writing, bureaucracy, and statehood is subject to considerable historical variation (Goody 1986: 87–112), James Scott (2009: 220–237) advanced the argument that for the upland peoples, embracing writing was tantamount to spatial fixation, taxation, and military service; it was synonymous with becoming part of larger political entities, subjugated to such external powers as the Buddhist kings. Hence, accepting script and thereby becoming more like the lowland rulers could be potentially dangerous because it could threaten the highlanders' internal social order and lead to the establishment of new power relations enmeshed in statehood and the domineering forms of lowland civilization. In other words, in such contexts, imitating the state could fail as a result of the desire to remain outside a state-ruled society and so evade its perceived dangers.

Dangerous States

As with the Nambikwara chief, promises of imitation as a source of power could also be alluring to European colonizers; equally they could fail and become blind to the consequences and traps of 'becoming Other'. Newspapers, artistic images, and literary novels made imitations by agents of colonialism into ingredients of a pervasive ambivalent imaginary of both the wonders of white supremacy and the perverse cruelties and madness of colonialism. It stands as revealing of the further political significance of imitation (as well as of the dangers and failures that it unleashed) that *European* mimicries of indigenous elements could also become the object of control and regulation, as Bastos's, Kohl's, and Roque's chapters outline in this book. Because they could threaten the boundaries upon which the difference between Self and Other in colonial relations was ideally to be established, the 'indigenization' of colonizers could be criticized and controlled. Thus, in taking on indigenous customs as models for individual behavior, or simply in accepting to participate in indigenous social life and rituals, the European agents could endanger not just the premises of their identity but also, in some instances, the grounds of the authority of the colonial state. In order to make these imitations less visible and to hide them from sources that could be reported back to central colonial administration, these forms of colonial mimesis could, for example, be claimed as mere temporary suspensions, as in the case of the governor analysed by Roque in his chapter. Or, to appropriate a term from archaeologist David Wengrow (2010: 19), they were carried out as "camouflage borrowing"—that is, cultural exchanges in which apparently 'foreign' influences are simply presented as 'indigenous' elements. But as our collection suggests, not all colonial imitations can be camouflaged, nor can all be successful.

Europeans in the colonies were often aware of imitating indigenous worlds as a practical possibility. They could fear its dangers, but they could also manipulate its virtues. They could seek to take possession of the imagined alterity of indigenous cultures and societies in order to forge their own identities, to pursue religious conversion, to achieve commercial ends, or to extract some other form of colonizing power, including, as this book reveals, to support the state in the exercise of government. Mimetic strategies of colonial government abounded, but this does not signify mimetic domination and control of the 'natives' consummated successfully. One needs to remember that mimetic governmentality was not a self-fulfilling prophecy. Like many colonial projects, it was vulnerable and fragile. Sometimes, rather than signs of rational action, mimetic impulses could spring from feverish states of irrational excess, or even plain boredom. The colonizers' attempts to mime and even to faithfully represent the alterity of the so-called natives was an ambiguous project condemned to the creation of forgeries and failures. "Once the mimetic has sprung into being," Michael Taussig writes (1993: 43), "a terrifically ambiguous power is established; there is born the power to represent the world, yet that same power is a power to falsify, mask, and pose. The two powers are inseparable." Taussig's (1987) inspired writings on colonialism and shamanism further suggest that colonial mimesis flourishes most consequentially within a delusionary and fantastic realm of storytelling. In a comparable vein, in his work on African exploration Johannes Fabian (2000: 8) elaborates on the notion of ecstasis as an important dimension of the colonizing experience. Mimesis could similarly constitute an instance of this colonial ecstatic—another possible manifestation of 'stepping outside' or 'being beside oneself' that characterized so many European living experiences of being in the tropics.

Imitative strategies of governance, therefore, bear the risk of slipping over a fine boundary. Perhaps unsurprisingly, then, to embrace mimesis in colonial life was also a potentially self-harmful undertaking that could endanger and subvert the premises of the colonizers' double claim to being different and being superior to the 'native' mob. Stories of Europeans dangerously 'going native' are abundant, and they epitomize the tensions entailed in mimesis as an ambiguous form of colonial power. In his novel *Heart of Darkness*, Joseph Conrad ([1902] 1990) famously explored that prevailing European trope. In it, Kurtz's deflection from the colonial apparatus and subsequent transformation into a charismatic, god-like figure worshipped by the natives stand as evidence of both the fascination and anxiety that surrounded the mimetic transit into other, non-European cultures. Kurtz's transformation can also be read as an attempt at establishing a 'tribal counter state' based on sacrifices, excess, and violence, capable of eluding the idealized rationality of the West. And yet all this fantastic alternative world of power through mimetic immersion came into being as an inner struggle that led ultimately to tragedy. Kurtz's singular state of imitation was doomed to fail. "He struggled with himself, too," evoked Conrad (ibid.: 61). "I saw it,—I heard it. I saw the inconceivable mystery of a soul that knew no restraint, no faith, and no fear, yet struggling blindly with itself." Perhaps also for colonial governors in Roque's chapter, Orientalists in Ladwig's chapter, Tappe's law makers, Saraiva's karakul breeders, or Bastos's medical officials and planners, colonial state making through the mimesis of alterity was, like Conrad's allegory of Kurtz, a magnetic spell, yet a never-ending struggle with oneself.

Patrice Ladwig studied social anthropology and sociology and obtained his PhD from the University of Cambridge. He has worked at the University of Bristol, the Max Planck Institute for Social Anthropology, and the University of Zurich. His work focuses on the anthropology of Buddhism (Laos and Thailand), death and funeral cultures, colonialism, the link of religion to communist movements, and general social theory. He currently works at the Max Planck Institute for the Study of Religious and Ethnic Diversity and carries out research on economic modernization, religion, and ethics in the context of the Max Planck Cambridge Centre for the Study of Ethics, Human Economy and Social Change. E-mail: ladwig@mmg.mpg.de

Ricardo Roque is a Research Fellow at the Institute of Social Sciences at the University of Lisbon (Instituto de Ciências Sociais da Universidade de Lisboa). He is also an Honorary Associate in the Department of History at the University of Sydney. He works on the history and anthropology of colonialism, human sciences, and cross-cultural contact in the Portuguese-speaking world from 1800 to the twentieth century. He has published widely in Portuguese and English on the history of physical anthropology and colonial encounters in East Timor, Goa (India), and Angola. He has also published on the theory and ethnography of colonial archives. He is the author of *Headhunting and Colonialism* (2010) and co-editor of *Engaging Colonial Knowledge* (2012), *Crossing Histories and Ethnographies* (2019), *Lusotropicalism and Its Discontents* (2019), and *Resistance and Colonialism* (2019). E-mail: ricardo.roque@ics.ulisboa.pt

References

Clastres, Pierre. 1987. *Society Against the State: Essays in Political Anthropology.* Trans. Robert Hurley and Abe Stein. New York: Zone Books.
Conrad, Joseph. (1902) 1990. *Heart of Darkness.* New York: Dover Publications.
Fabian, Johannes. 2000. *Out of Our Minds: Reason and Madness in the Exploration of Central Africa.* Berkeley: University of California Press.
Goody, Jack. 1986. *The Logic of Writing and the Organization of Society.* Cambridge: Cambridge University Press.
Hechter, Michael. 1975. *Internal Colonialism: The Celtic Fringe in British National Development, 1536–1966.* Berkeley: University of California Press.

Lévi-Strauss, Claude. 1961. *Tristes Tropiques*. Trans. John Russell. New York: Criterion Books.

Michaud, Jean. 2017. "What's (Written) History For? On James C. Scott's *Zomia, Especially Chapter 6 1/2.*" *Anthropology Today* 33 (1): 6–10.

Oppitz, Michael. 2006. "Die Geschichte von der Verlorenen Schrift" [The story of the lost script]. *Paideuma* 52: 27–50.

Scott, James C. 2009. *The Art of Not Being Governed: An Anarchist History of Upland Southeast Asia*. New Haven, CT: Yale University Press.

Taussig, Michael. 1987. *Shamanism, Colonialism, and the Wild Man: A Study in Terror and Healing*. Chicago: University of Chicago Press.

Taussig, Michael. 1993. *Mimesis and Alterity: A Particular History of the Senses*. London: Routledge.

Thomas, Nicholas. 1991. *Entangled Objects: Exchange, Material Culture, and Colonialism in the Pacific*. Cambridge, MA: Harvard University Press.

Wengrow, David. 2010. *What Makes Civilization? The Ancient Near East and the Future of the West*. Oxford: Oxford University Press.

INDEX